WHEN HAPPILY EVER AFTER ENDS

how to survive your divorce—
emotionally, financially and legally

By Karen A. Covy, JD

SPHINX® PUBLISHING
AN IMPRINT OF SOURCEBOOKS, INC.®
NAPERVILLE, ILLINOIS
www.SphinxLegal.com

First Edition: 2006

Published by: **Sphinx® Publishing, An Imprint of Sourcebooks, Inc.®**

<u>Naperville Office</u>
P.O. Box 4410
Naperville, Illinois 60567-4410
630-961-3900
Fax: 630-961-2168
www.sourcebooks.com
www.SphinxLegal.com

This publication is designed to provide accurate and authoritative information in regard to the subject matter covered. It is sold with the understanding that the publisher is not engaged in rendering legal, accounting, or other professional service. If legal advice or other expert assistance is required, the services of a competent professional person should be sought.

From a Declaration of Principles Jointly Adopted by a Committee of the
American Bar Association and a Committee of Publishers and Associations

This product is not a substitute for legal advice.

Disclaimer required by Texas statutes.

Library of Congress Cataloging-in-Publication Data
Covy, Karen A.
  When happily ever after ends : how to survive your divorce--emotionally, financially and legally / by Karen A. Covy.-- 1st ed.
      p. cm.
  Includes index.
  ISBN-13: 978-1-57248-548-8 (pbk. : alk. paper)
  ISBN-10: 1-57248-548-5 (pbk. : alk. paper)
  1. Divorce--United States. 2. Divorce settlements--United States--Popular works. I. Title.
HQ834.C75 2006
306.89--dc22   2006008120

Printed and bound in the United States of America.

VP — 10 9 8 7 6 5 4 3 2 1

This book is dedicated to my father, Stanley Covy,
without whose wisdom and loving support
I would never have known
what to say.

ACKNOWLEDGMENTS

I would like to thank the entire staff at Sphinx Publishing, including Michael Bowen, Sarah Brittin, and my fabulous publicist, Genene Murphy. I would also like to thank Dianne Wheeler for having the courage to take a risk with a new author, and for taking the time to help me become one. Finally, I would like to thank my mentor, Kim Clark, as well as my family and friends, who encouraged and supported me while I wrote this book.

Contents

The Realities of Supporting Your Child
Custody, Visitation, and Child Support—
   How They Relate and How They Don't
Fighting Over Money—Again

Your Divorce Does Not Have to Ruin Your Children's Lives
Your Children are Not Pawns in the Chess Game of Your Divorce
Communicating with Your Spouse is the Most Important Thing
   You Can Do for Your Children
Your Children Have Two Parents
You May be Able to Control Your Children, but
   You Will Never be Able to Control Your Spouse
When it Comes to Your Children, Always Take the High Road
Fighting Hurts Your Children
The Reality of Getting Along with Your Children's Other Parent
Fighting Over the Kids is a Never-Ending Battle

What Goes Around Comes Around, So Take the High Road
Dealing with Your Divorce

Introduction

The concepts in this book are simple, yet radical—and they are not for everyone. Many people will scoff at them, while others will laugh. Having been a trial attorney for over twenty years and a divorce attorney for more than eleven, I've had the benefit of seeing exactly what litigation does to people over time. I have witnessed what happens when love turns into hate and hope turns into bitterness—and what I've seen day after day has made me believe that there has to be a better way to end a marriage.

The stories in this book are composites of what has happened to real people in real courtrooms. I've watched judges struggle to handle social and psychological issues that the court system was never designed to address. I've seen high-powered lawyers fight for hours over who gets a $100 vacuum cleaner or who spends an extra half hour with the children on Christmas. I've stood by in courtrooms as people raged in anger, sobbed in despair, or were hauled off to jail in handcuffs. All of this has been done in the name of *justice*—in the name of what is right. After watching people litigate every conceivable personal, social, moral, and ethical issue in public courtrooms before judges who are imposing what are at times arbitrary laws, I can only say that much of what I see has nothing to do with either righteousness or justice.

This book is not an indictment of the judicial system or lawyers. I am a lawyer—I practice family law. I believe in the judicial system. I know that, for the most part, the lawyers, clerks, sheriffs, and judges who are a part of this system do an incredible job in cases that are often very emotional and difficult to deal with. However, the reality is that judges are human. Lawyers can only do so much. In spite of everyone's best efforts, the system is still far from perfect. Going through a divorce still ranges from being mildly unpleasant to being sheer hell. What people often don't realize is that how they get through the divorce process, and whether they emerge with their integrity and their sanity intact, depends not so much on the judges and the lawyers, but on themselves.

The simple truth is that divorce stinks. It doesn't matter how amicable you try to make it, how civilized you attempt to act, or how rationally you approach the situation. Going through a divorce is a lot like getting hit by a Mack truck on a deserted highway in the middle of winter—it's cold, it's lonely, and it hurts like hell. If you didn't see the truck coming at you in the first place, it can leave you shocked and confused, as well as in excruciating pain. However, no matter how devastating or unexpected the collision, no matter how intense the agony it causes, you can still collect the pieces of your life and knit them back together in ways that you never would have dreamed possible while you were still married. Doing so, however, requires that you act in exactly the opposite way that most people want to act during a divorce—it requires that you have patience, perspective, and compassion.

Having patience with yourself, your spouse, and your divorce is not easy. In our society, which values instant gratification, we delude ourselves into believing that we are entitled to have what we want and have it now. However, human emotions are not nearly so predictable. They take time to work through and time to resolve. Finances take time to separate. The courts take time to process cases. You must give yourself, your spouse, and your children the time it takes to emotionally process and financially adjust to a very different life than the one you created as a married couple. If you do, your divorce will be considerably less stressful than if you insist on getting through the process on your timetable. If you don't, you will likely face ten times the amount of resistance that you ordinarily would have encountered, and in the end, your divorce will probably take about the same amount of time anyway.

Not only do you need patience, you also need perspective. Maintaining perspective means looking at the big picture, and making conscious choices about what is really important and what is honestly in your best interests and the best interests of your family. It also means letting go of what's not. That includes giving in on some things that may seem important at first glance, but upon reflection, only matter to you because they provide a means to control your spouse or your children, or to make your spouse suffer.

Finally, getting through a divorce sanely and with integrity also requires that you approach the situation with as much compassion as you can muster—for yourself, your family, and if you can manage it, even for your spouse. That is not to say that you are ever going to repair your relationship or save the marriage. It does not mean that you should excuse your spouse's bad behavior or allow yourself to become a doormat while your spouse rakes you over the coals financially and emotionally in divorce court. What it does mean is that you try to understand not only your own fear and pain, but also your spouse's fear and pain. You don't have to agree with your spouse, believe your spouse, or trust your spouse. You don't even have to like your spouse. However, if you can at least understand your spouse and keep yourself from demonizing him or her, your own experience of divorce will be qualitatively different than if you storm through the process in anger, grasp greedily for every penny you can get, or wallow in self-pity as you become the consummate victim.

No matter what choices you make or how you conduct yourself during your divorce, it's still going to hurt. You're going to be angry, sad, scared, and lonely. No matter what you do, your divorce is very likely going to take longer, cost more, and be more aggravating than you would have liked. However, if you approach your divorce with patience, perspective, and compassion, you just may be able to get through the process with your head held high, while leaving you and your family considerably less traumatized than if you had engaged in the *War of the Roses*.

🙟 🙟 🙟

Disclaimer

The characters in the stories in this book are purely fictional. The stories are loosely based upon real cases; however, for ethical reasons, the names, facts, and all identifying characteristics have been changed to protect the identities of those involved. Many of the stories are composites of several different cases put together. Some of the stories are based upon cases I have seen in court or learned about from other attorneys, even though I did not represent anyone involved in the case. Any resemblance any of these stories bears to any past or present client I may have had during the course of my career is purely coincidental.

The only alternative to coexistence is co-destruction.

Jawaharlal Nehru
First Prime Minister of India

ፃ ፃ ፃ

Kindness
It's Kindness, Human Kindness
That the World Needs Most Today...
Not Quite So Much Talk of Duty
But a Friendly, Kindly Way.
Sometimes the Good Are Selfish
And the Righteous Stern and Cold...
But the Kind Are Always Welcome
For Kindness Never Grows Old
And There is No Force More Potent
Than a Gracious Act or Smile...
It's the Kindly Men and Women
Who Make Our Lives Worthwhile.

—*Author Unknown*

This saying can be found on a plaque
on the bench of Judge Gerald C. Bender,
Circuit Court of Cook County, IL.

The Reality and Unreality of Divorce

Americans, who make more of marrying for love than any other people, also break up more of their marriages, but the figure reflects not so much the failure of love as the determination not to live without it.

—Morton Hunt, Psychologist and Author

There is a rhythm to the ending of a marriage just like the rhythm of a courtship—only backward. You try to start again but get into blaming over and over. Finally you are both worn out, exhausted, hopeless. Then lawyers are called in to pick clean the corpses. The death has occurred much earlier.

—Erica Jong, Author

The Reality of Marriage

Very few people dream of divorce as they walk down the aisle to be married. Yet, according to the U.S. Department of Health and Human Services, over 50% of American marriages will end in divorce. Psychologists and historians have all kinds of theories about why so many marriages don't live up to the promise of *until death do us part*. Those who are either contemplating a divorce or living through the divorce process are usually less concerned about what the divorce rate says about American society and more worried about how to survive the process with their lives, their families, and at least some of their sanity reasonably intact. In order to survive the emotionally charged, financially devastating, and psychologically destructive process known as *divorce*, it is important to understand a little about marriage, a little about divorce, and a lot about human nature and relationships.

In our society, marriage is a contract. Webster's New Universal Dictionary defines marriage as:

> 1. *the social institution under which a man and woman establish their decision to live as husband and wife by legal commitments, religious ceremonies, etc.* 2. *The state, condition, or relationship of being married; wedlock:* **a happy marriage**.

While anyone going through the torture of a divorce might dispute the definition of marriage as "happy," they would probably agree that their marriage was a legal commitment, which they now seek to end by a legal divorce.

At its most basic, a *marriage* is simply a legal relationship that binds two people together in a socially acceptable way. In order to get married, you must first get a license to do so from the state. Then, you must have a judge, minister, or some other legally sanctioned person perform a ceremony, after which he or she must register the event with the proper authorities. If you don't go through this process, fill out the appropriate paperwork, or comply with the proper rules, you will not be legally married. It doesn't matter how much you love your significant other, whether you live with that person, whether you merge your finances, or whether you act exactly the same way that every other married couple in the world acts. If you do not go through the proper legal procedures to be married, you will remain legally single.

The same thing is true in what are referred to as *common-law marriages*, where the mere fact of living with someone as if you were married eventually creates the legal relationship of marriage. First of all, you need to realize that many, if not most, states do not recognize common-law marriage any more. In those that do, in order to become married, you still have to follow certain rules in order to proclaim that your relationship is, in the eyes of the law, a marriage. You must live with your common-law spouse for a certain number of years and must also do whatever else your state requires in order to be considered legally married. Thus, whether you choose to get married in a ceremony or opt for a common-law marriage, if you want to be married, you must still abide by the laws creating the institution of marriage.

The Reality of Divorce

If marriage is the legal coupling of two people, then divorce is simply the legal uncoupling of that same pair. Yet, as anyone who has been divorced knows, there is much more to marriage than a legal license to live together—and much more to divorce than the end of a legal relationship. Marriage is a relationship on multiple levels—legal, financial, emotional, familial, and psychological. Divorce is no different. Financial issues often create legal problems. Family relationships become case studies in psychological drama. Seeing divorce as strictly a legal problem simplifies it to the extreme. At the same time, because divorce is a legal event, the legal aspects of it are an enormous part of what constitutes a divorce.

Since the law creates marriages and the law dissolves marriages, it is not surprising that many people assume that courts are the best places to go to deal with all of the marital problems that arise when they are getting divorced. They assume that a judge will find a way to fix their finances, separate their assets, divide their debts, and deal with their children. People also assume that this is all done quickly and fairly, in a way that gives them everything they want and grants them a new lease on life. Unfortunately, that's not exactly the way our justice system works.

Contrary to popular belief, our court system was only designed to resolve legal disputes. Most courts do that job remarkably well. Divorce, however, involves all kinds of different issues, only some of which are legal. It involves relationship problems, complicated tax issues, financial planning questions, asset valuation disputes, and child development dilemmas, just to name a few. Courts were never intended to resolve all of these types of issues. No judge can teach you how to communicate with your ex-spouse, how to divide up your friends, or how to go about living your new life after your spouse has left you for your former best friend. No lawyer—and no judge—can be with your family twenty-four hours a day to make sure that your former spouse brings back the children from weekend visitation on time, doesn't use foul language when the kids are around, or doesn't introduce your 5-year-old to a new boyfriend or girlfriend before the ink is dry on your divorce decree. Courts simply do not have the capacity to handle these types of day-to-day family problems. Unfortunately, many divorcing couples expect them to do just that.

If you believe, as many people do, that all judges are like King Solomon and that the court system will fix all the broken pieces of your life, you are going to be sorely disappointed. It's not that divorce judges aren't good people, that they don't know the law, or that they don't care about you. The truth is that judges are human. They can decide the law. They can divide up your assets. They can even throw you or your spouse in jail, given the right circumstances. However, they cannot fix your life. They cannot solve your financial woes. They are not responsible for making sure you get through your divorce with your sanity or the rest of your life intact. The only one who has the power to do all of those things is *you*.

Your Attitude Determines How Well You Will Get Through the Process

It goes without saying that divorce is traumatic. Of all the possible events that can cause emotional pain to a human being, death and divorce rank at the top of the list. In a way, a divorce is a death—the death of a marriage. For many, it is also the death of a dream—a dream that was only supposed to end with the death of a spouse. Unlike physical death, in which the one we loved is gone forever, the death of a marriage happens while the one we used to love continues to live and breathe and drive us mad. The pain of having to bear that loss, let alone bear it with any kind of grace, is excruciating. Yet, while divorce undeniably ends a marriage, it only sometimes ends a relationship. The truth is that for most people—particularly those with children—divorce is not the end of a relationship at all. It is simply a change in status.

While most people believe that after they get divorced they will be done with their spouse for good, nothing could be further from the truth. The only thing that divorce does is end the legal relationship known as marriage. It separates two people whom the law had previously looked at in many ways as one. After you are divorced, you can no longer file joint income tax returns with your former spouse. You are no longer responsible for your former spouse's debts, and you do not have any legal claim to his or her assets or estate. However, to think that after you are divorced you will have no feelings for your former spouse or that you will never have to deal with him or her again is unrealistic. The fact that your legal relationship ends does not mean that every other kind of relationship you had with your former spouse will also end. For example, even after your divorce is final, you may have to manage, sell, or pay off your former spouse's interest in the home you once shared together. You may have bank accounts and credit cards to separate or close, and retirement accounts to divide. One of you may be dependent upon the other for financial support (alimony) for years after your divorce is over. If you and your spouse have children together, you will continue to have to interact with each other as parents for the rest of your lives. Any or all of these kinds of ties continue to bind you to your former spouse and force you to have a relationship with him or her, whether you like it or not. With that in mind, if you go through your divorce and act like you're never going to see your ex again, you are bound to create problems for yourself in the future.

Your Attitude Affects Your Behavior, and Your Behavior Affects Everything Else

Once you understand that divorce is only a change in status, not an end to your relationship, you quickly realize that the way you treat your spouse while you are going through your divorce matters much more than you ever dreamed possible. If you allow yourself to vent all of your anger and outrage at your spouse during your divorce, you are not creating the foundation for a decent relationship afterwards. Although it may sound crazy, when going through a divorce, abiding by the golden rule makes all the difference in the world. If you do all kinds of horrible, awful things to your spouse during your divorce, there is no telling what your spouse will do to you and what kinds of craziness you will have to live with both during your divorce and long after. It's that simple. It doesn't matter who you are. If you ignore, abuse, take advantage of, or otherwise mistreat your spouse during your divorce, you cannot realistically expect to have things work out well for you afterwards when you have to talk about who picks up or drops off the kids, or whether your spouse would be willing to kick in a few extra bucks for a project your oldest child is doing at school. If you spend your divorce fighting so intensely that you create a hatred of biblical proportions with your former spouse, your divorce process will be a lot like surviving the plagues—you may get through it, but the scars will be with you forever.

It is even more important that you treat your spouse like a human being at all times if you have children. The emotional and psychological damage you will do to your children by abusing your spouse during your divorce (and even afterwards) can damage them forever. No matter what kind of a scoundrel your ex may be, he or she is still—and always will be—your children's other parent. Nothing you can do will ever change that fact, or the fact that your children need to have healthy relationships with both of their parents. They love both you and your ex. They want everybody to be happy and they do not want you to fight. Even if you're not fighting about them, if you're fighting with your spouse it affects your children. For that reason alone, you should strongly consider treating your spouse with respect rather than contempt.

Respecting your spouse during your divorce also means understanding the stages of divorce and allowing your spouse to go through those stages at his or her own pace. When people go through a divorce, they go through stages of grief in much the same way as they do when someone close to them dies. They go through denial, anger or rage, bargaining, and depression. If a person works through all of these stages, he or she ultimately ends up accepting the situation and embracing his or her new life. If a person gets stuck in one stage or another, he or she may remain angry, fearful, or otherwise emotionally unbalanced. Knowing this, and giving your spouse the time and space he or she needs to work through these stages, is one of the most important things you can do—not only for your spouse, but for yourself as well.

Once you understand that both you and your spouse will go through various stages of emotions while you are getting a divorce, you should be able to deal with those emotions a little more sanely. If you normally consider yourself a mature, well-grounded, and happy person, yet find yourself to be constantly angry and mean for awhile, know that you are not alone. If you see your usually laid-back (some would say lazy), spacey, and decidedly unfinancial spouse suddenly become greedy and money-grubbing, know that it is normal and it probably won't last forever. If you've always prided yourself on being independent, yet suddenly feel grasping and needy, and find yourself trying to negotiate with your spouse to save your marriage in spite of overwhelming evidence that all your spouse wants is a divorce, go easy on yourself. All of these reactions are normal. Most of them arise, to some degree, in every person who goes through a divorce. What separates the people who get through their divorce well from those who don't is how they deal with these emotions, and whether or not they can work through them to get to a place of mature acceptance, rather than simply allowing themselves to wallow in negativity and pain.

Just as it is important that you give your spouse a break and treat him or her with respect while you are going through a divorce, it is also important that you do the same for yourself. You don't need to—and shouldn't— turn yourself into a doormat for your spouse's abuse at any time during your divorce. You don't need to sacrifice yourself and your needs for him or her, even for the sake of making your divorce go smoothly. Yes, you will need to compromise, but even compromise has its limits. You need to take care of yourself emotionally, socially, financially, and legally. If you don't do that, you will suffer the consequences of your inability to stand up for yourself for years to come. However, there is a fine line between standing up for yourself and taking advantage of your spouse. If you lie, cheat, or otherwise take advantage of your spouse during your divorce, you will suffer consequences. They may not be immediate, and they may not be direct—but they will happen. The trick is to adopt an attitude of respect for both yourself and your spouse, and then to act accordingly.

How Not to Act During a Divorce:
The Story of Robert and Vanessa

Robert and Vanessa got divorced when their children, Alyssa and Alexander, were very young. Robert was a charming, dedicated high-school teacher with a bit of a wandering eye. Vanessa was a beautiful, frail woman who was terrible at managing money and refused to work outside the home, even though her family could barely survive on Robert's salary. When Robert had an affair with a coworker, Vanessa, who was deeply religious, was devastated. Still, Vanessa refused to agree to a divorce, preferring the role of martyred wife. Robert was tired and frustrated by Vanessa's attitude, and what he perceived as her growing emotional instability and financial irresponsibility.

Robert and Vanessa had nothing when they divorced—no money and no property. All they had was their children. So, for three years, they fought over the kids, each determined to gain sole custody. They burned through what little money they had, racked up attorneys' fees they couldn't pay, and dragged each other through court battles until neither one could stand to see the other, or afford to fight the other, anymore. Then they settled on joint custody, mostly because they couldn't agree to do anything else. The children were to live with Vanessa, while Robert got a lot of visitation time.

Both Robert and Vanessa soon remarried. Robert moved to a city three hours away. Vanessa became pregnant with her new husband's child, and became very ill. She had to stay in bed constantly, and couldn't care for Alyssa and Alexander. Robert agreed to take the children until Vanessa was back on her feet. Vanessa recovered in a few months, but didn't ask for the children back for three years. By the time she did, Robert balked. The children had been in school in his city for years. They had friends, activities, and a full life. Vanessa went back to court.

Vanessa filed an *emergency motion* for the return of her children. Of course, Vanessa didn't tell Robert that she had filed that motion, and didn't bother telling the judge that Robert wasn't there because he didn't know he was supposed to be there. The judge only heard Vanessa's side of the story. Not surprisingly, he immediately ordered the sheriff to go get the children and forcibly bring them back to Vanessa's house.

When the sheriff came and removed Alyssa and Alexander from their home, they were completely traumatized. Robert ran into court the next day to try to undo what Vanessa had done, only to learn that there were certain court procedures he needed to follow, and he couldn't get a hearing date for a week. Meanwhile, Alyssa refused to go to school, Alexander got into daily fights with Vanessa and her new husband, and Vanessa found herself on the verge of a nervous breakdown. Needless to say, when the judge finally heard Robert's story, the children were ordered to go back and live with Robert until the judge could sort out what was best for them.

What happened to Robert and Vanessa, while perhaps a bit extreme, is unfortunately not at all unique. From the beginning of the divorce, each party felt wronged, each party felt betrayed, and each party translated his or her anger and frustration with the other into a fight over the only thing they had in common—their children. During their divorce, they treated each other with disrespect and thinly veiled disgust. Robert was rigid and condescending. Vanessa played the role of victim, doing whatever she could to make Robert look like the bad guy. While both of them claimed that the only thing they were concerned about was their kids, in reality, what they were really preoccupied with was themselves.

Change Your Own Behavior and You Will Change the Entire Course of Your Divorce

Although they didn't realize it at the time, Robert and Vanessa set the tone of their relationship as parents during their divorce. By refusing to cooperate with each other and focusing their anger on each other's parenting skills, rather than focusing on the infidelity and financial neediness that were the real issues bothering them, they fell into an emotional pit and they were never able to pull themselves out. They became entrenched in a parenting chess game in which their children were the pawns, but neither one saw it that way. Each parent perceived the other as misguided, incompetent, or manipulative. Each struggled in their own way for control, not just of the children, but of each other. Once they became settled in that behavior, their manipulation became their relationship, and their relationship seriously damaged their lives.

When they started their divorce, Robert and Vanessa never dreamed that they would still be fighting ten years later. Yet, that is exactly what they ended up doing. They fought over every aspect of their children's lives—where the children went to school, what activities they participated in, and whether they went to church. They created an elaborate visitation schedule that meant the children spent a huge part of their childhood in the back seat of a car, just so neither parent missed spending an extra half hour with them. Through all of the fighting and the endless court battles, the ones who ended up suffering were the children.

As with many divorcing couples, Robert and Vanessa didn't understand that both of them were responsible for creating and sustaining their never-ending battles. Unfortunately, when two people fight so bitterly, their relationship is bound to deteriorate to the point that everything becomes a fight. That is one of the biggest problems with treating your spouse during your divorce as if you are never going to see him or her again in your life—you create a horrible, tension-filled relationship that you then have to live with for years to come.

Even though you may not realize it at the time, everything you do to your spouse during your divorce will come back to you in one way or another after the divorce is over. If you don't control your emotions while you are going through your divorce, you will very likely be fighting for a very long time. If, during your divorce, you attack your spouse in court, accuse him or her of all sorts of treachery, and tell all your friends how horrible he or she has been, you can't expect to calmly discuss your child's grades or upcoming soccer game with your ex after you're done. Human beings and human relationships don't work that way. The good new is, if you change the way you think about your divorce, change the way you act during your divorce, and understand the universal laws that apply to your divorce, you can dramatically change both your experience with the divorce process and your life after it's done.

2

The Universal Laws of Divorce

To decide to be at the level of choice, is to take responsibility for your life and to be in control of your life.

—Arbie M. Dale, Author

While we may not be able to control all that happens to us, we can control what happens inside us.

—Benjamin Franklin, Scientist, Inventor, Philosopher, and Statesman

People pay for what they do, and still more, for what they have allowed themselves to become. And they pay for it simply: by the lives they lead.

—James A. Baldwin, Author

The rules of divorce have changed as often as the civilizations that created them, with each particular culture, state, or government determining what constitutes grounds for divorce, how property is to be divided between former spouses, and who is responsible for raising and supporting the children. In spite of all the different laws that have governed the dissolution of marriage, certain universal laws apply in every divorce. These laws, which aren't part of any statute or case law, transcend both conventional wisdom and prevailing court rules. They are unwritten, largely unacknowledged, and very often ignored—yet, they apply unfailingly to everyone. They are the laws of responsibility, control, and karma.

The Law of Responsibility

The law of responsibility is simple and clear. You are responsible for your own actions. It doesn't matter if you are angry or hurt. It doesn't matter if you are the injured party, if you were wronged, or if getting a divorce was not your idea. It doesn't matter if you are an emotional basket case or a financial wreck. You are still—first, last, and always—responsible for everything that you do.

UNDERSTANDING THE LAW OF RESPONSIBILITY: THE STORY OF GEORGE AND ADELE

George, a handsome, charming self-employed contractor, had been married to Adele, a very wealthy, self-made millionaire, for a few years before their marriage fell apart. Adele was very smart, worked hard, and had the Midas touch—every company she created turned to gold. George, on the other hand, was a big dreamer and a great talker, but hadn't made ten cents in his entire life. In spite of being a financial disaster, George loved living the high life—a life that he never could have afforded if it weren't for Adele. At first Adele loved George, but she soon got tired of supporting him and she filed for divorce. George, however, had no intention of leaving the marriage peacefully or cheaply.

Knowing that George had a temper, and that he intended to fight for what Adele regarded as her money in the divorce, Adele retained a high-powered attorney, and immediately took the offensive. Although George had done nothing wrong, she filed for an order of protection, claiming she was afraid of him. When the police served George with the order, George let his temper flare, and ended up getting himself thrown in jail and kicked out of the house indefinitely. George then stopped working, claiming that since he ran his business out of his house and he couldn't get into his house, he lost all his jobs and couldn't make any money. Adele responded by cutting off George's allowance and refusing to pay for his car, his boat, his credit cards, his country club membership, and every other bill she had always paid for him in the past. George, who had no money of his own, also never made the payments. His bills went past due, his car got repossessed, and his credit tanked.

George ended up developing bleeding ulcers, which ultimately caused him to have a mini-stroke. Adele then became responsible for paying all of his medical bills, as well as thousands of dollars a month in maintenance, since George was now clearly unable to work. What's more, several of George's bills were also in Adele's name, so in the process of ruining George's credit, Adele seriously damaged her own. George and Adele each blamed the other for all of their troubles, and neither could admit or see the role they both played in wreaking havoc on their lives.

Contrary to what George and Adele chose to believe, everything they did was both their own choice and their own responsibility. George took it for granted that Adele would pay his bills, just as she had always done. When she stopped, George became outraged. He couldn't understand that if he wanted to drive a Mercedes, he needed to get a job and pay the bill. For her part, Adele allowed George to be financially irresponsible for years, and then when she'd finally had enough, abruptly pulled the rug out from under him in a way that ended up costing her a fortune and damaging her own credit. Each one was responsible for creating the mess that was their marriage, and each one was responsible for causing the debacle that became their divorce.

RESPONSIBILITY IN YOUR OWN DIVORCE

Taking responsibility in your divorce means owning your own baggage and admitting the role you played, both in the demise of your marriage and in the process of your divorce. "But," you may protest, "I didn't do anything wrong." Maybe that's true. Maybe the only thing you are guilty of is marrying a louse. The bottom line is, you married the louse. No one stood behind you with a shotgun at the altar. No matter how innocent you may be, you still played some role in creating your present situation. If you can admit that, you can deal with it much more rationally than if you insist that everything in your life is your spouse's fault.

It is, of course, only natural to want to blame your spouse for all of the pain and heartache you are feeling when you're in the middle of a divorce. However, if your divorce is less than amicable, chances are that it's not only your spouse who is causing problems. You, too, are involved in playing the game. The problem is that you probably don't see it that way. Perhaps your spouse cheated on you or hurt you deeply in some other way, so you now feel justified in hurting him or her back. Maybe you feel that you're better able to handle money than your spouse, so it's only right that you should decide how the assets are divided. Maybe you think your spouse never spent any quality time with the kids anyway, so he or she shouldn't be allowed to take them every other weekend now. Whatever your issues are, at their base is two people who are both acting and reacting in ways that are creating an emotional conflict. Both of you are fueling the fight, yet each of you is likely blaming the other for being the one who won't stop.

The problem with blame is that it doesn't solve the problem. As long as you're spending time and energy blaming your spouse for whatever mess you feel that you're in, you are diverting energy away from solving the problem and into continuing the conflict. The fight becomes not just the means to an end, but an end in itself. Until you can view your behavior for what it really is and admit that you are playing a role in the ongoing battle, you are going to be powerless to stop it.

Digging deeply into your emotional issues during a divorce isn't easy or pleasant. However, if you want to emerge as a whole human being at the end, you have to do it. You may want to enlist the aid of a good counselor or therapist in this process. There is no shame in getting help, and there is nothing more important to you or your family than taking care of yourself during this difficult time. It's only by taking care of yourself that you will be able to care for anyone else. That is the essence of responsibility.

Responsibility applies not only to the emotional aspects of your divorce, but to the financial ones as well. You must take responsibility for your own finances—your income, your expenses, your assets, and your debts. In order to do so, of course, you must know what you have, what you spend, and what you owe. That means you have to pay attention to things like bank statements, retirement accounts, and credit card bills. If you've never paid attention to any of those things during your marriage, it's all the more reason to start paying attention to them during your divorce. You can't possibly know whether you can support yourself if you don't know how much money you bring in each month and how much money you spend. You can't know whether the settlement your spouse is proposing is fair unless you know exactly what assets the two of you have to divide. Once you know what your financial situation is like, then you can deal with it. Until that time, you are not only ignorant—you are powerless.

At this point, you may be thinking to yourself, "I hate all that financial stuff. My lawyer can sort that out for me, right?" Wrong! This is your life! How do you expect your lawyer to figure out what's going on in your life if you don't even know? Your lawyer doesn't get your mail. Your lawyer doesn't know your spouse. Your lawyer is not going to have the time or the resources to subpoena every bank statement, every credit card bill, years' worth of income tax returns, and all the records from every financial transaction you or your spouse has made in the past three years. What's more, if you have the kind of spouse who is purposely trying to hide assets, unless you do a little sleuthing on your own, your lawyer may never find all of your money, even by subpoenaing every financial record possible.

Being responsible also means taking the time to learn and under-stand the legal process and what you're supposed to do. That's not to say that you need to spend hours on the Internet researching the law. It simply means that you need to ask your lawyer to keep you up to date on what's happening in your case. If you don't understand something, ask questions. If your lawyer won't take the time to explain the legal process to you, fire him or her and get a new lawyer who will.

If you need to be in court, show up on time and appropriately dressed. If the judge orders you to do something, do it. Nothing will get you in serious trouble more quickly than blowing off a court order. It doesn't matter if you don't like or agree with that order. It's a court order—if you don't follow it, you can end up being held in contempt of court, paying your spouse's attorney's fees, paying fines to the court, or going to jail. In the end, it's far easier for you to just do what you're supposed to do.

Finally, responsibility means protecting your children from as much of the emotional turmoil of your divorce as you can. Divorce is hard on children. When their parents divorce, children have to adjust to a new living environment, a new family structure, and the realities of what is often a very different financial situation. They also have to adjust to a whole new set of rules and roles. Suddenly their parents are not even superficially on the same page, leaving them with a crumbling emotional foundation and confused social rules. It is even worse when they are forced into the role of *go-between* for their parents, trying to keep the peace in a war-torn family. As a parent, you need to realize that you are responsible for how your children get through your divorce and how they cope with life afterward.

The Law of Control

Control and responsibility go hand-in-hand. Not only are you responsible for your own actions, but you alone control those actions. The flip side of this universal reality—which is every bit as important to understand and much harder to accept—is that the only one you can control is yourself. At times, if they are still young, you may be able to control your children. But that's about it, and even that won't last forever. You cannot control your spouse. You cannot control your situation. You cannot control the court system. While most people claim to understand that they can only control themselves, when it comes to divorce, they just can't seem to stop themselves from trying to control their spouse.

CONTROL IN ACTION:
THE STORY OF ARTHUR AND KATHY

Arthur and Kathy had been married for six years when Arthur filed for divorce. Arthur was a banker with a *type A* personality. Kathy was an artist and stay-at-home mom of three children, ages 6 months, 2, and 4. Arthur was convinced that Kathy didn't understand how to spend money wisely. Throughout the course of their marriage, Arthur had been the sole wage earner, and he had been in charge of managing their checkbook and paying their bills. If Kathy wanted money for anything, she had to ask him. Not surprisingly, Arthur didn't think things should change, even after he filed for divorce.

When Arthur moved out, he had all of the household bills forwarded to his new home. He paid Kathy's mortgage, utilities, and insurance, just as he always did. He wouldn't give Kathy a dime in cash, nor would he put her name on his checking account. She never even saw any of the bills. Arthur also told Kathy, straight-faced, that she should give him a grocery list each week, and he would buy the groceries he thought she needed, as well as the kids' clothes and whatever the kids needed. Arthur made it clear that he thought Kathy was a flake and that he wasn't going to let her spend his money foolishly. Kathy, who finally got the courage to stand up for herself, thought otherwise.

Kathy demanded that Arthur give her child support and maintenance, and let her manage her own money, just like every other divorcing woman. Arthur responded by telling Kathy that if she wanted her own money, she should get her own job—even though Kathy hadn't worked in years and their youngest child was still in diapers. You can imagine Arthur's dismay when the judge agreed with Kathy, and ordered Arthur to turn over more than half his income every week so that Kathy could support herself and the kids, and handle her own bills.

It may seem like Arthur's extreme need to be in control is not only rare, but downright pathological. However, the truth is quite the contrary. All of us want to believe that we are in control of our environment. All of us want the security of knowing that we're going to be okay, and the way to know that is to control what happens to us. All of us think that the good intentions that motivate our behavior make that behavior not controlling. We look at our rationale rather than our behavior and conclude that we are not trying to control our spouse at all. We're just trying to make sure that the bills get paid, the kids get fed, or whatever we think is supposed to happen, happens. What we don't realize is that forcing things to happen our way is the very definition of control.

Learning to control yourself while giving up trying to control your spouse is one of the most difficult tasks you face during your divorce. So much of your life is already out of control when you're going through a divorce that the mere thought of giving up what little control you may have left is petrifying. Of course, there are some things you shouldn't give up control over. Like Kathy, you need to insist that, as much as possible, you control your own income, your own expenses, and your own life. Before you can control any of that, you must first control yourself.

STAYING IN CONTROL OF YOURSELF

When most people think of *self-control*, they typically think of things like keeping themselves from spending too much money, drinking too much alcohol, or eating everything chocolate that comes their way. Keeping control over yourself during a divorce, however, obviously means much more. It means controlling your emotions, your behavior, and the manner in which you deal with your spouse. It means doing your best to not put yourself in situations where you know your spouse will push your buttons. It means controlling your reaction when, in spite of your best efforts, you find your spouse picking a fight with you over the same issue you always argue about, and you just want to scream. It means forcing yourself to talk to your spouse in the same manner that you would talk to any other human being, and not in a disrespectful tone that you know will send him or her rocketing into the stratosphere. Screaming at your spouse, ignoring your children, purposely running up giant credit card bills, or destroying your spouse's family heirlooms out of pure spite are all counter-productive. Resist the temptation. Control yourself.

NOT CONTROLLING YOUR SPOUSE

As important as it is for you to control yourself, it is equally important for you to stop trying to control your spouse. To do that, though, you first have to recognize when you're being controlling—and that isn't always easy. For example, many people try to forbid their former spouse from introducing the children to any person of the opposite sex until their former spouse marries that person—and even then they'd prefer that their children never met the new spouse. Custodial parents want noncustodial parents who blow off visitation time with the children to have to pay them a fine. Noncustodial parents want to force custodial parents to produce receipts for every item they buy for the children, just so the noncustodial parent can see that child support payments are really being used completely for the kids. In all of these and countless other circumstances, what one parent is trying to do, possibly without even being aware of it, is to control the other parent.

The reason most people don't recognize their behavior as controlling is because they think they are only doing what's best for the children. They look at their motivation instead of at their actions. They forget (or don't want to admit) that their former spouse is also an adult and presumably also wants to do what's best for the children. Just because the spouse's ideas about what's best may be different than theirs, that does not give them the right to have everything done their way. Most of the time, there is more than one right way to do anything. Insisting that things be done your way is not about doing what's right—it's about control.

People try to control each other in many different ways, but in a divorce and after a divorce, the two things people use the most to control their ex are money and children. Not only are these two things that most people hold dear—money (because they need it to survive and also because it gives power and control) and their children (because they are their children)—but they are precisely the two things that most married couples share. It's very easy, therefore, to fight about them. When you find yourself in the middle of a battle royale about paying the children's uncovered medical expenses, it might be wise to take a step back and examine what really lies at the heart of that issue. Are you angry because your children were sick and your spouse never told you? Or is it that you think your spouse purposely took your child to the emergency room to treat a cold just to stick you with a bill that the insurance company wouldn't cover? If you're the parent who took the child for medical treatment that you knew wouldn't be covered by insurance, why did you do it? Was there a true emergency? Or did you do it because you weren't paying the bills anyway, so why should you care? Is your issue really your children's welfare, or is your issue a simple need for control?

In order to deal with your own control issues, you need to take a good, hard look at what you're fighting with your spouse about, then examine your motives. What is really upsetting you? If you can understand your real issues and admit your real problems, you'll go a long way toward solving them. At the very least, you will be able to deal with them in a much more productive way. If you can then go one step further and understand what your spouse's real issues are, you will put yourself in a position to look at your problems with brand-new eyes. When you do that, you may be able to see solutions that had never occurred to you before.

When it comes to controlling your spouse, the best advice is—give it up. Divorce is compromise. No matter what you want, or what you think you want, you're not always going to get it. That applies to pretty much every aspect of divorce, from dividing the things you accumulated during the marriage, to agreeing on the way you raise your children, to dealing with the way your spouse treats you after your divorce. You can either stress about that and turn yourself into an emotional crazy person, or you can understand that you can't change your ex, and just let it go.

The Law of Karma

For many people, the word *karma* has all sorts of mystical connotations. They think karma is some kind of crazy, New Age spiritual thing, or something that the Beatles dreamed up in the 1960s, probably when they were doing a lot of drugs. In reality, the concept of karma doesn't necessarily have anything to do with mysticism, the Beatles, or psychedelic drugs. Simply stated, karma is the law of cause and effect—*what goes around comes around*.

The law of karma is the law of justice. It is the cornerstone of what we believe our court system is supposed to do. If people commit crimes, they are supposed to be punished. If people injure others in a car accident, they're supposed to compensate the injured persons for the injuries they caused, or face a judge or jury in court. If people enter into contracts, they're supposed to live up to their end of the deal. If they don't, they can be sued and a judge can make them do what they were supposed to do, or make them pay for not doing it. That is karma.

Most people want to believe that what goes around comes around. They want to believe that their spouse is going to get what's coming to him or her, hopefully sooner rather than later. However, we all know of people who got divorced and got the shaft. So, before exploring the law of karma any further, you first need to understand a few other universal truths. People get away with things in a divorce. People lie. People cheat. People do horrible things to their children and to their spouses. Sometimes, they get away with it, it looks like they get away with it, or they get away with it for awhile. However, one way or another, even if it takes years, what they do always comes back to haunt them. Always.

KARMA HAPPENS:
THE STORY OF MELISSA AND TONY

Melissa, a beautiful and naïve young woman, was married to Tony, a talented and successful businessman. Tony had an international import/export business, and he made a good deal of money. He had money and property all over the world. Tony and Melissa lived the high life, which was not at all evident from looking at the income stated on their tax returns. However, Melissa never paid much attention to the financial details of her life with Tony—all she knew was that Tony gave her a life she could have otherwise only dreamed about. Unfortunately for Melissa, Tony was apparently providing the same kind of life to several different women at once.

When Melissa filed for divorce, she immediately got custody of their son and exclusive possession of the mansion in which she lived. Tony had to keep making the payments on the house, the cars, the boat, his son's private school, and everything else. In her jilted rage, Melissa, who had never been a low-maintenance woman to begin with, rang up credit card bills that rivaled the national debt of certain small countries. Tony responded by folding his business, allegedly because of the bad economy and new import regulations, and the couple soon spiraled into debt. By the time they divorced, their multimillion-dollar marital estate had dwindled to a paltry hundred thousand dollars.

Melissa accused Tony of purposely wrecking his business just so he didn't have to pay her in the divorce, a charge that Tony vehemently denied. She also accused him of hiding income and assets in other countries from which she could not obtain financial records. Both Melissa and Tony hired high-powered divorce attorneys, who fought with the skill of a finely tuned military machine. They sifted through mountains of paperwork and complex financial deals, each lawyer trying to prove that his or her client was right and the other party was wrong. In the end, Melissa got most of what was left of the property and Tony got all of the debt. Still, what was left was only a small fraction of what they once had. Melissa was bitter and angry, but there was nothing more she could do—or so Tony thought.

Melissa had no intention of letting Tony off that easily. It took her awhile, but she eventually organized the tangle of financial paperwork she had obtained during the divorce case, and presented it to some investigators at the IRS. Suffice it to say, not only was Tony unable to restart his business after the divorce, but he found himself doing time in federal prison for income tax evasion.

Although she was still bitter, Melissa was ecstatic that Tony finally got what he deserved—and she was only too glad to have helped bring a criminal to justice. However, Melissa also reaped what she sowed. Michael, their son, who was just turning 12 when his parents divorced, deeply resented his mother for sending his father to jail. Over time, Michael's relationship with Melissa disintegrated, he ran away from home several times, and he ended up with a drug habit and serious behavioral issues.

Sometimes, as Tony learned, the law of karma strikes fast and furious. Other times, as Melissa discovered, it evolves over time. Either way, it happens. Always. If you treat your spouse with hatred or violence, then one way or another, that hatred or violence will come back to you. If you insist on holding your spouse to the letter of the law, so too will you be required to dot every "i" and cross every "t" later on in your life. On the other hand, if you treat your spouse with kindness and respect, in spite of his or her bad behavior, you may be pleasantly surprised when your kindness and respect returns to you. Even if your spouse never returns your kindness and continues to act like a jerk, somehow, somewhere, at some point in your life, what you have done *will* come back to you. In the meantime, while you may still have to deal with your spouse's ignorant behavior, at least you will be able to look yourself in the mirror and know that you took the high road and truly tried to do what was best.

No matter what you think about the law of karma, the simple truth is, it exists. As any physicist will tell you, every action has an equal and opposite reaction. Every action has consequences—and every action you take is your choice. Your choices are your responsibility. Your choices are under your control. Your choices create your karma. The difficulty for us as human beings is that we don't always see the reaction we cause. Sometimes the consequences take time to develop, so we assume that the consequences don't exist, or that what happens to everyone else won't happen to us. If our bad behavior doesn't immediately cause us problems, we assume that we got away with it. We assume that we can treat our spouses badly behind closed doors, hide assets, or fill our children's heads with nonsense about what horrible people our exes really are, and we can get away with it. In the long run, though, the only thing we get away with is our own deception.

3

Creating a Productive Attitude in Your Divorce

When you're in the muck you can only see muck. If you some-how manage to float above it, you still see the muck but you see it from a different perspective.

—David Cronenberg, Filmmaker

It all depends on how we look at things, and not how they are in themselves.

—Carl Jung, Psychiatrist

To say that divorce is difficult is the ultimate understatement. Even an amicable divorce can temporarily turn the most stable, rational human being into an unreasonable, pseudo-psychotic wreck. Knowing that divorce is difficult and navigating through those difficulties without becoming a raving lunatic are two entirely different things. You can know in your head that you need to respond calmly and rationally to your spouse's demands, and still find that after thirty seconds of what you had intended to be a mature conversation, your spouse has pushed every button you have, and the two of you are locked into the same fight you've had a hundred times over the life of your marriage. The key to changing your reaction and changing the course of your divorce is to change your own attitude first. Once you do that, either your spouse will also change in response to the difference that exists in you, or your spouse won't change and you'll just be able to handle him or her better. Either way, you come out ahead.

Perspective

Changing your attitude isn't easy. We all see life in our own particular way. As anyone who has ever investigated an accident will tell you, if you question ten people who witnessed the same event about what they saw, you will get ten different versions of what happened. We all see what we want or what we expect to see, and we filter out the facts that are inconsistent with our view of the world. This is even more true when our *reality filters* are clouded with the emotions that arise in a divorce. The paradox is that the more emotionally clouded your viewpoint is, the more emotionally difficult your divorce will be. The first key to maintaining your sanity is to maintain your perspective.

Webster's Dictionary defines *perspective* as "the faculty of seeing all the relevant data in a meaningful relationship." Certainly, nothing could be more crucial during a divorce than being able to see all the relevant data in what was once your very meaningful relationship. Yet, the emotional reactions a divorce triggers almost immediately obscure your ability not only to see the facts around you, but to determine which of those facts are relevant, and then to think clearly enough to put those facts together in any sort of meaningful way.

In order to maintain even a minimal amount of perspective while you're going through a divorce, it is absolutely essential that you understand both the changing nature of your relationship to your spouse and your reaction to it. Even if your immediate pre-divorce relationship left much to be desired, presumably at some point in the past you had a good relationship with your spouse—you did things together, you went places, and you talked. When your marriage began to dissolve, all of that changed. You found that you no longer wanted to go places or do things with your spouse, or your spouse no longer wanted to go places and do things with you. After you filed for divorce, your relationship changed yet again. By that point, not only did you not want to go anywhere with your spouse, but you no longer wanted to see, talk to, or even think about your spouse. Once your divorce is over, your feelings toward your spouse will likely change again.

Once you understand the ways in which your relationship with your spouse is changing, you must then change the way you deal with your spouse and with your relationship, so that you can keep up with those changes. Changing the way you deal with your spouse or your relationship with your spouse, however, requires you to change yourself. For most people, that's scary and very difficult. Most of us don't want to change. We don't like to change. One of the primary reasons we don't like change, whether in ourselves or in someone else, is that we can't control it.

Nowhere are the effects of change, and the lack of control it brings, more obvious than in a divorce. Suddenly you find that your spouse, who couldn't manage to stay up long enough to watch the nightly news before you filed for divorce, is now out until the wee hours of the morning—and there's nothing you can do about it.

It's not just your spouse you can't control—for awhile, you can't seem to control anything. Your kids are acting out and you're worried sick that they are going to be scarred for life by everything you do. You can't go places or buy things the way that you used to because money has become incredibly tight. Many of the people you used to count as friends are either taking sides or staying away. Nothing is the same, and quite frankly, you're no longer sure you can control the family pet, let alone anything else in your life. How well you react to these changes determines both how easily you will get through your divorce and how well you will adapt to your new life thereafter.

Your Attitude Colors Everything Else:
The Story of Tamela and Mickey

Tamela was a meek, quiet woman who married Mickey, a blustering brute of a man, when she was only 18. Tamela loved Mickey, and paid no attention to his overbearing, boastful behavior—until one day, she found that he had secretly gambled away their retirement accounts. Then, Tamela snapped.

Tamela threw Mickey out of the house, refused to let him see their kids, and immediately filed for divorce. Convinced that Mickey was going to gamble away their fortune, she had her attorney freeze every asset they had, including Mickey's business accounts, which made it nearly impossible for him to keep working. By the time Mickey's lawyer was able to free up enough of the assets to enable Mickey to make a living, his business was in trouble.

Mickey might have been a gambler, but he wasn't a bad guy. He admitted he had a problem, started counseling, went to Gamblers Anonymous, and tried his best to make amends—but Tamela wouldn't give him a chance. She refused to let him near her or the children. What's more, she made sure the children didn't want to be near him. She told them that they'd better work hard and get good grades, because their daddy had gambled away all their money and they probably wouldn't be able to go to college now. She told them that, from now on, they had to survive without Mickey.

Mickey eventually got to see his children, but his relationship with them was never the same. Meanwhile, once word got out about his gambling problem (which Tamela made sure happened), Mickey's struggling business took a complete nosedive. By the time they divorced, Tamela got about one-tenth of what she and Mickey had shared while they were married. Plus, their kids were a mess, Tamela was a nervous wreck, and the family ended up losing the house.

Tamela and Mickey's divorce was ugly right from the start. By gambling away their retirement fund, Mickey shattered Tamela's confidence in him. However, by not separating Mickey's addiction from his good qualities—as a father, as a businessman, and as an otherwise decent human being—Tamela made the situation between them one hundred times worse. Of course, Tamela refused to accept her role in the situation, and instead blamed Mickey for everything. What she didn't see was that his gambling destroyed their marriage, but her vindictiveness and lack of perspective destroyed the rest of their lives.

Getting Past the Obstacles that Make You Lose Perspective

It's never easy to maintain your perspective when you're in a difficult and emotional situation. Divorce is nothing if not difficult and emotional. However, you can still maintain your perspective during and after a divorce if you take the time to understand both what makes you lose your perspective and how to get it back.

The first obstacle to maintaining your perspective is mistrust. Because marriage is such an intimate relationship, trust is an integral part of it. When a marriage starts to fail, trust is usually one of the first casualties. Suddenly, you feel that the very person with whom you once shared your most intimate secrets is unfit to view your weekly pay stub— even though it is exactly the same as the last fifty pay stubs you received, and your spouse knows it. You become suspicious of everything your spouse says or does. You search every seemingly ordinary action, discussion, or decision your spouse makes for a hidden agenda. You find yourself transformed from a loving couple into a pair of people who each act like the other just walked out of a Tom Clancy novel.

Mistrusting your spouse is understandable and very often well-founded. Divorce often involves betrayal, and it's difficult to trust someone who just stabbed you in the back (or who you think just stabbed you in the back). However, trust is the cornerstone of effective communication. Unless you establish at least a base level of common ground from which you and your spouse can work to wrap up the details of your divorce, the process is going to be a nightmare. If you have children together, unless you and your spouse can maintain at least a minimal level of communication, not only will getting through your divorce be difficult, but living the rest of your life in peace will be impossible.

At this point you are probably thinking, "What? Trust my spouse? After all that's happened? You've got to be crazy!" Admittedly, in some cases, trusting your spouse would be crazy. However, before you make yourself paranoid thinking that everything your spouse says or does involves an ulterior motive, take a good, hard look at what you know to be true of your spouse, what you no longer know to be true, and what you just plain don't know. Your spouse may be acting erratically toward you while still maintaining a solid, stable, loving relationship with your children. Or, your spouse may have abandoned both you and the children in search of a second childhood or an extramarital affair, but is still faithfully upholding his or her financial obligation and is paying for the children's expenses. Look at the facts. See what's there. Test the waters. If your spouse says he or she is going to pay the bills on time, give him or her a chance and see if it gets done. If it gets done, great. If not, then you can insist on having more control in managing the finances. However, to act before there is a problem and to assume that your spouse will not fulfill his or her obligations before he or she even has the opportunity to do so only causes resentment.

It's important at this point to distinguish between establishing a base level of trust with your soon-to-be former spouse and being a complete dupe. It's all well and good to say you shouldn't be suspicious of every little thing your spouse says and does. It's quite another thing to give your spouse the benefit of every doubt when the facts in front of your face and the voice of common sense in your head are telling you otherwise. If you walk into the living room and find the expensive painting that once adorned your wall is gone but nothing else has been touched, it is irrational to assume you were just burglarized by a thief with very good taste in art. It is just as ridiculous to believe your spouse's story that he or she suddenly decided to get the picture reframed, but, not to worry, it will be back in a few weeks. Neither of those explanations makes sense. At the same time, it doesn't make sense to question whether your spouse really just walked the dog when he or she has only been gone for ten minutes and there's mud on his or her shoes. You need to navigate between carefully analyzing the facts as they are and acting like you are in a relationship with a counterintelligence agent.

The loss of trust that occurs in divorce also creates another obstacle to maintaining your perspective. It is called the *personalization of reality*. That's the term that describes the tendency of people who are going through a divorce to see everything their spouse does in every instance as being motivated by the desire to hurt, aggravate, lie to, hide from, or otherwise get back at them. Just like chronically mistrusting spouses, those who personalize reality see the world through slightly paranoid glasses. They are suspicious of everything their spouse does, says, or thinks. Objective reality, as the rest of the world knows it, does not exist for them. People who are suffering from the personalization of reality literally view everything that happens during (and sometimes even after) their divorce as having been caused, controlled, or at the very least influenced by their spouse, regardless of whether or not that's true.

IT'S NOT ALWAYS ABOUT YOU: THE STORY OF JERRY AND SUE

Jerry, a businessman and father, lived in Illinois. His ex-wife, Sue, and daughter, Cherise, lived in New York. Cherise was scheduled to fly to Chicago to spend a weekend with Jerry not too long after September 11, 2001. Needless to say, Sue was extremely reluctant to put Cherise on a plane flying out of New York at that particular point in time. Instead of understanding that the world had changed, and postponing or rescheduling his visitation so that Cherise wouldn't have to be on an airplane in such turbulent times, Jerry became outraged. In his mind, Sue's concern over flying Cherise to Chicago was merely a pretext for her to keep Jerry from spending time with his daughter. Jerry rushed into court to demand that the judge order Sue to put their child on a plane at a time when most adults in this country were afraid to fly. Needless to say, the judge did not share Jerry's view, and Cherise stayed home.

Like Jerry, it's not unusual for you to personalize reality when you are going through a highly charged, emotional time. Once someone you love betrays you, the pain and mistrust you feel runs deep and lasts a long time. When you and your spouse become locked into a game of *an eye for an eye*, after awhile you probably have very good reasons for thinking that your spouse is purposely doing things to hurt or undermine you. While that kind of thinking may be realistic in some cases, it is more often caused by an overabundance of suspicion than it is by a spouse who is truly bent on exacting vengeance in every circumstance. What's more, if you believe that everything your spouse does is aimed at making your life miserable, you will create and perpetuate a relationship of fear and mistrust that not only will affect your own life and your own perspective, but the lives of your children and all of those around you.

The final, and perhaps the biggest, obstacle to maintaining your perspective while you're going through a divorce is the sheer emotionality of the whole process. One minute you hate your spouse, the next you're worried that you still love him or her. One minute you're not sure you're doing the right thing, the next you're so frustrated with your spouse that you want to pull every hair out of your head. You're on an emotional roller coaster, and it's hard to maintain your perspective when the world around you is spinning. To make it stop, you need to remember the universal laws.

You are responsible for your own life. You choose how to act and react. You need to keep your own emotions under control in order to be able to clearly see what's really going on around you. You can't possibly maintain your perspective when you're swirling around in a rage that would put a Tasmanian devil to shame. You can't see the wonderful opportunities for creating a new life that are opening up to you if you're stuck wallowing in self-pity over the fact that your marriage failed. Get over it! Take control of yourself and start to reframe your perspective.

Maintaining your perspective is always easier if you have someone else around who can act as your reality check. Maybe it's a counselor, a family member, or a good friend. No matter who it is, it helps to be able to talk to someone outside your situation to see if that person thinks you are justified in being so mad or if you're overreacting. Of course, in order to be a good reality checker, whoever you choose has to be somewhat independent and unemotional. If your sister starts foaming at the mouth every time you mention your ex's name, perhaps she wouldn't be the best person to give you a fair, unbiased view of your ex-spouse's behavior when your ex does something that makes you lose control. Try to choose someone who has a good head on his or her shoulders and will tell you the truth—not just what you want to hear.

Understanding Limitations Keeps Things in Perspective

Another key to keeping life in perspective during your divorce is understanding the limitations of everyone and everything involved— you, your spouse, and the institution of divorce. Divorce is about change, but there are some things divorce will never change. If your life was a mess before you were divorced, recognize that, while losing your spouse may be a step forward in getting it back on track (if your spouse was actually part of your problem), it doesn't ensure that everything will be wonderful and you will instantly be happy the minute the gavel comes down and the judge pronounces your marriage dissolved. If your spouse was obsessive or abusive during your marriage, don't expect him or her to be any less so during—or even after—your divorce. If you think that a court of law is the place to go to fix all the problems you have with your spouse and your children—not to mention your finances and your lifestyle—think again. Everything has its limits.

The first set of limitations you must recognize is your own. You are human. Divorce is emotional. There are going to be times when you're a wreck. There are going to be times when you reach levels of anger and frustration you never knew existed. There are even going to be times when you do some really stupid things. Accept that. Instead of trying to push yourself past your limits or pretending that you're in control when you're about to burst into more pieces than a supernova, give yourself a break. Get a baby-sitter for the evening and spend some time alone or with friends, or go watch a good movie. (Although you should probably stay away from anything romantic unless you're a true masochist.) Join a gym or read a book. Do something—anything—that clears your head and restores your perspective.

Another helpful hint for dealing with your own limitations is to enlist the aid of your friends and family—form your own support group. It doesn't need to be formal and it doesn't need to be big. It just needs to be supportive. Surround yourself as much as possible with people who are positive and optimistic—people who care about you and are willing to help you through the painful process of divorce. They can be relatives, friends, or professional counselors. However, there is one group of people you do not want to have in your support group—your spouse's relatives.

It may sound obvious that your spouse's relatives do not belong in your personal divorce support group. However, you would be amazed at the number of people who feel closer to their in-laws or their spouse's siblings than they do to their own family. Before you spill your guts to one of your spouse's relatives, though, remember—

blood is thicker than water. You may think that's just a cliché. You may think it doesn't apply to you. Don't fool yourself—it does. When push comes to shove, almost everyone will stand with their family—even if they admit their family doesn't deserve it. While your in-laws may love you dearly and think their own child is a complete disgrace, their child is their child, and you are an outsider. So when you're selecting supporters and confidants, don't choose someone who is related to your spouse.

Once you have established your support group, you can use your supporters not only for emotional support, but also to provide a reality check when you're not sure you're seeing the facts clearly yourself. When your child comes home from visitation and gushes to you about how cool your ex's new significant other is, and your ex had promised you he or she wouldn't introduce the kids to the new squeeze until after the divorce was final, talk to your friends and get their perspective, before you rip your ex's throat out. Work through your emotions and take a little time to cool down. Then, when you're calmer and you can think clearly, decide what to do.

You will notice that, implicit in the scenario outlined, there are several unspoken, yet critical, elements—time, thought, and decision. Nothing will cause you to blast through the limitations of your good behavior faster than reacting to an emotionally charged situation in the heat of the moment without thinking about what's really best for everyone involved. When your spouse does something that pushes your buttons, stop. Breathe. Count to ten (a hundred, if you need to). Don't react right away. Instead, take the time you need to think about what has happened, and then decide what to do. That might not feel as good as reading your spouse the riot act, but it will probably be considerably more productive.

You also need to recognize your financial limitations. While you are going through a divorce, and for a considerable period of time thereafter, your lifestyle is not going to be what it was when you were married. You are taking the income that used to support one household and stretching it to support two. Obviously, your standard of living is going to suffer. You can either accept that fact and try to live within your new means until life gets better, or you can ignore it and fall deeper into debt—it's your choice.

The concept of choice in the context of a dissolving family's finances is one that many people have a difficult time understanding, especially if they weren't the ones who wanted a divorce in the first place. It is far easier to blame your soon-to-be ex-spouse for the decline in your standard of living, rather than admit that you, too, played a role in your present situation, and more importantly, that you are free to choose how to react to it. It's even tougher when you see your children's standard of living suffer. There may not be enough money to keep them in private school, summer camp, or music lessons. Before you launch into a tirade against your spouse—particularly one that your children might overhear—think about what you have, what you need, and what you can do to get through these tough times.

Instead of blaming and alienating your ex-spouse for the financial pinch you have to live with while you're going through your divorce, see if you can't sit down and work with him or her to create a plan that will optimize everyone's lifestyle, given the money that's available to go around. Make a budget. List your income and expenses, and have your spouse do the same. Then, compare the two budgets. You may be surprised, once you do that, to see that both of you are wasting money on things that you don't consider to be high priorities, and that, with a little creativity, you can stretch what you have in ways that at least come closer to meeting everyone's needs. (To learn more details about creating a budget, see Chapter 7.)

Creating a budget is a practical exercise that not only helps you recognize your own financial limitations, but can also enlighten you about your spouse's limitations as well. This is particularly important in a divorce, when concerns over your personal survival generally outweigh any thoughts of your spouse's well-being. At some point in the process, everyone going through a divorce thinks their spouse is better off than they are. For most people, getting divorced means learning (or relearning) to survive on their own—a prospect that can be as overwhelming as it is scary. Everyone is afraid they won't have enough money to make it, and no one wants to be responsible for supporting someone to whom they are no longer attached. Regardless of which side of the support equation you find yourself on (the supporter or the supportee), you can't help but wonder if the person on the other side is really suffering as much as you are. In the end, it is the suffering—not the money—that's the real motivator.

No one wants to suffer, much less to suffer alone—especially if you believe that the person responsible for your suffering is living on easy street. Either consciously or not, you do whatever you can to ensure not only that you are okay, but that you are *really* okay. You go for the extra cushion and pad your budget just so that you don't have to live quite as frugally as you want your spouse to think you have to live. You want to make sure you don't have to suffer, while secretly hoping that your spouse does. The problem with divorce is that, while you're going through it, everyone suffers. Not everyone does so visibly, but everyone feels the emotional and financial strain of divorce in some way. Expecting your spouse to either pay you buckets of money or to agree not to ask you for money when he or she is incapable of paying the bills without your support is not realistic. What's more, the law in your state may regulate the amount of support that you either have to give or are entitled to receive in a way that you don't think is fair. If you understand and can accept your spouse's and your own financial limitations, as well as what the law requires for support, you will be a long way toward accepting reality. Once you accept reality, then you can start looking at realistic ways to change and improve it.

Not only do you need to be aware of your spouse's financial limitations in your divorce, but you also need to understand your spouse's emotional limitations as well. It is unrealistic for you to expect your spouse not to be hurt, not to be angry, and not to lash out at you from time to time. You can't expect your ex to admit that he or she was wrong, to confide in you about his or her new life, or to treat you with anything warmer than polite civility while your case is still pending in court, no matter how amicable your divorce may be. Emotions, just like everything else in this world, have their limits.

Another limitation you need to understand is the limitation of time. No matter how hard you try, you often cannot control the timing of your divorce. Believe it or not, divorce cases have a natural rhythm that flows through them until they're done. That rhythm is influenced by the court system and the court rules, but it exists independently of the law. It's more of an emotional rhythm than a legal one. That rhythm is created by all of the various people involved in a divorce, including the lawyers and the judge. It is created by a combination of their needs, their emotions, their personalities, and their workloads. You are only one part of your case, and only one of the many people who create the flow of your case. This means that you alone cannot control how fast or slow things happen in your divorce. You can influence the pace of your divorce, but you can't necessarily control it.

Getting divorced is like dealing with death—you need to go through many stages before you can accept and adjust to what's happening in your life. You need to grieve. You need to mourn the loss of your relationship and create a new identity for yourself as a single person—and so does your spouse. Unfortunately, you and your spouse probably won't go through that process at the same speed. As a matter of fact, in all likelihood, one of you (usually the person who files for divorce) will have already mourned the relationship and moved on before the other one realizes that the marriage is really over. That creates an automatic timing problem—one person is ready to race through the process and into a new life, while the other is still trying to adjust to the idea that he or she is getting divorced.

What's the best way to deal with this inherent pacing problem? Be patient. If you have already dealt with the emotional pain of ending your marriage, but your spouse still wants to patch things up, try letting him or her be instead of pushing your spouse to get divorced quickly. Give him or her some breathing room. So what if it takes you an extra six months to get divorced? If giving your spouse the time he or she needs to work through emotional issues means that the two of you can settle your divorce amicably instead of going through the *War of the Roses*, isn't that a better choice? In the long run, your divorce will probably take about the same amount of time anyway, so you might as well go with the flow rather than beating your head against a wall.

When dealing with a timing problem, it helps to step out of yourself for a moment and put yourself in your spouse's shoes. If you were the one who needed more time to resolve things, wouldn't you be grateful that your spouse gave it to you? Treating your spouse the way you would want to be treated (even if you don't think your spouse deserves it) will go a long way towards making your own life, and your future, much easier. On the other hand, if you are the slower spouse, you also need to understand that there is a limit to anyone's patience. If you need to get counseling to help you through the process, then do it. If you need to separate your finances and learn to run your own budget, or maybe get a better-paying job, then do it—but do it quickly. Remember, even though you may have your own emotional processing to do, you still need to respect your spouse's need to move on with his or her life.

The limitations you must acknowledge while going through a divorce extend not only to you and your spouse, but also to the institution of divorce itself. Contrary to how you may feel or what you may want, getting a divorce does not and cannot right all of the wrongs that you feel were done to you during your marriage. What's done is done. For the most part, it doesn't matter who made the most money, who ran up the biggest bills, or who had the extramarital affair. What matters is what exists right now. You, your spouse, your lawyers, and the judge can only deal with the facts as they are at that moment. The court system, too, has its limitations.

Understanding the limits of the court system is not nearly as difficult as you might think. The first thing that you need to remember when dealing with the court system is that it is a giant system governed by very specific rules. You either need to know what the rules are, or preferably, find an attorney who knows them for you. While you have an absolute right to represent yourself, you don't have the right to ask the judge, the court clerk, or your spouse's attorney to educate you about the rules and your rights. If you own nothing, want nothing, and have nothing your spouse wants, you can probably muddle through the legal system on your own. However, if you have children, if you own anything of value, or if you have a spouse who is itching for a fight, you need a lawyer. Proceeding without one will not only tax your own limitations, it will stress the entire court system's limitations as well.

The next thing you need to keep in mind is that the court is not a self-motivating machine. If you have a problem you want to address, you must bring it to the court's attention. Until you do, the judge doesn't know the problem exists. If your spouse left you five years ago and you never bothered to file for child support during that time, don't complain to the court that your deadbeat spouse hasn't paid you a penny while you've been struggling to raise the kids alone. You didn't raise the issue five years ago, so there was nothing for the judge to address. What's more, not only do you have to raise an issue before the judge in order to get it resolved, but you must also present evidence to support your position. You can't expect the judge to believe that everything you say is true just because you said it. You need receipts to prove what you paid for. You need tax returns to prove what you earned. The judge doesn't have a crystal ball, and cannot know what you made or what you paid for unless you bring proof.

Another limitation of the judicial system is that, theoretically at least, judges have to follow the law. This means that even if living with your spouse qualified you for sainthood, you are only going to get from your spouse what the law says you are entitled to receive. For example, if you supported your spouse for years because you thought he or she was going to come into a big inheritance someday, and the ingrate filed for divorce before his or her parents died, you are not entitled to receive 100% of the marital assets and a future piece of the inheritance just because you suffered through all those years while your spouse was poor. You are also not being cheated out of *your* inheritance just because your spouse is divorcing you—it's not your money, and it never was. Staying married was your choice. You are responsible for living your life and making your choices.

A final judicial limitation worth noting is that courts are places for resolving legal disputes—they are not social service agencies, counseling centers, or crisis management facilities. If you and your spouse can't agree on what day it is and you expect the judge to negotiate a perfect settlement for you, you're being unrealistic. If both you and your spouse insist on irritating each other by doing whatever you want regardless of what the judge says, don't expect the judge to be impressed with either person's behavior. If you think that the court is going to supervise every detail of your children's parenting just because you and your spouse can't even be in the same room together, let alone talk about the kids, think again. Everything has limitations. The sooner you accept that, the saner you will be during your divorce.

4

The Universal Laws
and the Litigation Process

The law isn't justice. It's a very imperfect mechanism. If you press exactly the right buttons and are also lucky, justice may show up in the answer. A mechanism is all the law was ever intended to be.

—Raymond Chandler, Author

He who would not go to hell must not go to court.

—Proverb

Stepping into a divorce court is a little like falling down the rabbit hole—just like Alice, you feel like you've entered a different world. The court rules are arbitrary, the laws aren't written the way you think they should be, and the judge's rulings don't always make sense. You don't understand how the system works, why everything takes so long, and why you can never get a straight answer from your lawyer whenever you ask what you think is a fairly simple question. Welcome to Wonderland!

As frustrating as getting through the court system may be, you can navigate your way to the end of your case with much more ease—and much less grief—once you understand a little bit about the law and the court system. However, since each state has its own set of divorce laws, and each court system has its own set of rules, explaining the details of every state's divorce laws and the manner in which each court system across the country works is well beyond the scope of this book. To really understand the laws of your state and the court system in your area, you need to discuss your case with a qualified divorce attorney who practices in the county in which you live. However, since every state has now adopted some form of no-fault divorce law, it is important that you understand, before you get divorced, what *no-fault* really means.

The Reality of No-Fault Divorce

Most people think they know what no-fault divorce means. They are familiar with the term *irreconcilable differences*, which lies at the heart of no-fault divorce, and they believe that if they get divorced based upon irreconcilable differences, they can end their marriage for any reason they want, including the fact that they simply they don't get along. While that is generally true, the concept of no-fault divorce means much more than that. (It is only *generally* true because each state has its own specific requirements regarding how much time you must live apart from your spouse, as well as other requirements, in order to qualify to get a divorce based upon irreconcilable differences. In order to understand the law in your state, you need to consult with your own attorney.)

No-fault divorce not only means that you can now get divorced without having to prove that anyone was at fault in causing your marriage to end, but it also means that marital misconduct no longer counts when you're dividing marital property or awarding support. It doesn't matter if your spouse lied, cheated, stole, or did any one of a hundred other horrible things to you during your marriage. He or she is still going to be awarded a fair share of the marital assets when you divorce. If he or she is not self-supporting, you will probably be ordered to pay spousal support in some amount for some period of time—no matter what your spouse did to you, and regardless of whether you like it or not.

It's not surprising that once people understand that *no-fault* means that the laws will be fair to both of the parties in a divorce, regardless of who caused the marriage to dissolve, they don't like it. The idea of having to give half of your marital assets to, or having to support, the person who just ruined your life, destroyed your family, and betrayed your trust, somehow seems wrong. Yet, before no-fault laws existed, divorces were often even uglier and far more dangerous than they are today.

When *fault* mattered in a divorce, people spent small fortunes on private investigators trying to accumulate evidence to prove their spouse was unfaithful, just so their spouse wouldn't get alimony or a fair share of the marital property in the divorce. You can imagine the chaos that occurred when a private investigator burst into a room to catch a cheating spouse in the act of cheating. Not only was doing that sort of thing ugly and sleazy, but it was also dangerous—when a private investigator broke down the door with a camera in hand, the people inside the room weren't exactly happy about it. Tempers flared, fights broke out, and bad things happened to lots of people.

When spouses stood to gain a lot of money just by proving their divorce was not their fault, getting divorced became an enormous chess game in which spouses who were willing to do whatever it took to prove (or make it look like) their spouses were rotten human beings, and who had the money to fuel that kind of insanity, won their cases. Those who didn't have access to money, or who chose not to destroy their spouses and their families just for the sake of gaining an advantage in their divorce, lost. What's more, during a divorce, both spouses would routinely ruin each other's reputations and each other's lives by alleging in court records (which are public documents) that their spouse was a drug addict, a compulsive gambler, an abuser, or was guilty of some other kind of horrible act that provided grounds for divorce. Even if the allegations weren't true, just by making the allegations the damage was often done. In fact, people had to make those kinds of allegations in order to be able to get divorced in the first place. If one spouse wasn't at fault in causing the marriage to fail, neither one of them could get divorced. Even in the most amicable of divorces, one spouse was forced to make up a story about how the other spouse had done something that gave him or her grounds for divorce. At some point, making people go through that kind of craziness just to get divorced simply didn't make sense anymore. At that point, the laws changed.

Divorce 101—Your Case from Filing to Judgment

Understanding a little bit about divorce law is not the only important piece of legal information you need to know in order to get through your divorce sanely. You also need to know something about the litigation process. Again, while each jurisdiction may be slightly different, cases generally follow the same basic pattern.

A divorce case starts when you file a *Petition for Dissolution of Marriage* or a *Complaint for Divorce* in court. After you have filed the Petition, the sheriff (or some other appropriate person) must then serve your spouse with the Petition and with a *Summons*, which requires your spouse to appear in court and answer the Petition by a certain date. On or before that date, your spouse or your spouse's attorney needs to appear in court and file a response to your Petition. If your spouse fails to appear and ignores your Petition, you may then get a default judgment against him or her. If your spouse does appear, then the case begins its normal course through the court system.

The two most intense periods in most divorce cases are the beginning and the end. In the beginning, one party has to take the initiative to start the case. That means either you or your spouse has to stop talking about a divorce and has to actually do something to get the process started. However, for some reason, no matter how much you and your spouse may have talked about, screamed about, or threatened each other with getting a divorce, when one of you actually files for divorce, the other is often shocked. Even if the divorce itself was no surprise, there is something about seeing in writing that your spouse wants to divorce you that suddenly makes the situation real. Because of the shock and the reality of the situation, emotions tend to run very high when a divorce first begins. You suddenly find yourself committed to a path that feels very strange—even though it may have been what you've wanted for years. Maybe because of the strangeness or shock, you suddenly see your spouse differently. No longer is he or she just your spouse. He or she is now the other party in a lawsuit against you.

Being involved in a lawsuit with another person immediately makes you distrust that person. The American legal system is an adversarial system—that means there are two sides to every case, and one side opposes the other. Even if you and your spouse agree on everything in your divorce, as far as the court system is concerned, you are opponents. Being legal opponents makes you feel like real opponents, and the reality of being in a case against each other makes you instantly distrust each other in a way you may not have done before. Unfortunately, that distrust causes nothing but problems, and often contributes to changing what started as an amicable divorce into a fight of epic proportions.

If your spouse reacts poorly to your divorce right from the start, you may find that you need to immediately go to court to ask the judge to protect you, freeze your assets, or order your spouse to provide you with enough money to keep you and your children from starving. If your spouse starts playing games with your money, or erupts violently against you or the children the minute you file for a divorce, then like it or not, you need to go to court and deal with the situation immediately—no matter how much you wish that everything would just work out so you could be done with your divorce right away. If, for example, you find that your spouse has left you high and dry, and you don't have enough money to pay your bills and put food on the table, don't wait until the house has gone into foreclosure or your creditors are hauling you into court in a collections case before you tell your lawyer there's a problem. Take care of it right away. Courts are notoriously slow, so if you have a problem now, or you see that you are going to have a problem soon, don't wait until you are in a crisis to bring it to the judge's attention.

Once you've made it through the initial craziness at the beginning of the case, you will probably settle into what seems to be a whole lot of nothing going on. You may have to file discovery responses of some sort—financial disclosure statements, income and expense affidavits, or answers to written *interrogatories* (questions). You may have to produce reams of financial paperwork from years past or appear for a deposition. If you are like most people, you're probably going to be wondering why you have to go through all of this nonsense and why your spouse's attorney insists on making you jump through more hoops than a circus lion just to get a divorce. You also may be wondering why everything you do seems to take so long. Don't despair! Divorce is a process, and unless you and your spouse can agree to work things out, you may have to experience every step of the process in order to get through it. On the other hand, if you and your spouse have both had enough (because your spouse will probably have to answer all the same discovery requests that you have to answer), there is nothing to stop the two of you from coming to terms and working out a deal so that both of you can stop the insanity. As a matter of fact, that's often exactly what happens.

The second most difficult time in the course of a divorce case comes at the very end. By the time you've been fighting for a couple of years, everyone is tired, angry, and fed up with the whole process. Sometimes this works to your advantage, and you may find that your spouse wants to be done so badly that he or she is willing to agree to things he or she never would have agreed to in the beginning. The same thing may be true of you. When you're tired and frustrated, and you just want to get on with your life, you may suddenly find that the things you thought were so important in the beginning of your case just don't matter that much anymore. So you give in a little, your spouse gives in a little, and you settle—in principle.

Most people assume that once they agree with their spouse on the basic terms of the settlement, their case is done and they can just walk into court and get it over with. Unfortunately, that's not how the system works. Even if you agree with your spouse in principle, until the terms of your agreement are written down, signed, and approved by the court, you don't really have an agreement at all. At any step along the way your agreement can explode. Either what's in writing isn't what you thought you had agreed to—or you think what's in writing is fine, but your lawyer disagrees or your spouse changes his or her mind before the deal is sealed—and you have to start from scratch. That's when the real fireworks start.

While time can work in your favor at the end of your case, it can also work against you. The longer your case drags on, the more time you and your spouse have to aggravate each other, and the more your patience wears thin. You push each other's buttons, drive each other crazy, and sometimes one of you crosses a line. When that happens, the person who just got pushed too far often becomes angry, irrational, and no longer willing to make a deal—at all. If that person, be it you or your spouse, has enough time to cool down, sometimes you can still pick up the pieces of your agreement—but sometimes you cannot. Sometimes, the explosion is so huge or it happens so close to your trial date that there is no time to cool down and no way to turn back, so you go to trial and let the chips fall where they may. Sometimes that's your only choice—and sometimes it's your best choice—but, most of the time, it's a bad choice. No matter what, it is always—*always*—a risky choice.

The Realities of Litigation

Litigation is expensive. It takes a long time, it costs a lot of money, and it causes you and your family untold amounts of grief and aggravation.

In the beginning of your divorce, you may be so angry with your spouse that you are willing to fight to the death over every penny you have. However, once you start getting bills from your attorney, you will soon realize that if you keep fighting with your spouse, it won't matter who wins because the only people who will have anything once the case is over is the lawyers. You may also realize that even though your spouse is cheating you in the divorce and hiding income or assets that you know exist, if you insist on fighting about it, you will spend three times as much in accountants' and lawyers' fees as what you will gain in income or assets. What's more, none of that begins to describe the emotional turmoil that you have to live through when you're constantly fighting with your spouse, both in and out of court.

Most people underestimate the emotional cost of a bitter divorce. Nothing rips up your insides faster than being stuck in a major court battle for years at a time. Either you can't eat at all or you're constantly stuffing yourself with food, you can't fall asleep or sleeping is all you want to do. You're stressed, you're exhausted, and you feel really lousy most of the time. In short, your divorce makes you sick—and the longer it drags on, the worse you feel.

Everyone knows that divorces can take a long time, but most people don't believe that their divorce will take a long time. However, there is one truism about divorce that applies to everyone—divorce always takes longer and costs more than you ever imagined. Even if your divorce is fairly amicable and you and your spouse are able to work out an agreement on everything, it can still take months to get through the process. If you and your spouse insist on fighting—and you actually have something to fight about—your divorce can easily go on for years. Even if you don't have anything to fight about, but you and your spouse still can't seem to reach an agreement, your divorce can go on for years. Due process and the principles of fundamental fairness require that every party to a case has enough time to fully develop and present his or her side. What's more, in many cities, courts are overcrowded and overburdened. When you put all that together, you'll find that if you want to fight, even the simplest case can take a very long time.

How to Fight Forever Over Nothing: The Story of Laura and Evan

Evan and Laura had been married for less than a year when Evan decided to call it quits. He and Laura had no children, few assets, and nothing to fight about. Unfortunately, Evan had left the house without taking the motorcycle his parents had given him for a wedding gift, as well as a few other sentimental items. Meanwhile, Laura, who had been supporting Evan while he went to school, was angry because she had refinanced her house before the marriage and had used a portion of the money she received from the refinance to pay for Evan's tuition and buy him a used car. Laura refused to return Evan's motorcycle to him, claiming that, as a wedding gift, she was entitled to half of it. She also refused to give him anything else from the house until he paid back the money she paid for his tuition and gave the car she bought for him back to her. Evan thought Laura was being absurd—the motorcycle was his personal gift from his parents. He also hadn't asked Laura to buy his car—that was her idea. It had been her gift to him—a gift she gave him even before they were married. As for the tuition, Laura never mentioned that it was a loan until after Evan filed for divorce.

Laura and Evan's divorce should have been easy. They really had very little to fight about. But Laura was mad. She didn't want the divorce and thought Evan had given up on their relationship far too easily. She had her lawyer file all kinds of *discovery requests*—written lists of questions about every asset Evan ever had, every debt he ever owed, and every penny he made in the past five years. Answering that discovery wasn't particularly difficult—Evan was 22 years old and owned almost nothing of value.

However, answering took time. Dealing with the lawyers took time. Trying to settle the case took time. Then, when Laura refused to settle, waiting for a trial date took time. When all was said and done, Laura and Evan's divorce—which essentially involved one disputed motorcycle, a beat-up old car, $8,000 in tuition expenses, and a few family photo albums—took almost eighteen months to resolve.

By anyone's estimation, Evan and Laura's case went on for seventeen months longer than it should have. They had nothing to fight about, yet they fought anyway. Because they fought, their case took time. No matter how angry or frustrated Evan got because the case was dragging on, no matter how many phone calls he made to his lawyer, and no matter how much he tried to push the case along, his case followed its natural course through the system, the same way every other case does—and there was nothing Evan could do to change that.

The Limitations of the Legal System

Not only does fighting in court take longer and cost more than you ever think it should, but many times you go through years of agony only to lose in the end. Of course, nobody in the heat of battle really thinks he or she is going to lose. Most people believe that they are right, their spouse is wrong, and anyone with half a brain can clearly see that fact. They are so angry with their spouse and so confident that the judge will agree with them that they are eager to have the judge decide their case—until the judge makes a decision they don't like. Then they scream that the judge is biased, the system is unfair, and their lawyer didn't do a good job.

While it's true that there are good judges and bad judges, most family law judges are intelligent, knowledgeable, and reasonably compassionate. They are also human. They hear hundreds of cases a week. They are faced with complex legal and social issues that people expect them to resolve on a moment's notice. They work in the eye of an emotional tornado, and often have a courtroom full of frustrated, angry, and emotionally distraught people. It only stands to reason that even the best judge will sometimes render decisions you don't understand or don't agree with. What's more, while your divorce case may be the only case in your life, it's not the only case in the judge's life. Judges have to decide hundreds—maybe thousands—of cases a year. There is no way they can know even a fraction of the people involved in those cases on any more than the most superficial level. When you ask a judge to decide an issue because you and your spouse can't agree on what time of day it is, let alone anything of substance, you need to understand that you are asking a complete stranger to decide issues that may dramatically affect you and your family for the rest of your lives. Any way you look at it, that's rarely the best choice.

Another problem with letting a judge decide your case is that every issue you bring before the court takes time—usually more time than you think it should take. Most people believe that if their spouse does something that they think is wrong or hurtful—especially when it involves their children—they can run to court any time and immediately get the judge to order their spouse to behave. Unfortunately, that's not how the system works. Judges are busy. Litigants have to wait their turn to be heard. The courts have rules that require you to give a certain number of days' notice to your spouse before you can go to court, unless you have a real emergency. What's more, the judge's definition of what constitutes an emergency may be vastly different from yours. For example, your spouse may tell you the day before your child's birthday that every minute of your child's day has been booked, and you will just have to wait until the weekend to celebrate with your child. Doing that may be wrong, and it may be very disappointing to you and hurtful to your child. However, it is not an emergency, and it's extremely unlikely that a judge is going to allow you to barge into court—ahead of all of the other scheduled cases—and get a ruling on whether you can see your child for a few hours on his or her birthday. As far as the court is concerned, that's just not an emergency.

Americans are brought up to believe that if they have a dispute, the best way to settle it is to go to court. Court TV and legal dramas depict a court system that can deal with almost anything and be entertaining at the same time. Reality, however, is seldom like television. Particularly in the area of family law, there are a lot of things that the courts simply aren't equipped to handle. Courts are not social service agencies. They are not set up to baby-sit your children, make your spouse treat you kindly, or manufacture the money you need to survive. If your finances are a shambles, your children are a mess, and your personal relationships are not working, you don't just need a divorce—you need therapy. The only thing a judge can do is get you divorced, divide your assets, and decide the most basic issues involving your children's welfare. A judge cannot—and will not—fix your life.

The Laws of the Universe and the Reality of the Legal System

Every court operates according to its own rules. Each court follows its own state's laws, and each judge interprets those laws in his or her own unique way. The laws of the universe, however, do not change. Understanding those laws, and remembering them while you are going through your divorce, will help you maintain both your perspective and your sanity.

The first thing you need to acknowledge when you find yourself frustrated with the legal system is that in some way, however great or small, you are responsible for being there. While you may protest that had it not been for some absolutely unforgivable offense your spouse committed, you wouldn't be in divorce court in the first place, that is never the whole truth. The whole truth is that, no matter what your spouse did or didn't do, you played some role in getting yourself to where you are now. Maybe it wasn't as big or as blameworthy a role as your spouse, but it was a role. Once you can admit that and take responsibility for it, you will stop thinking of yourself as a victim, and get yourself to a place where you can once again stand tall and do whatever you need to do to get your life on the right track. However, as long as you continue to blame your spouse for all of your problems, instead of taking responsibility for them and trying to find a solution to them yourself, you will never be able to deal with your problems effectively and move on.

Taking responsibility doesn't just mean admitting that you are in some way responsible for your divorce. It also means acting responsibly while you are going through your divorce, and acting responsibly means acting with self-control. You can control how you act in court. You can control how quickly and to what extent you cooperate with your lawyer and the judge in order to move your case forward, and you can control (to a certain extent) what approach your lawyer takes when handling your case. If you want to settle and your lawyer wants to fight, you can either direct your lawyer to do what you ask or find a new lawyer. You can also control how you react to what your spouse does and what the judge rules. You can control how much you fight with your spouse. What you can't control is your spouse, the judge, or the legal system itself. If you can accept what you can't control, and control what you can, you will be well on your way toward getting through your divorce with your sanity and your integrity intact.

Karma, the last universal law, also plays a role in the court system. Because of the length of time it often takes to develop, it's usually easiest to see karma playing itself out in post-decree cases—those cases that have come back into the court system after the parties have already been divorced. That's when you often see the people who were miserable to their spouses screw up and become miserable themselves. You see the parents who poisoned their children's relationship with their ex back in court, begging their ex for help when their children suddenly develop behavioral problems they can't handle. You see parents back in court fighting over unpaid child support, fighting for more child support, fighting to pay less child support, fighting over visitation, or just plain fighting. That's when you realize that karma is real—what goes around really does come around. When you see these cases, you understand that resolving your case amicably, and in a way that leaves you and your spouse at least on speaking terms, makes all the sense in the world.

5

Alternatives to Court

He who goes to law for a sheep loses his cow.

—Spanish Proverb

Don't take the bull by the horns, take him by the tail; then you can let go when you want to.

—Josh Billings, Humorist

Even though the American judicial system pits the parties on either side of every lawsuit against each other, there is no rule that requires those parties to keep fighting until one of them keels over in defeat. As a matter of fact, most cases—including most divorce cases—settle. Some settle in court, with the help of a judge who meets with the lawyers and the parties, and tries to broker a deal between the two feuding sides of the case. Others settle out of court, either with the lawyers acting as negotiators for their clients or the clients working out a deal that they can live with themselves in order to avoid going to court. Increasingly, though, formal, out-of-court alternatives for resolving cases have been cropping up all over the country. Called *alternative dispute resolution*, or ADR, these systems provide the parties to a lawsuit with a means to resolve their conflicts outside the courthouse in a way that is faster, more efficient, and less costly than engaging in a lengthy trial. In divorce cases, the most common alternative dispute resolution system is mediation.

Mediation

Mediation is a dispute resolution technique in which a trained mediator sits down with the parties to a conflict and tries to help those parties work out a deal. Mediation is typically voluntary (although courts in some jurisdictions require it) and not binding. If the parties fail to reach an agreement in mediation, they simply return to court. The mediator can not force them to agree to anything.

A mediator is trained in helping people resolve their issues and settle their differences themselves. In the context of divorce or family law issues, the mediator is most often a family lawyer or some type of counselor—either a psychologist or a social worker. The mediator is supposed to be an independent, neutral third party. He or she is supposed to help both parties settle their case themselves. The mediator acts as a facilitator and tries to guide the parties into coming up with creative solutions for resolving their differences. He or she is not supposed to take sides with either party, although during the mediation, it might seem to one of the parties from time to time that the mediator is doing just that. The mediator often plays the role of devil's advocate—arguing for or against something—not to get the parties to do what he or she wants, but to get them to think of both sides of the issue. Often, if the parties can see both sides, they start to see their issues in a new light, and find a way to resolve those issues that leaves everyone as satisfied as possible under the circumstances. (Of course, no one is ever totally happy or completely satisfied with any divorce settlement. A good settlement is not one that makes everyone happy—it's the one that makes everyone the least unhappy.)

A mediator does not—and cannot—decide any of the issues in your case. He or she has no authority to order you or your spouse to do, or not to do, anything. A mediator's only job is to help you and your spouse settle your issues yourselves. If you can't do that, then the mediation fails and you go back to fighting in court. This means that in order for mediation to work, both you and your spouse have to want to participate and must fully cooperate in the mediation process.

Cooperation in mediation means, first and foremost, that you and your spouse need to honestly disclose all of your income, expenses, assets, and liabilities, both to each other and to the mediator. A mediator can't help you divide up your property if he or she doesn't know what you own. A mediator can't help you figure out if both you and your spouse will have enough income to survive after the divorce if he or she doesn't know what each of you earns and spends. A mediator also won't be able to help you calculate the proper amount of child support you should pay or receive without knowing how much money you and your spouse make and what your children need in order to survive. If you or your spouse is reluctant to come clean with accurate financial information, mediation isn't going to work.

Cooperation in mediation also means that both you and your spouse must come to the mediation with the intention of negotiating fairly. Both of you must be prepared to give and take. "I get everything, you get nothing" is *not* negotiation. That's bullying, and it has no place in mediating a fair settlement between equal parties. The same is true for the "it's my way or the highway" style of negotiation. If you aren't willing to give an inch on any issue at all and will only agree to settle if you get everything your way, mediation simply won't work.

The idea that the mediation occurs between two *equal parties* is also important. If you are in a marriage that involved any sort of domestic violence, mediation is not a good choice for you. That applies not just in cases of physical violence, but in marriages were there was verbal abuse as well. You can't mediate a settlement when you're scared to death of the person with whom you're supposed to be cutting a fair deal. If your spouse is constantly yelling at you, calling you names, and making you feel like you're less valuable than a doormat, forget about mediation. You will be far better off, and considerably less stressed-out, if you let your lawyer negotiate a settlement on your behalf.

Finally, in order for mediation to work, both you and your spouse have to want to go to mediation, and you have to want to make a deal with each other. Your attitude in the mediation process is key. If you are so angry that you would just as soon see your spouse boiled in oil as look at him or her, your chances of being able to sit next to him or her in a mediation session and calmly discuss the family finances are not good. If you think your spouse is a liar and a cheat, and doesn't give two hoots and a holler about your kids, you are probably not going to be able to work out the terms of a joint custody arrangement with him or her. You can't mediate with a heart full of hate. You either have to change your attitude or find a different way to resolve your case.

Mediation is not for everyone. Unless both you and your spouse are willing to provide the necessary financial information and openly participate in the process, it won't work. What's more, while mediation typically saves you money in the long run, it usually costs more up front, because the same person cannot be both your mediator and your lawyer. If you and your spouse have anything worth fighting about—children, property, retirement accounts—you're both going to need your own lawyers. The mediator is extra. Now you find you're paying three professionals instead of just two. What you need to understand, however, is that the savings you will reap from a mediated settlement will show up in the long run, and those savings will far outweigh what you pay the mediator to help you negotiate a settlement in the short term.

The reason you save money by using a mediator is that, in mediation, you and your spouse can create a much more flexible agreement—and one that meets more of each of your needs—than anything a judge would ever have ordered. To the extent that you and your spouse can create an agreement you can really live with, rather than a cookie-cutter agreement that your lawyer or the judge recommends, each of you is less likely to go running back to court to change that agreement as your life circumstances change in the future. Staying out of court saves you money.

Mediation can also save you money because the mediator may be able to help you find ways in which both you and your spouse can maximize your incomes or minimize your expenses simply by working together rather than against each other. The mediator may be able to point out tax advantages that both you and your spouse will benefit from if you agree to divide up your income or assets a certain way. The mediator may also force you and your spouse to deal with issues during your divorce that you would have preferred to sweep under the rug until after the divorce. While that might cause you to go through more emotional trauma as you fight out issues you would rather not have discussed, resolving those issues now keeps you from fighting with your spouse about them later. Again, that keeps you from having to go back to court to fight about those issues in yet another long and drawn-out court battle, which in turn saves you money. Finally, just having an agreement that you helped create makes it more likely that you (and your spouse) will abide by the terms of that agreement, rather than treat it like a useless piece of paper.

Mediated agreements tend to last longer than agreements reached after a long, drawn-out court battle in which both parties end up agreeing only because they're too tired (or too broke) to keep fighting. People don't normally need to redo mediated agreements every year or every other year. When they do need to redo them, they can usually work something out amicably with their ex, because mediation tends to preserve, rather than destroy, relationships. Mediation is not adversarial. Going through mediation actually helps to set the stage for your future relationship with your spouse. It helps you find a way to start working together as unmarried partners, rather than as spouses. All in all, even though you may think that you're spending more money on your divorce if you use a mediator, chances are, in the long run, you will really spend less.

In order to succeed in mediation, the most important thing you need to do is find the right mediator. Most of the time, that means finding a trained professional. While your parents, friends, or in-laws may have the best intentions when they offer to try to help you and your spouse work out a deal, using any of these people as your mediator is almost always a bad choice. They are not trained in mediation or negotiation, they are not unbiased, and they are not neutral. Using them as your mediators is a little like letting the wolf guard the hen house.

Whether you should choose a mediator who is a lawyer or one who has a background in psychology or social work depends upon your personal style and what you want to achieve in the mediation process. Typically, a lawyer will write a better settlement agreement—one that both your lawyer and your spouse's lawyer will be more willing to accept—than a social worker would write. However, a lawyer will also not have the same background in dealing with relationship issues that a counselor would have. If you're not good at standing up for yourself, or if you feel intimidated or overwhelmed by your divorce, you may be better off mediating your case with a social worker or psychologist. If you have trouble expressing yourself freely or aren't comfortable asking for what you want in a deal, you may be better off mediating your case with a social worker or psychologist. On the other hand, if you are concerned that you don't know your rights, or you need an agreement that covers all of your bases and is very explicit and well-written, you may be better off mediating your case with a lawyer. No matter what type of professional you choose, the most important thing is to find someone you are comfortable with, and who is qualified and certified to mediate your divorce.

The best mediators, of course, are the ones who have successfully mediated agreements for others in the past. When you are looking for a mediator, don't just open the Yellow Pages or go online. Talk to your friends and talk to divorce lawyers. Contact your local bar association or the Association for Conflict Resolution (**www.acrnet.org**). Do your homework. It will pay off immeasurably in the end.

Arbitration

An *arbitration* is a mini-trial that is held outside of court and in the presence of an arbitrator, who acts as the judge in the case. Typically, both parties in an arbitration are represented by attorneys, yet arbitration is much less formal than a full-blown trial. The court rules are relaxed, the process is streamlined, and consequently, arbitrations take about half as much time as and cost considerably less money than trials. After the arbitration hearing has been held, the arbitrator—who is typically a lawyer or a former judge—renders an opinion and decides the case.

Arbitration can be binding or nonbinding. In *binding arbitration*, the arbitrator's decision is final. It can be recorded in court as a judgment in the case. If one of the parties is unhappy with the decision, he or she may be able to appeal it, but cannot change it. In *nonbinding arbitration*, the arbitrator renders a decision, and if either party doesn't like it, he or she can reject the decision and go back to court.

The difference between arbitration and mediation is that most arbitrations are binding, while most mediations are not. In an arbitration, the arbitrator acts like a judge and decides whatever issues are before him or her. In a mediation, the mediator is simply a facilitator who tries to get the parties to reach an agreement. He or she has no power to order the parties to come to terms, and he or she does not have the authority to decide any of the issues in the case.

Arbitration is used a lot in deciding disputes involving businesses, contracts, and automobile collisions. It is not used very often in divorce cases. The reason is simple—if most people have issues that they can't settle themselves, they would usually rather have a judge decide those issues for them. They don't want or need an arbitrator telling them what to do. What's more, unlike in business contracts, which mandate that certain disputes be resolved by arbitration, there is nothing to force two people in a divorce case to go to arbitration rather than court. Going to arbitration is entirely voluntary. In divorce, unlike in business contracts, there is no automatic method set up for selecting an arbitrator. Obviously, both parties are going to want to pick someone as an arbitrator who they think will be sympathetic to their side. In commercial cases, the same contract that requires the two sides to go to arbitration also sets out the rules for picking an arbitrator. Since no such contract exists in divorce, no set means for selecting an arbitrator exists. Unless both sides agree on who will arbitrate their case, no arbitration can ever take place. Moreover, since arbitration is not often used in divorce cases, there is no ready pool of arbitrators to decide these kinds of cases, which makes arbitrating divorce cases even more difficult and less practical. For all of these reasons, most divorce cases aren't arbitrated.

Even though arbitration is not typically used to resolve divorce cases, there is no reason why it cannot be used. If you and your spouse can agree on an arbitrator and can agree to be bound by the arbitrator's decision, you may be able to proceed with their arbitration hearing in much less time, and with much less expense, than you would in a court case—especially if the courts in the area you live in are crowded. An arbitrator can be used not only to decide an entire case, but just to decide certain isolated issues. For example, if you and your spouse have agreed on all of the terms of a settlement except for one sole issue—say, the issue of whether you should divide your retirement accounts 50/50 or 60/40—you could submit that one question to an arbitrator. The arbitrator's decision could be made a part of your settlement agreement, and you would then be able to complete your entire case in court relatively quickly.

If you want to explore the idea of using an arbitrator to decide some or all of the issues in your case, the first thing you need to do is discuss the idea with your attorney. However, be prepared—most attorneys will balk at this idea. Attorneys are creatures of habit, and they like what's tried and true. They don't usually like doing what's never been done before. For that reason alone, most attorneys would never consider using an arbitrator to resolve anything in a divorce. If either your attorney or your spouse refuses to use an arbitrator for anything, you're done. You cannot force your spouse to participate in arbitration. Unless you and your spouse both agree that you want to arbitrate your divorce, and you both get your lawyers on board with that decision, the arbitration won't happen. If, however, you can get both attorneys to agree on arbitration, then you can resolve your case with this method.

Negotiation

Negotiation is similar to mediation, except it is typically done directly between the parties, their attorneys, or between both the parties and their attorneys in one big settlement conference. It can also be done with the help of a judge in a pretrial conference in court. During such a conference, the judge will get the parties and their attorneys together and will try to negotiate what he or she believes to be a fair settlement in the case. The judge will then try to persuade the parties to resolve their case, either based upon his or her recommendations or upon whatever other terms the parties can agree, without going all the way through trial. The judge acts much like a mediator in this conference, trying to help the parties reach an agreement on their own before trial. Unlike a mediator, however, the judge has the power to decide the case if the parties can't settle it themselves. Therefore, the judge's suggestions for settlement often carry more weight and are more difficult to ignore than a mediator's recommendations would be.

Negotiation is the way that most cases settle. If you and your spouse are on speaking terms and can work through your issues without ripping each other apart, you can negotiate a settlement yourselves. Usually, though, the lawyers are the ones who negotiate a settlement. For many people—particularly those for whom mediation is not an option—letting the lawyers negotiate their case is most often the best choice.

Lawyers are trained to negotiate. They do it every day. Theoretically, at least, they're good at it. They also don't have the same emotional stake in your case that you do. Because of this, they can be much more objective in negotiating a settlement for you than you can be in negotiating a settlement for yourself. After your case is over, your lawyer won't ever have to deal with your spouse again. Your lawyer doesn't care if he or she makes your spouse angry or upset. You, on the other hand, will have to continue to deal with your spouse for years after your divorce. So, while your lawyer is free to negotiate based purely upon logic, reasoning, common sense, and the law, you have to worry about not aggravating your spouse so badly that he or she becomes impossible to deal with for the next ten years. For all of these reasons, it's usually best to let your lawyer handle your negotiations.

If you do decide to negotiate your case directly with your spouse, you should still consult with an attorney first and make sure that you know what the law is, how it applies to you, and what kind of settlement you should be trying to achieve. You need to know what the law considers to be marital property, whether you live in a community property state, how much you should be paying or receiving in child support, and what joint and sole custody really mean. You also need to know what you and your spouse have, what you earn, what you owe, and what you spend. It is absolutely critical that, before you start negotiating with your spouse, you know everything you need to know about the facts and the law so that you can negotiate a settlement that is fair and makes sense.

Collaborative Law

Collaborative law is a new form of alternative dispute resolution that is being used to resolve family law cases. It is, quite simply, a *collaboration* between both of the parties in a divorce case, their attorneys, and whatever other professionals they may need to settle their differences without going to court. In order to participate in a collaborative law setting, both parties and both of their attorneys must agree not to fight in court. If either party does go to court, then the collaborative process ends, both of the parties' attorneys must resign, and each party has to find a new lawyer and start all over again. Both of the parties must also agree to make a full and fair disclosure of all of their assets, liabilities, income, and expenses, as well as any other pertinent information in their case. Both of the parties must be honest with each other, and both must agree to communicate respectfully with one another.

The goal of collaborative law is twofold—to reach an agreement and to stay out of court. To accomplish these goals, the parties can put together a team of professionals, including financial experts, real estate appraisers, mental health professionals, child development experts, and anyone else with whom they may need to consult to obtain information and resolve whatever issues they have. Of course, anyone going through a divorce is also free to hire these types of professionals, even if they are not using the collaborative law process to resolve their case. However, when people are fighting about their case in court, they each typically find and hire their own experts, who (not surprisingly) usually end up giving each party the opinion that supports that party's view of the case. Instead of helping the parties understand their issues and settle their case, the experts usually end up adding fuel to the fire. If the parties are using collaborative law, on the other hand, they work together until they can agree on a single expert, whom they hire together, and who will hopefully give them a fair and unbiased opinion that is within his or her area of expertise.

Once the parties have all of the information they need in their case, they meet together with their attorneys in a series of four-way settlement conferences, in which they try to resolve their issues and settle their case. Collaborative law works in much the same way mediation works, except that instead of both parties meeting with an independent mediator, they meet with each of their lawyers in four-way settlement conferences. During these conferences, everyone negotiates in much the same way as people negotiate in any other case, with one critical difference—no one threatens that if they don't get their way, they'll take the other side to court. Sure, if the parties truly can't reach an agreement they can still go to court and fight just like anyone else, but no one is motivated to do that. Since both attorneys will have to resign if the case goes to court, the attorneys are motivated to try to settle the case. Since both parties have agreed to try to use collaborative law in the first place, presumably, they are also motivated to stay out of court and try to work out their differences on their own. What's more, since both parties know that they will have to hire new lawyers (which will take more time and cost more money) if they decide to start to fight, they are even more motivated to settle their case amicably.

Collaborative law is not appropriate for everyone. It won't work if one person is consistently dishonest, won't provide financial information, or really doesn't want to settle the case. It won't work if one party is afraid of the other, or if either party has been guilty of any type of domestic violence against the other or against the children. It won't work if either of the lawyers is a shark who insists on fighting tooth and nail over every little issue in the case. In most other cases, however, collaborative law is a wonderful alternative to litigation. It focuses on settling issues rather than fighting to the death. It also works better for children, since they are not thrown into the middle of a lengthy court battle. It gives both sides a way to resolve their differences with dignity and integrity. It allows a divorcing couple to maintain the kind of civilized relationship that they will need in order to continue to deal with each other in the future. Overall, while collaborative law won't work in every case, in those cases where it does work, it provides a marvelous alternative to litigating in court.

Counseling

Most people think of counseling as a way to keep their marriage together. They think that counseling is what couples do when they're having problems and they're trying to work them out so that they don't get divorced. They find a good therapist, talk about their issues, and try to get their relationship back on track. Most people do not think that counseling is what couples do when they are already getting divorced or they've already been divorced. However, counseling can help in any of these circumstances.

If you are in the process of divorce, you can choose to go for counseling either to help you get through the process sanely or to try to reconcile with your spouse. If you hire a counselor to help you stay sane, then you just need to find a qualified person with whom you feel comfortable. If you don't want to go to a counselor, you can also hire a *divorce coach*—a person who will give you emotional support and practical advice to get through your divorce—instead of a counselor. Divorce coaches are typically not as highly credentialed as counselors, and are therefore less expensive. However, if you are seriously depressed, angry, or suicidal, or have had any sort of mental health issues in the past, you would be much better off going to a psychiatrist, psychologist, or licensed clinical social worker than you would be by simply consulting with a divorce coach.

If you decide you'd like to try to get back together with your spouse after one of you has already filed for divorce, then you should definitely find a counselor to help you do it. It is virtually impossible for you and your spouse to repair your own relationship without any help from a therapist or counselor after your relationship has fallen apart so badly that you are already in the middle of a divorce. It just doesn't happen. What's more, if you really want to save your marriage, you will probably need to attend counseling for a decent period of time. That having been said, counseling has saved many marriages, and it can definitely work. However, before you go running off to find a counselor, you need to make sure that your spouse really wants to give your marriage another try and is willing to invest the time it will take to do that. You can't make someone want to be married, and you can't stop someone from getting divorced. Instead of spending your time in couples counseling trying to save a relationship your spouse isn't interested in saving, you would be much better off finding a good therapist for yourself and getting on with your own life.

Even if you are not interested in trying to reconcile with your spouse, couples counseling may still help you in a number of ways. For example, if you and your spouse have children together, and you are having problems communicating with each other or working out your parenting issues, going to counseling to establish an effective and nonthreatening means of communicating with each other is an excellent idea. If one of your children is having emotional problems, is experiencing anger or depression, or is just having difficulty adjusting to your divorce, going to counseling as a family may be extremely helpful—not just for your child, but for everyone involved. Finally, if you find that you are having difficulty coping with your divorce, individual therapy can be a lifesaver.

Going to individual therapy is probably the single best thing you can do for yourself if you are going through a stressful divorce. Not only will your therapist become a part of the support network that is so important to help you maintain both your mental and physical health during a divorce, but he or she has the education and training to guide you through the process with much more sensitivity and insight than your friends, no matter how well-intentioned they may be. Your therapist can be your anchor and your reality check. He or she can make sure you keep things in perspective, and respect your limitations, while going through the divorce process. He or she can gently remind you that you are responsible for your own actions—even during your divorce—and that you can control those actions, but you can't control your spouse, your lawyer, or the judge. He or she can help you understand that what goes around comes around, even if you're too angry to believe that at the moment. In short, your therapist can help you get through your divorce with your sanity and your integrity intact.

6

The Reality of the Right Attorney

It is the trade of lawyers to question everything, yield nothing, and talk by the hour.

—Thomas Jefferson, Third President of the United States

The trouble with law is lawyers.

—Clarence Darrow, Lawyer

If you were to ask someone who's been through a divorce for the single most important piece of advice they could give you, you'd undoubtedly get a number of different answers. But the one answer you're likely to hear most often is, "Get a good lawyer." The truth is, not only do you need a good lawyer—you need the right lawyer. You need someone who shares your philosophy and approach to divorce, and someone upon whose judgment you can rely when your own is clouded or confused. You need someone who will listen to you and understand your concerns, then be able to clearly explain your choices to you. If you have a spouse who is violent or abusive, you need an attorney who won't be afraid to stand up to him or her in a courtroom. If you have a spouse who you suspect has hidden assets or is playing complicated financial games, then you need an attorney with the brains, the resources, and the determination it takes to look under every rock and follow every lead to find the truth. If you have a spouse who is fairly reasonable and with whom you would like to try to amicably resolve your issues, then you need an attorney who can work with you and your spouse to help you negotiate an agreement. The one thing most people don't need is a shark.

Sharks Don't Just Bite Your Spouse

The stereotypical divorce lawyer is slick, loud, and aggressive. He or she makes everything a fight, doesn't care how much pain or how many problems he or she causes, and is only interested in making money. This is the kind of lawyer who makes opponents shudder and clients smile. While there are plenty of divorce attorneys you will find who meet this description, there are even more who don't—and that's a good thing.

Contrary to what most people think about divorce attorneys, most are good lawyers, reasonable negotiators, and decent human beings. While they are capable of being tough when they need to be, they are not the kind of attorneys you typically think about when you hear the word "shark." In spite of what most people believe, hiring a shark to get you through your divorce is not always your best choice. As a matter of fact, except in extreme circumstances, it is rarely even a good choice. True, a shark will put on a fabulous show in a courtroom, and will likely drive your spouse into fits of rage and temporary insanity. However, it is equally true that, by the time the shark is through, you will have spent two or three times the amount you should have spent on your divorce. What's more, your shark will very likely have done so much damage to your relationship with your spouse—and maybe even with your children—that you may never be able to be in the same room with any of them again. Think it doesn't matter? Think again.

Starting a war without good cause and burning through a client's retainer in record time is bad. Leading clients to believe that they are going to get the sun, the moon, and the stars, and then leaving them high and dry as soon as their money runs out, is worse. Sharks do both. Instead of settling, people with shark attorneys fight. They fight during the divorce. They fight after the divorce. They systematically build a hatred and distrust between them that will last the rest of their lives, and in the end—many years and tens of thousands of dollars in attorneys' fees later—the only ones who win are the lawyers.

Choosing the Right Lawyer

In every community you can find lawyers who are sharks. You can find lawyers who are less than honest, not particularly bright, or too busy to pay attention to your case. You can also find lawyers who are hardworking, brilliant, and knowledgeable about the law. It is your responsibility to find a good lawyer. To do this, talk to people, find out who your friends or neighbors have used in the past, and get referrals. If you know someone who got divorced and was satisfied with his or her attorney, go talk to that attorney. Finding a lawyer who did a good job for someone else is the best way to find one who will do a good job for you.

If you don't know anyone who can refer you to a good divorce attorney in your area, you might want to check with your local bar association and ask for a referral for a few good divorce attorneys, and then pick two or three from that list to interview. You can also always try the Yellow Pages or the Internet—but if you do that, be careful. Just because someone has a huge advertisement does not mean they're the best lawyer. All it means is that they have the biggest advertising budget. As a matter of fact, as a general rule, the more an attorney advertises, the less likely it is that you will be happy with that attorney's services. So, do your homework, and don't hire just anyone. Meet the attorney, interview him or her, and make sure that the attorney you hire is someone you are comfortable with and someone you think will do the best job for you. Make sure that the attorney you hire will be the one handling your case—or will at least be in charge of supervising your case, even if a young associate will be the one doing the lion's share of the work. There is nothing worse than hiring the big shot lawyer in a firm, only to discover that the big shot's first-year associate is the one who is actually working on your case.

When choosing an attorney, you want to make sure that you choose someone who specializes in divorce work. You don't need someone who spends 100% of his or her time practicing divorce law, but on the other hand, you don't want someone handling your case who has only handled two divorces during the course of his or her entire career. This is not the time to hire your childhood buddy who mostly does real estate closings, but is willing to do you a favor and handle your divorce. You need an attorney who knows family law and practices it regularly in the city or county in which you live.

When you first meet with an attorney, remember—*you* are the client. You are interviewing the attorney as much as the attorney is interviewing you. If you are not comfortable talking to that attorney, or if your gut tells you this person is wrong for you, listen to your gut. There are lots of good divorce attorneys in the world. You don't need to hire someone you don't like or don't feel right about hiring. You also don't need to hire someone who takes an approach to your divorce that you are not comfortable taking. When talking to an attorney, find out what ideas he or she has for handling your case. Find out what approach the lawyer suggests taking in your case, and how long he or she thinks your case will take to resolve. Listen carefully to the lawyer's answers. Any lawyer who promises you that he or she can finish your case in a set amount of time or for a fixed amount of money, no matter what happens or how much you fight, is lying to you. No lawyer can guarantee what will happen in your case, and a good one won't even try. What you are looking for is a lawyer who is honest with you and who will tell you the truth—whether you want to hear it or not.

Another quality you should look for in your lawyer is the ability to listen to you. If you want to settle your case amicably, and the lawyer starts talking about all the ways he or she plans to find out where your spouse has hidden assets and all the court motions he or she can file to protect your rights, that lawyer is not listening to you. Of course, there may be times when your lawyer has different ideas about handling your case than you do, and the lawyer may be right. Sometimes you need to listen to your lawyer and do what he or she says. At the same time, it is also important that your lawyer respects your wishes and listens to what you're saying. If you don't feel your lawyer is doing that, then you need to find another lawyer.

Another important thing to consider when hiring an attorney is where that lawyer is located. Hiring a local attorney is almost always a good idea. Not only do divorce laws differ widely from state to state, but the court rules that govern the divorce process differ from county to county. Whether you can ever get anyone to admit it or not, in many places the *home court advantage* still holds weight. Local attorneys are familiar faces in the courtroom. The judges, clerks, and other attorneys know them, and know what to expect from them. What's even more important is that the local attorney knows what to expect of the other lawyers and the judge. He or she knows which attorneys are straight shooters and which ones aren't. He or she knows a bit about each judge's temperament and how the judge views certain issues. While that's still no guarantee that things will go your way, it usually gives you a fighting chance of getting a fair shake. Hire a local attorney, and with a little luck, you'll get through the divorce process with a minimal amount of grief and aggravation (other than the normal grief and aggravation that accompanies any divorce). Hire an outsider, and you may have to deal with everything from never getting a break from the other attorney or the judge, to improperly done paperwork and enormous amounts of wasted time while your lawyer learns the system.

Choosing a lawyer is the single most important decision you have to make in your divorce. The reason it is so important is simple—who you get to represent you affects every other aspect of your case. If you hire a jerk, your spouse's attorney will respond by being a jerk, and the two lawyers will end up fighting over everything from which party can keep the pink tupperware to which attorney gets to talk in front of the judge first. If you hire someone who doesn't know what he or she is doing, you may get through your divorce with a minimal amount of conflict, but when you're done, you're going to be wondering if anyone got the license plate number of the truck that just ran over you. If you hire a good lawyer who knows the law and tries to work out a settlement that keeps you and your spouse on speaking terms (at least for the benefit of the kids), you will end up getting through your divorce with a reasonably fair result and some semblance of your dignity intact.

When choosing a lawyer, it is important to consider not just the lawyer—his or her knowledge, attitude, experience, and philosophy—but yourself. You need to figure out what you have, what you want, and how much of a fight you anticipate (and are willing to engage in) to get what you want. Of course, there's also the issue of how much you want to spend.

Some people believe that the more a lawyer charges, the better the lawyer is. Wrong! It's true that more experienced attorneys charge more for their time. However, lawyers are like wine—you can pay a lot of money for a fancy bottle that tastes like vinegar, or you can find a good deal that fits your budget and your palate alike. Regardless of how much an attorney charges, you still need to make sure that the attorney has the skill and shares the approach to your case that you want. That being said, in some cases, you need an expensive attorney. If you have a multimillion-dollar estate, complicated financial dealings, and enormous custody issues, you need to find a lawyer who is capable of handling those kinds of issues. Lawyers like that aren't cheap. Of course, most people don't need that level of lawyering, but they do need someone who's competent and professional. Unfortunately, even average lawyers cost money. The bottom line, though, is that they are worth it. The money you spend on a good attorney is nothing compared to the money you will spend if you try to get through your divorce without one.

THE HORRORS OF HIRING THE WRONG ATTORNEY:
THE STORY OF JOEL AND NORA

Joel and Nora were married shortly after Nora got pregnant in their senior year of high school. Ten years and three kids later, their marriage fell apart. Joel was a factory worker who worked the night shift. Nora was a stay-at-home mom. They had a house that was mortgaged to the hilt, two beat-up cars, and three little kids—that was it. So, they went to a lawyer who advertised that he would do quick, uncontested divorces for a flat fee of $1,000. The lawyer represented Joel, and Nora represented herself.

In order to keep the divorce uncontested, both Joel and Nora agreed to terms that they never really thought about, and that the lawyer never explained. Even though they could barely stand to be in the same room together, they agreed to joint custody; even though Nora had no income at all, she waived maintenance; and, even though Joel was an active dad who spent a lot of time with his kids, he agreed to a visitation schedule that only allowed him to see his children while they were at Nora's house. Joel and Nora didn't work out any holiday visitation schedule or a vacation schedule. Their entire divorce judgment, including their marital settlement agreement and their joint parenting agreement combined, was seven pages long. (If done properly, these documents would usually be upwards of twenty-five or thirty pages.) However, as promised, the lawyer only charged Joel and Nora $1,000. They were divorced in less than a month, and within another month, they were back in court fighting about all the things they should have figured out before they were divorced, but had never bothered to discuss.

Nora, who figured out after the divorce that having Joel hanging around her house was a bad idea, tried to get him to stay away— he wouldn't. She brought her new boyfriend around, she had her parents harass him—she tried everything she could to make his life miserable—but Joel insisted on seeing his kids. He even offered to take them to his house for visitation, like every other parent did, but Nora wouldn't hear of it.

One day, Joel took them anyway, and Nora freaked out. She immediately filed for an order of protection against Joel, accusing him of physically abusing their children while they were out of her sight. As it turned out, the two oldest kids had gotten into a fight that day and their daughter's arm got a small bruise on it. Joel had given his son a time-out, kissed his daughter's arm, and that was it. Nora, however, convinced herself that there was more to the story, took their daughter to the emergency room, filed a police report, and got an order of protection against Joel.

When the case got to court, it immediately became clear that Joel and Nora couldn't agree on the time of day, let alone anything that involved their kids. Four years, several therapists, a guardian for the children, and tens of thousands of dollars later, they finally sorted it out—not that either one of them was happy with the result. Much to Nora's dismay, Joel finally got a visitation schedule that gave him every other weekend and one weekday afternoon with the kids. Unfortunately for Joel, he was forced to reimburse Nora for thousands of dollars of unnecessary medical bills for the kids, including the bills for the treatment for the alleged child abuse that the court found never happened. In the end, no one was happy.

Joel and Nora's case is a classic example of what happens when you push a case through just to get it over with, but never take the time to work out the problems that you know are going to arise the minute the case is done. In their divorce, Joel and Nora got exactly what they paid for—garbage. Of course, if they had retained good lawyers to begin with, they probably would have fought more in their initial case than they did with the bad lawyer. That's not because the lawyers would have caused the problems—it's because good lawyers would have made them deal with their problems. Had they done that, they could have solved those problems and moved on with their lives. As it was, they ended up fighting for years. They fought twice as long and twice as hard as they would have if they dealt with their problems during their divorce instead of afterwards. Both Joel and Nora had very different ideas about what was going to happen after their divorce and what the terms of their divorce judgment really meant. Unfortunately, that judgment was so vague and incomplete that it really didn't say anything at all. When life didn't turn out as they expected, they each fought with a vengeance for what they thought they had agreed upon. The problem was, they hadn't really agreed upon anything.

Aside from hiring a bad attorney, the quickest way to screw up your divorce is to do it yourself. Yes, you have the right to represent your-self. Yes, practicing law is not rocket science, and if you have a short marriage, no children, no assets, and no joint debt, you can probably muddle through the system yourself and do a minimal amount of damage. However, lawyers go to law school for a reason. If you don't know the law and you don't know the court rules, you can't expect to come out on top—especially if your spouse has a lawyer.

There are times in everyone's life when professional help makes a difference. Divorce is one of those times. People assume that they can search the Internet, download a few forms, learn whatever they need to know about the law, show up in court, and get themselves divorced. If that were true, everyone would be doing it—they're not. What's more, once you've really made a mess of your case, no lawyer in the world may be able to straighten it out. Some things just can't be changed. You're the one who has to live with the consequences of whatever you create. You can either take the time and spend the money to make sure that you have the best possible situation as you go forward into the rest of your life, or, like Joel and Nora, you can get divorced cheaply and suffer the consequences for the rest of your life.

So You Have an Attorney—Now What?

After you've hired an attorney, you should feel some sense of relief. You're moving in the right direction, hopefully with an attorney you can trust. What happens after that? What should you expect from your attorney, and what should he or she be able to expect from you?

The first thing you can expect from your attorney is communication. Your attorney is obligated to tell you what is going on in your case. Your attorney should send you copies of anything he or she files in court on your behalf. Your attorney should also let you know when your case is up in court and should advise you of any important developments in your case. If you haven't heard from your attorney in awhile and you're not sure of what's going on in your case, call your lawyer. You have the right to talk to your attorney (of course, you will pay for the privilege of doing so, but that's another issue) and you have the right to expect that your attorney will return your telephone calls—maybe not the same day, but certainly within a few days. If you leave a message for your attorney and don't hear anything back from him or her, call again. Attorneys, like everyone else, get busy and lose track of messages. However, in order to represent you properly, your attorney must communicate with you, and you need to make sure he or she does just that.

In addition to communication, the other thing you can expect from your attorney is that he or she will pay attention to your case, work on it, and move it along for you. Letting your file languish in a file cabinet somewhere does nothing for you. You need an attorney who has the time and makes the effort to work on your case, no matter how difficult it may be, and who does whatever it takes to move your case towards its eventual conclusion. At the same time, you have to understand that you are not the attorney's only client and there are many parts of your case that your attorney cannot control. Your lawyer has to wait for the judge to assign court dates, for your spouse to provide documents, and for your spouse's attorney to do what he or she is supposed to do as well. Even though your case is taking longer than you would like, it may not be your attorney's fault.

In addition to the things you can expect your attorney to do, there are certain things you should expect that your attorney cannot do. First, your attorney cannot do anything illegal or unethical, and should not ask that you do so either. Hiding assets, destroying documents, and filing motions in court that have no legal basis whatsoever are all things your attorney can't do. Second, your attorney can't guarantee how your case will turn out. Every case is different, and every couple is different. Just because your friend got to keep her house and her kids, and got awarded maintenance for ten years, does not mean that you will end up with the same result. You may have a very different situation from your friend, you may be in front of a different judge, or there may be other things about your case that are just not the same as your friend's case. Don't expect that your divorce will end up the same as anyone else's divorce—that's just not how the legal system works.

As with everything else in life, expectations go both ways. Not only do you have a right to expect certain things from your lawyer, but your lawyer has a right to expect certain things from you. The first thing your lawyer has a right to expect is that you will participate in your own case. You need to advise your attorney of what's going on in your life and what you're doing with the kids. You need to gather and provide your attorney with all of your financial information. You need to decide what you want to do and what you want to end up with after the dust settles and the judgment has been signed. No matter how good an attorney is, he or she is not going to know whether having visitation on a Tuesday night fits into your schedule better than Wednesday night unless you say something. If you don't take the time to send your attorney complete financial records or if you purposely hide information from your attorney or your spouse, your divorce judgment may end up either being inaccurate, unfair, incomplete, or wrong—simply because your attorney was working with bad information. If you can't decide what you want in your case, or if you don't want to take time off from work to go to court, then don't be surprised when the judge makes rulings that you don't like. If you don't care enough about your own case to stay involved in it, you can't expect to end up with a divorce judgment that gives you everything you thought you would get.

Another reason that you must participate in your case is because lawyers are human. They are busy, they are usually overworked, and they sometimes make mistakes. The cliché that *the squeaky wheel gets the oil* is, unfortunately, all too true. Unless your case is in a crisis or you're calling to ask what's going on, your file is likely going to sit in a drawer while your attorney works on other cases where a crisis exists or where the client is calling. That's just the way the world works. You need to communicate with your lawyer and you need to follow up on your own case. If you never call your lawyer, don't bother to read what your lawyer sends you, or don't ask questions when things arise that you don't understand, then chances are you are not going to be happy with how your divorce ends up. You can't sit on the sidelines and then complain when you didn't win the game. How could you win? You weren't even playing.

The final thing that your attorney has a right to expect from you is that you pay his or her bill. While that sounds fairly simple, you would be amazed at how many people believe they can hire a lawyer, and when their retainer runs out, just not pay any more and still have their attorney do a good job for them. That's not how the world works. Regardless of what you think of lawyers in general, you have hired your lawyer to do a job for you. If you don't pay your lawyer for his or her work, don't be surprised when your lawyer withdraws from your case and lets you do the job yourself.

What to Do When Your Lawyer Doesn't Work Out

No matter how much effort you put into finding and hiring just the right lawyer, it sometimes happens that you and your lawyer come to a parting of ways. Either your lawyer is not answering your telephone calls, not responding to your needs, or just not getting you what you want in the time you want to get it. When that happens, what do you do?

The first thing you need to do when you're unhappy with your lawyer is to try to figure out the reason you are unhappy. If your lawyer isn't doing what you want, examine whether your expectations are realistic. Maybe no lawyer in the world could give you what you want. If that's the case, then changing lawyers isn't going to do much good. On the other hand, if your lawyer isn't returning your telephone calls or if you just don't think your lawyer is doing a good job, you can always find a new attorney and move on. Sometimes getting a new lawyer and a new approach is just what you need to jump-start a case that has been sitting around at a stalemate for months. Other times, getting a new lawyer does nothing more than delay the case and cost you more money than staying with your original lawyer would have done. Still other times, getting a new lawyer is not even possible. If your case has been pending for a long time and you have a trial date that's coming up in the near future, the judge may not allow you to change lawyers. If you are thinking of changing lawyers, don't wait until the last minute to do it, or you may not be able to do it at all.

Aside from hiring a new attorney to represent you, you also have the option of consulting with a new attorney just to get a second opinion on your case. You can pay the attorney for a few hours of time, and have that attorney review your file and listen to your history, then give you an opinion as to what your options may be and how you should proceed in your case. What's more, if you bring the second attorney all of your paperwork yourself, rather than asking that he or she get it from your current attorney, then you can get a second opinion without ever having to tell your current attorney what you are doing. That way, you won't jeopardize your relationship with your current attorney in case you decide you want to have him or her continue to handle your case.

Once you go for a second opinion, you may find that the second attorney gives you the same advice as your first attorney. If so, at least you will have the peace of mind of knowing that your present attorney is doing the right thing. If, however, the second attorney gives you advice that is very different from what your first attorney advised, you may want to bring up those ideas with your present attorney and discuss them. Your attorney may be open to trying a different approach. On the other hand, if your attorney rejects your ideas out of hand or isn't comfortable doing what the second attorney advised you to do, then you may want to fire your first attorney and go with the new one. The one thing you don't want to do, though, is fire your first attorney before you hire a new attorney, or worse yet, fire your first attorney and go through the process alone.

Being unrepresented in your divorce, particularly if your spouse has a lawyer, is not just a bad idea, it's usually a disastrous one. You don't know the law, you don't know the court rules, and no matter how smart you may think you are, if you don't know the court system, you are not going to do well. No matter how much you may dislike or disagree with your present attorney, it's best not to fire him or her until you have someone else lined up to take your case. Nine times out of ten, any lawyer is better than no lawyer at all.

7

The Financial Realities
of Spousal Support

Alimony is like buying oats for a dead horse.

—Arthur Baer, Comic and Columnist

Alimony—the ransom that the happy pay to the devil.

—H. L. Mencken, Writer and Political Commentator

There's an old adage that money and sex cause most marital problems—if either one is missing for long, a marriage is in trouble. Imagine, then, how much more trouble there is when a marriage is over, the sex is gone, and one spouse still demands that the other continue to pay support. The whole concept of supporting someone who is no longer related to you (and who you probably no longer even like) seems vaguely un-American. At the very least, it is frustrating and unpleasant. It's not surprising, then, that of all the issues that arise during a divorce, issues of *spousal support* (also known as maintenance or alimony) are among the most difficult to resolve amicably.

Alimony Today

The past few decades have seen far-reaching changes both in the American family structure and in divorce law. While in the past, it was usually the man who paid to support his ex-wife, in today's world, that's no longer necessarily true. If a woman is better educated, has a better job or better job prospects, or makes more money than a man, she is just as likely to have to support her ex-husband after they are divorced as he would be to support her if their financial circumstances were reversed. The same thing is true in so-called nontraditional families, in which the husband stays home to raise the children while the wife works to support the family. Whether one spouse is obligated to support another now depends less upon that spouse's gender and more upon both parties' finances, jobs, health, education, and children, and the laws of the state in which they live. Regardless of who is supporting whom, if you are the person making the support payments, you probably aren't happy about it—and the reason you're not happy about it has a lot to do with your ideas about divorce.

If you view divorce as an end to your relationship, then that is exactly what you want—an end to your relationship. You want to be done. You don't want to share your life, your home, your money, or anything else with your former spouse. If you could get away with it, and it didn't hurt your children, you probably wouldn't even share them. It's not surprising that with this kind of a view of marriage, paying spousal support for months or years after you've gotten divorced irks the living daylights out of you. It's even worse if the reason you got divorced in the first place was because your spouse lied to you, cheated on you, spent you into the poorhouse, or was simply the one who wanted the divorce when you didn't. When you are the spouse who has been wronged, paying spousal support to your ex for months or years after your divorce feels like you are rewarding your ex for his or her bad behavior. However, that is essentially what the concept of no-fault divorce is all about.

In most states, the law now holds that both you and your spouse are entitled to receive your share of the marital assets when you divorce, regardless of who did what to whom during the course of your marriage.

You are also both entitled to have enough money coming in to allow you to survive and get on with the rest of your life—at least for a while. That does not necessarily mean, however, that you are entitled to have your spouse pay you enough money so that you can survive without having to work for the rest of your life. Spousal support is not Social Security—you are not entitled to get it just because you were married. Unless you are elderly, disabled, or unable to work for some legitimate reason, you have an obligation to at least try to support yourself. By the same token, if you earn three times as much as your spouse and have a higher education, and you've been married for twenty-five years, don't delude yourself into thinking that you're going to be able to get divorced without paying a penny in spousal support or giving your ex anything more than a straight 50% of your assets. That's just not going to happen.

To determine whether spousal support will be an issue in your case, and if so, how much money will be involved, you need a lawyer. You cannot handle your case yourself. There are way too many factors that can influence a judge's decision to grant or deny support for you to be trying to make your case without a lawyer's help. Even with a lawyer, however, things might not turn out exactly as you would like.

MAINTENANCE GONE WRONG: THE STORY OF PHILLIP AND JULIE

Phillip and Julie married while they were in college. Julie got pregnant almost immediately and dropped out of school. Phillip graduated and worked in the family business, where he earned a nice living. Julie, however, managed to consistently overspend their budget, and the couple was swimming in debt. Ten years and three children later, Phillip had enough. He filed for divorce.

Phillip and Julie's divorce was bitter, and ended up going to trial. Since Julie hadn't worked in ten years, was unskilled, lacked a degree, and still had small children at home, the judge ordered

Phillip to pay her maintenance and child support. Unfortunately for Phillip, the judge didn't specifically say when the maintenance would end.

In time, Phillip remarried, and the children grew up, went to college (which Phillip paid for), and left. Julie remained single, and for the most part, penniless. She never went back to school, she changed jobs often, and she blew through every penny she ever had, including a sizeable inheritance she received when her parents died. Meanwhile, Phillip kept paying Julie $250 a month in maintenance. He often thought about taking her back to court to end his payments, but there was never a good time to do it—Julie was regularly unemployed and never financially stable. Meanwhile, Phillip had gotten a master's degree, was earning a huge salary, and had become a very wealthy man. Two hundred and fifty dollars a month wasn't going to break him. You can imagine Phillip's surprise when, thirteen years after their divorce, Julie took Phillip back to court for an increase in support.

It seemed inconceivable to Phillip that any judge would order him to pay even more money to a woman from whom he had been divorced for thirteen years, and who had done nothing during that time to educate herself or improve her life. What's more, Phillip had been supporting Julie for longer than he had been married to her. Phillip figured that he'd done his share. He filed his own motion to end maintenance forever, and he forced the case to go all the way to trial. As it turned out, that may not have been his best decision.

At trial, Julie presented herself as the uneducated, unskilled, slightly ditzy, and financially irresponsible person she was. Instead of being angry at her, however, the judge was sympathetic—here was a middle-aged woman who would clearly never be able to support herself without some help from someone. Phillip was that person. The judge ordered Phillip to pay Julie $500 a month in maintenance—and still didn't set a date when Phillip's payments would be done.

Needless to say, Phillip was appalled. The judge's ruling didn't make sense. However, appealing that ruling would have been expensive and most likely useless. The judge had broad discretion in this kind of a case, and it was unlikely that the decision would have been reversed on appeal. What's more, paying Julie $500 a month was not going to break a millionaire—and the judge knew it.

What happened to Phillip seems outrageous. It seems like the judge was biased and that the decision was wrong. Yet, the decision was final and Phillip had to live with it. A different judge might have decided the case differently, but Phillip didn't have a different judge. So, he found out the hard way that when you're dealing with an issue over which the judge has a lot discretion—like maintenance—you cannot predict what a judge will do or how your case will turn out. For that reason alone, when maintenance is an issue in your case, you are almost always better off dealing with that issue yourself, and resolving it in a way that ends your obligation forever, even if that means paying more to do it than you think you should ever have to pay.

Fear, Support, and the Will to Survive

Regardless of whether you are the potential supporter or the potential supportee, before you can make any kind of decision regarding support, it helps to understand the emotions that surround this issue. Otherwise, you will find yourself locked in a battle with your spouse over dollars and cents when the real issue (believe it or not) has nothing to do with money.

No one ever wants to support their ex-spouse. Most people who are facing the prospect of having to pay spousal support see the issue in terms of their spouse's laziness or greed. They believe that their spouse just wants to make them miserable, take them to the cleaners, or leech off of them when the spouse could be supporting him- or herself. In some cases, all of that is true. In most cases, however, it's not laziness or greed that motivates one person to seek support from his or her ex-spouse—it's fear.

Few things are stronger than the human survival instinct. If you don't make a lot of money, and you're faced with the prospect of no longer having the money your spouse makes to keep food on the table and a roof over your head, you get scared. You feel that your very existence is being threatened—so you react by fighting with every fiber of your being to make sure that your soon-to-be ex-spouse supports you, whether he or she wants to or not. If, in addition to feeling threatened yourself, you have children who stand to suffer by the sudden lack of funds, you will fight that much more. What you may not realize is that your spouse may be feeling just as threatened as you are.

Although most people who are going through a divorce with a spouse who makes more money than they do don't feel a lot of sympathy for that spouse, the truth is that, unless your spouse is independently wealthy, he or she probably feels just as pinched for cash as you do. Regardless of how much money your spouse makes, when your spouse opens a paycheck and sees half of it gone for child support and maintenance, he or she is going to be in shock. Your spouse is also going to wonder how he or she is supposed to pay the bills and still survive on half as much money (or less) than he or she had before. What's more, your spouse is not just feeling threatened—he or she is feeling angry. From your spouse's perspective, he or she is working like a dog just to have to give a huge chunk of his or her earnings to you—while you (at least in your spouse's mind) have done nothing to earn that money yourself. Your spouse very likely sees you as being greedy, lazy, and just looking to make a buck. Meanwhile, you think your spouse is the most selfish, greedy, and insensitive creature who has ever walked the face of the earth for not understanding that there's no way you can make it on your own, at least for awhile, until you can put your life back together and start supporting yourself again. Not surprisingly, when you're locked into that kind of an emotional standoff, it is hard to get anything resolved.

If you understand that fear (and admittedly, sometimes greed) lies at the core of the support issue, you are on your way to resolving your support conflict with your spouse. If you can manage to handle your fear and view your spouse as another human being with whom you are still going to be in an ongoing relationship, you will be a little less likely to drive yourself insane with rage every time you either have to shell out your hard-earned money or receive a support check that is considerably less than what you think it should be. The bottom line is that, one way or another, you will be much better off if you act from a place of balance and self-control rather than one of fear and emotional reactivity. While there may be little you can do to make your former spouse less greedy or self-absorbed, there is a lot you can do to take control of your own emotions and combat your fear that you will be destitute after the divorce. The first thing you need to do is get the facts.

The Law of Responsibility and the Reality of Support

Before you can accurately determine whether or not you will have to pay, or may be entitled to receive, spousal support, you first have to understand what spousal support is and what it's not. Spousal support is not an entitlement. Just because your spouse earns more money than you do does not mean that you are automatically entitled to receive a portion of his or her earnings—even if the kids are going to be living with you. If you are the custodial parent for your children, you will be entitled to receive child support. Technically, that is money you are supposed to use to support your children. Spousal support is money you use to support yourself. Unlike child support, which virtually every custodial parent is entitled to receive in some amount, spousal support is not guaranteed.

Spousal support is never set in stone. It can change at any time. Whether you receive spousal support depends upon your financial situation and that of your soon-to-be ex-spouse. If you suddenly win the lottery and become independently wealthy, or you find a new true love and remarry, your spouse can petition the court to end support payments to you, even if your divorce decree said he or she was supposed to keep paying you for the next ten years. Similarly, if your former spouse suddenly loses his or her job and no longer earns the same amount of money, he or she can ask the court to lower or eliminate your support payments, even if you don't earn one penny more than you did on the day of your divorce, and even if you were relying on the support money you thought you were going to be receiving in order to pay your bills. Of course, support can work the other way around, too. As long as your support is *reviewable* (that is, the end date is not set in stone), and sometimes even if it's not supposed to be reviewable, if you lose your job, become ill, or can no longer pay your bills for some other legitimate reason, your former spouse might end up paying you more money or paying you money for a longer period of time than what was originally ordered in your divorce judgment. Nothing about spousal support is ever guaranteed.

Spousal support is not free money. Any support you receive from your ex will be taxable income to you and tax deductible to your ex. While that is not true of child support (which is not taxable income to the custodial parent), it is true of spousal support. Since your spouse will not be withholding part of your support payments and depositing them with the federal government to pay your federal and state income taxes, you are going to have to save some of that money to pay the taxes yourself. Otherwise, come April 15th, you may find yourself in a real bind when you don't have enough money to pay the taxes you owe to the government.

Receiving support is not like winning the lottery. The purpose of support is to make sure that, after your divorce, you and your spouse both have enough money to survive. The purpose of support is not, however, to make sure that you are supported in the style you would like to have been supported in, but could never afford during your marriage. While it's true that in some states, under certain circumstances, the courts will consider the lifestyle you enjoyed during your marriage in determining how much money you will be entitled to receive for support after you are divorced, getting a judge to order your former spouse to pay you loads of money every month so you can stay home and do nothing is not realistic. Unless you had a long marriage, you married a multimillionaire, or you're permanently disabled while your spouse maintains a high-paying job, don't expect to rake in huge amounts of cash for the rest of your life. The law just doesn't work that way.

Spousal support is rarely a slam dunk. No matter who you are, what your financial circumstances are, or how clear it is to you that you should be receiving support, a judge may decide differently. The law regarding spousal support is not black and white. The issues of whether you should get support, how long you should get it for, and how much support you should get, are all negotiable. If you and your spouse can't agree on those issues, then ultimately a judge will decide them for you. However, as Phillip and Julie's story shows (p.89–91), judges don't always do what you think they should. No matter how strong your case may be, a judge can always decide against you. With that in mind, taking a hard-line position on support and insisting that your spouse pay you every penny you think you deserve is rarely your best choice.

SUPPORT SURPRISES:
THE STORY OF SARAH AND SAM

Sarah and Sam were high school sweethearts. They married at 18 and had two boys. Sarah stayed home and raised the kids, while Sam supported them and went to night school. Eventually, Sam worked his way up the ladder at a trucking company, and by the time they were getting divorced, he was doing quite well.

Consequently, Sarah had never felt driven to get either her GED or a job. She did, however, get herself a boyfriend, which was the reason Sam filed for divorce.

Sarah's goals in the divorce were clear. She wanted the house, the car, and the kids, and she wanted Sam to keep supporting her for the rest of her life. She was less than pleased to learn that it was unlikely that a judge was going to find her unable to support herself when she was only 33 years old and in perfect health.

Sarah decided that the best way to keep herself from having to go to work was to go back to school. She enrolled in an art history program at the local community college. By going to school part-time, Sarah figured that it would take six years before she graduated. Adding in another year to give her time to get a job, which she figured would be difficult with a major in art history, she decided that, at the very least, Sam owed her seven years of maintenance, maybe more. The judge decided differently.

At a pretrial conference held early in the case, the judge recommended that Sarah get two years of maintenance, an extra 10% of the marital assets, and that was it. Try as she might, Sarah's lawyer could not convince the judge otherwise. But Sarah was not to be daunted.

Sarah decided that if she was only entitled to get two years of support after the divorce, she would just drag out the case and keep from getting divorced for as long as possible. So she fought over everything—the kids, the cars, even the dog. Sarah and Sam fought about every item of personal property in the house, right down to the silverware. Two years later, they finally ran out of things to fight about. While Sarah still wasn't happy about the prospect of only getting two more years of maintenance, at least she felt she had made Sam sorry he had fought her in the first place.

You can imagine Sarah's surprise when the judge told Sarah at trial that, as far as she was concerned, Sarah had gotten her two years of maintenance while the case was pending. Sarah had dropped out of school and hadn't even tried to get a decent job. After much arguing, the judge finally granted Sarah an extra year of support, but at a much lesser rate. The judge also gave Sarah the extra 10% of the assets, just as she had said at the pretrial conference. However, after subtracting all the money Sarah and Sam had spent on lawyers, 10% wasn't what it used to be.

You are responsible for your own financial survival. If, like Sarah, you decide to sit back and let your spouse support you just because he or she can, then, like Sarah, you may find yourself in a tough financial spot when the gravy train ends. If you're like most people, being financially responsible means that you need to have a job. What's more, to be really financially responsible, you need to have the best job you can possibly get, or go back to school so that you can get a better job in the future. While it may be tempting to take a job earning minimum wage at the local grocery store just so your spouse has to pay support and you can make your ex suffer, doing that doesn't make sense. Most people are not entitled to receive support for the rest of their lives. They only get support for a few years, if they even get that. Why would you want to waste the time in which you are getting financial support by doing some menial job rather than using the opportunity to go back to school or get the training you need to get a job that will pay you more? In the end, your support will run out. Then, like Sarah, you'll be left to support yourself, regardless of whether you have the means to do so or not.

What should you do if you've already got the best job you can get, and you are only going to be getting support for a few years? First of all, don't squander your money. Make a savings plan. Invest some of your support money for a rainy day. See if you can pick up a part-time job to earn a little extra cash. Be careful about what you spend. Try to live within your means. Stay out of the stores. Cut up your credit cards. Do whatever you need to do—and whatever you can do—to make sure that your financial future is as secure as it can be. Remember—your finances are your responsibility.

Make a Budget

In order to figure out what you may be entitled to receive (or what you may have to pay) in spousal support, you have to know what you and your spouse have, and what you and your spouse owe. You have to know how much money both you and your spouse make, and you have to know the average amount of your monthly bills. In short, you have to make a budget.

Few people are thrilled with the prospect of making a detailed, itemized budget of their monthly living expenses. Making a list of all of your income and expenses is tedious and time-consuming. However, this is the first thing you need to do in order to get a grip on your current financial situation—regardless of whether spousal support will be involved in your case or not. You can't know whether you will have enough money to support two households until you know what supporting two households will cost. Creating a budget will provide you with crucial information about how much money you have and where it is going. If nothing else, creating a budget can be a real eye-opener.

If you and your spouse are on speaking terms, you can do a budget together. If you and your spouse can't be in the same city together, let alone speak to each other, then do a budget yourself. If you don't have access to your spouse's financial information, at least list your own income and expenses. If you have never done the bills during your marriage and don't know what your expenses are, find out. Open your mail, keep track of your bills, and make a trip to your bank. If necessary, have your lawyer get whatever other information you need and can't get yourself. (Keep in mind, though, that you will be paying your lawyer to do this for you, so you are better off doing as much as you can on your own.) Do whatever you have to do to try to figure out how much money you have coming in and how much money you have going out each month.

Making a budget takes time, but it's not advanced nuclear physics. With a little effort, anyone can do it. You have to remember, however, that the budget you create will only be as good as the information you use to create it. If you don't know what your income and expenses are, and you leave half the items blank just because you don't feel like looking for the information, your budget will be both inaccurate and useless. If, on the other hand, you invest the time to fill out your budget carefully, it will be an invaluable tool for helping you figure out how much money you (and your spouse) need to survive, how you can fairly divide up your assets and your debt, and how you can structure your finances so that both you and your spouse can move on with your independent lives as soon as possible.

If you've never done a budget before, you might want to follow the example listed in Appendix A. Start by listing your gross monthly income and your spouse's gross monthly income on a piece of paper. It will help to list them separately. If either of you gets an annual bonus or earns money based on commissions, you may want to look at the average amount that comes in each month from that income as well. To do that, examine the amount you or your spouse earned in bonuses and commissions in the past year, and divide that amount by twelve. That will give you an average monthly bonus amount. If the amount of the bonus or commissions varies widely from year to year, then take a three- or five-year average in order to be more accurate. After you've added up all of your income, then subtract from that number everything that comes out of each of your paychecks each month—including payroll taxes, Social Security, health insurance, 401(k) contributions, and union dues. After you've subtracted all of your deductions, you will be left with a net income per month—your take-home pay.

After you've figured out your income, you need to move on to your expenses. If you and your spouse are still living together, you're only going to have one set of expenses. If you're living apart, you will each have to list your expenses separately. Whatever your situation may be, do your best to state your expenses accurately. While you may be tempted to inflate your own expenses and deflate your spouse's expenses just to give yourself a little cushion, resist that urge. Try to be honest and accurate. If you're not, your budget will be useless, and you will be the one who's hurt in the end when your spouse or his or her attorney pokes holes in your numbers and makes it look like you're purposely lying about everything. Even though that may seem like a risk worth taking, keep in mind that once the judge doesn't believe you, the increased possibility of him or her ruling against you may cost far more than the few dollars you stood to gain with your inflated financial statement.

In addition to being accurate, when listing your expenses, you also need to be complete. Don't forget the cost of things like insurance premiums, license plates, vacations, and other items you only buy or pay for once or twice a year. Remember to figure in the average amount you spend for unanticipated expenses, like doctors' bills and car repairs. Include even the small items, like the children's allowances, that aren't much when you pay them, but add up to a lot at the end of the month when you're trying to figure out where your money went. Take the time to write everything down, and be as thorough as you can. When you're done, add up all your expenses, then compare those expenses to your net income and see what you get.

If you and your spouse worked together on a budget, you will both immediately see whether you have enough money to go around or not. If you worked on them separately, you will need to exchange your budget with your spouse (which you should be able to do through the court system if your spouse won't cooperate at all). When you look at both budgets, you will get a good idea of whether you will need or have to pay maintenance or support.

While making a budget is a long process, looking at a budget somehow makes your income and expenses much more real. If you are the higher-earning spouse, you may not feel so taken advantage of once you see how much your spouse is going to have to spend just to pay the household bills each month. If you are the lower-earning spouse, you may be surprised to see that you are not going to be as bad off as you thought—or that your spouse is not going to be as well off as you thought. Even if the results of doing a budget show that there's not enough money to go around, at least you will know how much you will be short each month. Armed with that information, you will be able to try to figure out how you can fill the hole. Maybe you will need to stop contributing to your retirement plan for awhile so you can have the extra cash, or maybe you will realize that you have to find a way to earn more money or cut out expenses for luxuries. No matter what your financial situation, there are always things you can juggle in order to make the most of your money for the benefit of you, your spouse, and your children. Without the right information, though, you can't even begin to solve your financial problems.

Controlling Your Emotions while Supporting Your Ex

Once you know how much you (and your spouse) earn and how much you (and your spouse) spend, you should be able to start to figure out whether or not one of you is going to have to support the other. Sometimes it's a close call. For example, if one of you earns more than the other, but the higher-earning spouse is also going to have to pay child support, that may even things out. Maybe each of you earns enough to live comfortably, even though one of you will clearly be more comfortable than the other. If you had a short marriage and you're both gainfully employed, you may not be entitled to receive support (even though your spouse earns more than you do). On the other hand, if you've been married awhile, you may look at your budget, look at your spouse's budget, and know for sure that if you get divorced, you are going to have to support your spouse.

There are many situations in which paying spousal support is inevitable. For example, if the last job your spouse had before quitting to raise your children ten years ago was working as a cashier at the local grocery store, while you've been steadily employed at a good-paying job since the day you were married, chances are, you're going to have to pay spousal support after you are divorced. The same thing is true if your spouse isn't well educated and you are a double-degree professional, if your spouse is disabled, or if your spouse has some sort of medical or psychological problem that would prevent him or her from getting a well paying job. You will also likely have to pay support if you have small children at home and your spouse can't earn enough to pay for day care and still bring home enough money to pay the rent. In all of these situations, as well as many others, it is extremely likely that you are going to have to continue to support your spouse for some period of time after you're divorced. You can either accept that fact and deal with it, or become angry and fight about it. The one thing you're probably not going to be able to do, though, is change it—at least, not in the short term.

No one likes paying spousal support. However, instead of acting out of spite and purposely quitting your job, lying about your income, or running away from your responsibilities, you need to realize that you will be much better off if you accept your situation and do your best to limit your exposure in the long term. If you try to avoid paying support by doing anything dishonest and anyone finds out (which, believe it or not, happens a lot), you will probably end up paying more in support, attorney's fees, and possibly even fines for contempt of court, than you ever would have had to pay if you had simply been straight with your spouse from the start. What's more, if your dishonesty involves lying to the government as well as to your spouse, you may end up facing charges for income tax evasion on top of everything else. (Remember the story of Melissa and Tony from Chapter 2.) You would be amazed at the number of cases the IRS is able to build using tips from disgruntled spouses in divorce cases. All in all, while lying, cheating, or doing other underhanded things may keep you from having to pay support or from having to pay as much support as you would have paid if you had been honest, the consequences for your dishonesty are simply not worth it. Remember, even if your strategy works, and you fool the judge, the lawyers, and your ex-spouse, karma happens.

The real key to limiting your support obligation lies not in lying to make your situation seem worse than it is, but in doing what you can to make your spouse's situation better. Although doing anything to improve your soon-to-be ex-spouse's life is the last thing you probably want to do, the truth is that the better off your spouse is, the less you will have to pay in support. Therefore, instead of spending your time hiding your income, you would be better off spending your energy helping your spouse become self-supporting.

There are two ways to increase your spouse's earning potential and financial situation—helping your spouse increase his or her education and skills to get a better job, and giving your spouse assets in the divorce that will either generate income or reduce your spouse's expenses after the divorce is over. For example, if you and your spouse have a decent amount of equity in your home, and your mortgage payments are relatively low, allowing your spouse to keep that home so he or she can afford to live on less money might make sense. Even if giving your spouse your home means giving more of the marital estate than what you will get, it may be well worth it if doing that saves you from having to pay spousal support. Obviously, though, this kind of strategy only works if you have enough assets to make it work. If your home is the only thing you own, and giving it to your spouse means that he or she will get all of the marital assets and you will get nothing, that is not a viable option. On the other hand, if you own rental property, have an investment portfolio that pays interest, or have any other kind of property that generates an income, you may want to consider giving that property to your spouse and keeping assets such as retirement accounts, stocks that appreciate in value but don't pay dividends, or other long-term financial investments that aren't current moneymakers for yourself.

Along with creatively dividing your assets so that your spouse can be financially stable, the other thing you can do to help minimize your support obligation is help your spouse maximize his or her income or earning potential. That means that you need to help your spouse find a good job, or support your spouse while he or she goes back to school and gets the training necessary to get a better paying job. Even if that means that you have to give your spouse a little extra money to help pay for his or her education, do it! If that is what it takes to increase your spouse's earning potential, it will be well worth it in the long run. You may also have to pitch in for baby-sitting or day care services while your spouse is at school. Whatever you have to do in the short term to improve your spouse's long-term earning capacity—do it! As long as your spouse's educational pursuit is legitimate and will lead to getting a better job and earning more money, you will be better off by supporting that pursuit than you will by being miserly and trying to let your ex sink or swim. Remember—in the end, both you and your spouse will be better off if you focus on your mutual survival rather than on your individual destruction.

8

Dividing Your Stuff and Paying Your Debts

Money often costs too much.

—Ralph Waldo Emerson, Philosopher

Money has never made man happy, nor will it, there is nothing in its nature to produce happiness. The more of it one has the more one wants.

—Benjamin Franklin, Scientist, Inventor, Philosopher, and Statesman

Money is just a way of keeping score.

—H.L. Hunt, Oil Magnate

In theory, dividing up assets and liabilities should be the least emotional part of any divorce. It doesn't involve heart-wrenching issues like child custody, or the emotionally charged issues of visitation and parenting. All you're dealing with is money and the things money can buy. While no one would deny that many people become attached to their stuff (not to mention their money), dividing it up seems like it should be easy enough. You just figure out what everything is worth, argue about who should get how much of whatever there is, and you're done. Right? Wrong.

Money, Money, Money

Of all of the issues in divorce, the one people end up fighting about the most is money. First of all, different people can have very different ideas of what the same thing is worth. One person values it at what it would cost to replace, while the other values it at its original price, less depreciation. One person cares more about sentimentality, while the other is only interested in dollars and cents. Even if two people agree on what their assets are worth, dividing them can still be difficult. One person wants to put a dollar value on every single item of personal property in the house, then divide the stuff into two piles of equal value. The other person is more concerned about each person taking what he or she wants or needs, without worrying about what anything costs. One person wants credit for everything he or she brought into the marriage, while the other thinks that everything should be divided equally no matter who had it first. Then there's the problem of cash flow.

Many people are *cash poor*. They have all of their money tied up in their house or their retirement fund, and there's not enough cash left for one person to buy the other one out without having to sell the house or cash out a big chunk of the retirement account. Each party is afraid he or she won't be left with enough assets to survive, and both parties are angry at having to give their ex-spouse what used to be all theirs. Each person suspects that what their spouse is getting is actually worth more than what their spouse claims, while what they're keeping is actually worth less than what it seems. As a result, no one is happy, everyone is scared, and both parties are suspicious of the other. When you add to that the issue of *hidden assets*—those items that somehow seemed to have mysteriously disappeared as soon as the word *divorce* was mentioned—the situation only gets worse.

In order to make sense of money issues, you need to remember one very important and seemingly contradictory truth—most of the time, when you're fighting with your spouse about money, money is not usually what you're really fighting about. Money is power. Money is control. Money is security. Having money enables you to buy what you want, and not having it makes you vulnerable and insecure. When people fight over money, they are fighting over their own fear, their pain, their need for control, and very often, their greed. People fight out of spite. A wife wants the new car the couple just bought, not because she needs state-of-the-art transportation or because she can afford the payments, but because her husband is a car fanatic and she always felt like he loved the car more than he loved her. A husband wants the bedroom dresser, not because he needs a place to put his clothes, but because taking one dresser breaks up the set and his wife will never be able to replace it. People fight over every conceivable piece of property, often spending three and four times what something is worth just so their spouse won't get it. Why? Because they're not really fighting about the money.

MONEY MAY NOT REALLY BE THE ISSUE: THE STORY OF NICK AND ANGELA

Nick and Angela's marriage hadn't been going well for years. Nick was hotheaded and jealous, and Angela wasn't much different. Neither of them had good jobs, and money was always an issue. They seemed to sink deeper into debt with each passing month, and the more their debt grew, the more their tempers flared. One day, Nick decided he didn't want to fight anymore and he filed for divorce. That's when the real fighting began.

Angela felt that Nick's temper—which not only caused their constant fighting, but had gotten Nick fired from every decent-paying job he'd ever had—was what broke their marriage apart. As far as Angela was concerned, she had thrown her heart, soul, and the best years of her life into her marriage, and she was entitled to everything she could get. Nick, on the other hand, just wanted half of what he and Angela had, which wasn't much. The only thing they owned was a little house with a big mortgage and a bunch of credit card bills. If they sold the house and paid the bills, all that would be left would be two old cars, some mismatched furniture, and their personal stuff. Angela wanted it all.

Angela refused to settle on any terms. She literally wanted everything Nick had, including the clothes on his back. Nick responded by insisting he get everything in the divorce that he knew Angela loved—the one-of-a-kind waterfall painting in the living room, the irreplaceable antique dresser Angela found at a flea market, and half of Angela's figurine collection. Neither Nick nor Angela would give in. Eventually, their case came up for trial.

Before starting the trial, the judge tried to get Nick and Angela to compromise and be reasonable. When he saw that it was impossible, the judge calmly told Nick and Angela that they were perfectly entitled to a trial, and that he would be more than happy to give them their day in court. However, as the judge who would be deciding the case, he felt they should both know that he was bound to follow the law—and the law said that, in this case, Nick was entitled to receive 50% of their possessions (although not necessarily the possessions Nick said he wanted). The judge said that, since he didn't know what belonged to who, if the case went to trial he would probably order the sheriff to go to Nick and Angela's house, impound all of their property, and hold a public auction to sell it all—everything from their tupperware to their underwear. Then the judge said he would take the proceeds from the sale and give half to Angela and half to Nick. That was what he thought was fair. Of course, that was not at all what Angela and Nick had in mind. The judge then took a brief recess for lunch. By the time he came back, Angela and Nick had found a way to divide their property themselves, and the case settled.

Obviously, Nick and Angela were not really fighting over their various pieces of personal property. Those things just gave them something tangible to fight about. What they were really fighting about was their own desire to get their way and make the other person suffer. The judge was smart enough to see that, and gave both of them a reason to stop fighting and settle.

You Can't Divide What You Don't Know Exists

Determining how to divide your assets in a divorce requires the same type of analysis as determining whether you or your spouse will need spousal support after the divorce. The first thing you need to do is get the facts. That means you need to figure out what you have, what you owe, and what you need. Only then can you divide what you've got in a way that makes sense.

To get a clear picture of what you own and what you owe, you need to start by making a list of all of your assets (what you own) and all of your liabilities (what you owe). This is similar to doing a budget, only instead of listing your income and expenses, you are listing your assets and your debts. A sample asset and liability list is included in Appendix A. You don't necessarily have to follow the format listed in Appendix A, or any other specific format, when compiling your list (unless the court in your jurisdiction requires you to use a special form). What you need to do is list things as completely as possible in a way that makes sense to you, so that you can clearly and easily see what you and your spouse have to divide.

Putting together a list of your assets and liabilities is fine—if you know what you have. However, what should you do if you don't know what your assets or your debts are? What if you've never been good with numbers, so you just let your spouse deal with all of the money issues during your marriage? What if your spouse was the controlling sort and never let you see any of your financial information? Worse yet, what if your spouse always hid that type of information from you? It's simple—figure it out!

Finding and compiling financial information may be tedious, but it's not brain surgery. If you are like most people, you have access to all the information you need—you just have to look at it. Open your mail. Go to your bank. Dig out copies of your tax returns. Talk to your financial advisor. Ask your employee benefits department for copies of your retirement account information. Find your recent credit card statements. If you can't find any statements, call the credit card companies and get copies of the statements sent to you (preferably at an address other than your home in case your spouse intercepts your mail). Call one of the credit bureaus or go online, and get a copy of your credit report. Do whatever you can to get the information you need—including asking your spouse for it! Believe it or not, sometimes it is that simple. Sometimes it's not, but it never hurts to try. (For a list of the types of financial documents and information you should be putting together, see Appendix B.)

Finding Hidden Assets

If you are like most people, gathering financial information is a pretty boring, but relatively simple, task. All you have to do is open the file cabinet, sort through mountains of paperwork, and figure out what you need. However, if you have a spouse who has been purposely hiding money or other assets from you, you can search the entire house and still not find the papers you need that will tell you what you really have. If you find that's true for you, then you are going to have to do a whole lot more than look through your bank statements in order to get a fair shake in your divorce.

Before you automatically assume (as many people who are going through a divorce do) that your spouse is hiding money from you, you need to determine whether that assumption is based in reality or is just a part of normal divorce paranoia. To do that, ask yourself a few questions. Have you been actively involved in your finances during your marriage? (In other words, do you know what you and your spouse make? Do you know what you and your spouse spend? Do you have a general awareness of the value of what you own and what you owe?) Is your spouse an employee who gets a paycheck every week? Did you and your spouse file joint income tax returns every year while you were married? Do you have access to all of your financial information?

If you've answered yes to all of these questions, chances are, no matter how paranoid you might feel, your spouse is probably not hiding money from you. That's not to say that your spouse couldn't have stashed away a little nest egg somewhere. However, if you've paid attention to money during your marriage, and you know how much comes in and goes out every month, there is probably not too much your spouse could have hidden from you. On the other hand, if you've answered no to these questions; if you've been financially clueless throughout your marriage; if your spouse is self-employed or works for cash; or, if your spouse has never shared any financial information with you, then you might have a problem.

The first thing you need to do if you reasonably suspect that your spouse is hiding money from you is try to gather as much information about your finances—and your spouse's finances—as you possibly can, given the situation you are working with. Do everything you would do even if your spouse wasn't hiding information—open your mail, go through your file cabinets, find your tax returns, and dig out the documents that are buried in the back of your closet. Even if your spouse has been purposely trying to hide information, you will still be amazed at what you can find if you just look. Call your credit card companies and get duplicate bills. Go online and pull your credit report. (You can get a free credit report at **www.annualcreditreport.com**, **www.equifax.com**, and **www.experian.com**.) Go to your bank and talk to your banker. Get copies of your bank statements. Get copies of your mortgage statements. Be creative. Look at the list of documents you need, and then see if you can figure out a way to get them. If you need to hire an attorney, an accountant, or a private investigator to help you, do it. Just understand that the more information you can put together yourself, the better off you're going to be and the less money you are going to have to pay someone to do the work you could have done yourself. You're also probably in a much better position to find information than your attorney, as you're the one who gets your family's mail, voice mail, and email.

No matter how much you dig to find your financial information and figure out where your money is, there are two circumstances in which your spouse can effectively hide money from you with relative ease and probably without getting caught: if your spouse owns his or her own business or if your spouse primarily deals in cash. If your spouse owns a business, there are a hundred ways to make sure the business doesn't show a profit or appears to suddenly be losing money while he or she is going through a divorce. Unless you are willing to hire a forensic accountant and spend tens of thousands of dollars on fees, as well as several years of your life in court, you will never be able to find everything your spouse has hidden. The same thing is true if your spouse has typically conducted business in cash. If your spouse gets paid in cash, pays others in cash (and not with a credit card), and hasn't been 100% honest with the IRS on income tax returns, he or she is also in a fairly good position to hide income and assets from you. What's more, you may even know that he or she is lying to you. However, if you've participated in the lies and have filed joint income tax returns claiming that your spouse only earned $30,000 a year when he or she really earned $60,000, you're going to be hard-pressed to convince a judge that you're now being truthful about what your spouse earns, even though in the past, both of you lied.

HIDDEN ASSETS GONE WRONG: THE STORY OF ADAM AND MARY

Adam and Mary led a simple life. Adam worked as a painter and Mary was a manicurist. Both were immigrants. They worked very hard and saved enough money to buy a small apartment building. Mary managed the property while Adam worked two jobs. In time,

Mary and Adam sold the property and bought two buildings, then two more. By the time Mary ran off with their mortgage broker, she and Adam owned a half dozen properties and two laundromats. Mary had managed them all. Adam, who didn't have a head for business, and had never paid attention to what Mary was doing with their money, didn't even know where the properties were located when Mary left.

By the time Adam filed for divorce, his financial affairs were a wreck. It turns out that, in anticipation of her divorce, Mary had started skimming money from the rents she collected on the buildings and stopped paying the mortgages at the same time. As a result, several of the buildings went into foreclosure. Most of the buildings were not in great neighborhoods, few of the tenants had written leases, and all of them paid their rent in cash. Adam had no way of determining how much rental income was really coming in and whether, as Mary claimed, the monthly rent suddenly wasn't enough to pay the monthly expenses. The same was true for the laundromats, which mysteriously stopped making money and had all of their equipment break down at about the same time that Adam filed for divorce.

Adam and Mary's divorce was a nightmare. It took their attorneys years to sort through their finances, sell all the buildings, wind up the businesses, and try to divide what was left between the two of them. Meanwhile, Adam spent thousands of dollars on attorneys, accountants, and private investigators, trying to piece together the truth about what Mary had done with their money. Of course, Mary had no bank accounts, no property, and no investments in her name. It was impossible to prove that she had any money at all. Although that didn't stop Adam from looking for it, it did keep him from finding it. Unfortunately for both Adam and Mary, Adam's digging around for the truth, coupled with Mary's financial wheeling and dealing, tripped some trigger with the IRS, which decided to audit their income taxes. Since neither Adam nor Mary had ever been 100% honest in declaring income, and neither of them had ever kept really good records, they soon found themselves facing much more than just a divorce.

Finding hidden money is time-consuming, frustrating, and expensive. Looking for it, as Adam and Mary discovered, sometimes has unanticipated consequences. What's more, unless you had the good fortune of finding a mysterious bank deposit slip, credit card receipt, or other telltale record lying around, you may not even know where to look. Sure, your attorney can subpoena documents, but before your attorney can do that, he or she has to know where to send the subpoena. An attorney can't very well send a subpoena to every bank in the state and hope that one of them turns up an account in your spouse's name. The same kinds of problems pertain to accountants. Sure, if you want to pay an accountant to pore over every financial record you or your spouse has generated in the past five years—including bank statements, tax returns, credit card bills, retirement accounts, business records, and anything else you can think of—you can do that. Maybe the accountant will even find a discrepancy in all of your records. Maybe. However, unless you are reasonably sure that your spouse has hidden hundreds of thousands of dollars, you are probably going to end up spending twice as much money in accounting fees looking for your spouse's hidden assets as you will ever get, even if those assets are found.

Understanding Your Finances

Getting information about your finances is step one. Making sense of the information you have once you get it is step two. For some people, that part will be easy—either because they have been actively involved in managing their own finances and they understand how money works, or because they don't have any assets so there is nothing to understand.

If you have nothing to divide, you have nothing to worry about. If, however, you have assets to divide and you find yourself staring like a deer in the headlights at your retirement account statement, your investment portfolio, or the detailed statement of your spouse's employment benefits package, then you may need to get help figuring your finances out. Even if you think you understand what you've got, you still may need help in order to understand what to do with what you've got and what your options are for dividing what you've got in a way that makes sense. To figure all that out, you need to understand a little bit about the law.

Property 101

When it comes to dividing property in a divorce, there are two kinds of states: community property states and noncommunity property (or common-law title) states. At present, the only community property states are Arizona, California, Idaho, Louisiana, Nevada, New Mexico, Texas, Washington, and Wisconsin. Puerto Rico is also a community property jurisdiction. In a community property state, anything a married couple acquires during their marriage is generally considered to be community property. It doesn't matter whose name the property is in or whose money was used to buy the property. It does not matter if one spouse earned a huge salary and contributed enormous amounts to the marriage, while the other spouse sat home and watched soap operas all day and contributed nothing. Both spouses are deemed to own an equal and undivided share of all of the property they acquired during their marriage, other than assets one spouse received as a gift or inheritance, or those that one spouse had before the marriage. In a community property state, marriage is considered to be a partnership. When the partnership dissolves, the court will divide the partnership assets equally.

In a noncommunity property state, ownership of property was traditionally determined by whose name was on the title to it. In other words, if you put your family home into your husband's name because you had bad credit, yet you contributed your earnings to pay the mortgage, taxes, insurance, and other household items, the house would still be deemed to be your husband's property when you got divorced—not yours. The result of this kind of law is obviously harsh and no longer makes sense in today's world. As a result, most noncommunity property states have now adopted *marital property* laws that operate in much the same way as community property laws.

If you live in a state that has adopted some type of marital property law, then it probably won't make much difference whose name is on the title to any particular piece of property. If the court finds that the property is marital, it will divide that property between you and your spouse. Even if your house is in your husband's name alone, if the two of you bought the property during your marriage, and you paid the mortgage with money that either one or both of you earned during the marriage, your home will still be considered marital property and will be divided between you. Anything that is nonmarital property—for example, property you inherited and have kept separated and in your own name—will belong completely to you (or completely to your spouse, depending on who owns the property).

The court in a marital property state will divide marital property *equitably* or in *just proportions*, rather than exactly *equally*. That means the court may not split property 50/50 between you and your spouse. Instead, the court may consider a variety of factors in dividing your marital property, including the amount of time, effort, and money you and your spouse each contributed to the marital estate, the length of your marriage, the relevant economic circumstances you and your spouse will have after you are divorced, the relative values of what you and your spouse will be receiving in the divorce, the effect of any premarital agreement you may have with your spouse, and whether you or your spouse will be receiving maintenance, among other things. All of these factors may lead the court to decide that either you or your spouse should get more than 50% of your marital estate. On the other hand (in theory at least), each of you should get all nonmarital property that is yours. Obviously, then, determining what is marital property and what is nonmarital property can be very important.

While a variety of factors can influence whether property is marital or nonmarital, the distinction between these two kinds of property is fairly simple. Marital property is property that belongs to the marriage. In general, marital property includes any property that you or your spouse earned during your marriage, regardless of whose name the property is in. It includes the home you bought during your marriage, your retirement plan, your spouse's retirement plan, and whatever else you accumulated during your marriage. Nonmarital property is property that belongs solely to either you or your spouse. Nonmarital property may be property that was yours before you were married, property that you inherited and kept in a separate account while you were married, or property that is designated as nonmarital property according to the terms of a prenuptial or premarital agreement you made with your spouse. While there are exceptions to every rule, nonmarital property is typically not divided between you and your spouse in a divorce. The owner of the property simply gets it as his or her own separate property.

Classifying property as marital or nonmarital, or as a mixture of marital and nonmarital, however, is not always easy or obvious. Sometimes things you think are marital property are really non-marital, and vice versa. To make matters even more complicated, there is also the issue of *mixed* or *commingled* property. This is property that is partially marital and partially nonmarital, or property that has all the funds so mixed up that you can't tell what's what anymore. Sorting out that kind of property so you can divide it in your divorce can be a real challenge.

In some cases, separating the marital and nonmarital portions of property is relatively easy. In others, it seems easy, but really is not. For example, if you had an investment account with $50,000 in it when you got married, and three years later when you get divorced, you have $75,000 in that account, then you might think the $25,000 is all marital property. However, whether that is true depends on where the $25,000 came from. Was it all appreciation, or did you put marital funds in to make the account grow? If you added in marital funds, how much of the $25,000 is interest on marital funds and how much is interest on nonmarital funds? All of those facts matter, and all of them can make the issue of what is or is not marital money very confusing. The bottom line is, if you really want to know what's marital property, you need to talk to your lawyer.

Valuing Your Assets

After figuring out what you have, the next step before dividing it is figuring out what it's worth. With some assets, knowing their value is easy. Money in the bank is money in the bank. If you want to know how much is there, all you have to do is look at your bank statement. Figuring out the value of other assets—such as real estate, small businesses, or pension plans—is trickier. What's more, in order to understand the value of those kinds of assets, you need to know not only what they are worth, but how much you owe on them. Your *equity*, which is the amount you are left with after you subtract what you owe from what you own, is what matters. For example, your home may be worth $200,000, but if you owe $185,000 on your mortgage, your equity is only going to be $15,000. That's the amount that gets divided in your divorce.

Valuing many assets requires the assistance of an expert. For example, if you want to know what the value of your house is, you need to find a real estate appraiser who can look at it, evaluate it, and tell you what it's worth. You might also consult with a real estate broker who won't necessarily give you a *certified appraisal*, but will be able to tell you what other comparable homes in your area have sold for, and thus give you a pretty good idea of what you could get for your house if you were to sell it. (A broker's estimate of the value of your home is not as official as an appraiser's certified valuation, but it's usually much quicker and cheaper to obtain.)

If you want to know the value of a pension, you will need to hire an actuary, who will review the terms of the pension plan, look at the amount the employee (you or your spouse) contributed to the plan, look at the employee's age and salary, how many years it will be before the employee is eligible to retire and start collecting money from the plan, and so on. After considering all of that, the actuary will crunch numbers and come up with an amount that the pension plan is worth in dollars and cents today. (Using an actuary is only necessary to determine the value of true pension plans—plans that have no set dollar value, but that pay you a certain amount of money per month when you retire. Other types of retirement plans—such as 401(k), 403(b), SEP, SIMPLE, or IRA accounts—have a defined dollar value all along and don't need to be valued by an expert. These types of plans typically provide you with a statement each month or each quarter, and they clearly tell you how much money you have in the plan.)

Valuing a small business also requires an expert. To value a business, you will usually need to hire an accountant, who will examine the books, records, tax returns, profit and loss statements, balance sheets, and other financial information from the business for the past few years, and will then use that information to evaluate what the business is worth. Needless to say, doing this is very time-consuming and expensive. Depending upon the size of the business and the willingness of your spouse to voluntarily turn over records, getting a business valued can cost thousands of dollars (just for the accountant) and take months to complete. It's not surprising, then, that many people don't bother to do it.

Whether or not you go through the trouble of independently valuing each and every asset you and your spouse own before you get divorced is a personal decision. Whether doing so is right for you depends on what you own, how much you own, what it will cost you to value what you own, and whether or not it's worth the grief and aggravation that it will take to value what you own. Most attorneys, of course, will advise you that it is always best to value everything. They are absolutely right in telling you that. The only way you can know for sure what something is worth is to have it valued by an independent expert. However, you are also absolutely within your rights to decide that you don't need to know, or that you don't want to know, the precise value of each and every piece of property that you and your spouse own. You may be perfectly content keeping your pension without bothering to value it, and in exchange, letting your spouse keep his or her pension or business without valuing it, because you and your spouse have decided that is fair and that's what you want to do. You may agree that spending thousands of dollars valuing your spouse's small business isn't worth it, as long as your spouse is willing to give you something else that you really want without fighting about it. Keeping the peace has value. Getting divorced without spending tens of thousands of dollars on experts and attorneys has value. In the end, determining what is most valuable—your money, your peace of mind, or some reasonable combination of the two—is your personal decision.

Fighting Over Your Debt

The flipside of fighting over assets is fighting over debt. Some people are not fortunate enough to have any assets to fight about. They've mortgaged all of the equity out of their houses, they've maxed out their credit cards, and they've lived a lifestyle they can't afford. Then, when they find themselves facing a divorce, they want to start a new life. They also want their spouse to pay for the old one. However, just as you are not entitled to receive 100% of the assets when you leave a marriage, so too are you unable to walk away from 100% of the debt. If you have run up credit card bills that would rival the national debt, you need to understand that paying off that debt will be your responsibility after you get divorced, just as it would have been if you stayed married. If your spouse—not you—ran up the debt, understand that paying that debt, or at least a portion of it, is probably still going to be your responsibility. That may not seem fair, but that's the way it is. You can fight with your spouse about it, blame your spouse for it, or try to manipulate your spouse into paying it—or you can just admit that you were the one who married your spouse in the first place, and since the law says that his or her debts may be your debts, you must deal with your problem.

The fight over who pays more of the debt is definitely less pleasant than the fight over who gets more of the assets, but it's really the same fight, just in reverse. Therefore, the same basic principles that apply to identifying and dividing your assets apply to identifying and dividing your debts. You need to figure out who you owe, what you owe, and whose name is on whatever it is you owe. Once you've done that, you can then start to figure out whether you or your spouse should pay the bill.

Before you can begin dividing up your debts, you first need to know what they are. Just as you made a list of your assets, you need to make a list of your debts. To do that, you need to gather up all of your bills, your mortgage, your home equity loan or line of credit, your credit card statements, and any paperwork regarding any loans you may have, and make a list of your debts. (Appendix A provides you with both an asset and a liability list you can use for reference.) Put all of the bills you and your spouse owe on the list, regardless of whether those bills are in your name, your spouse's name, or both of your names. Make sure you also list the total amount you owe on each bill, as well as the monthly amount you are obligated to pay.

In evaluating your debt, it is very important that you have complete and accurate information. In order to get that information, you may need to call the bank, the credit card company, or whoever you owe the debt to, and ask for current statements. You can't use outdated information. You need to know how much you owe now. You also need to know how much you and your spouse owed before you were married.

Of course, if your nonmarital debts have already been paid off, you don't need to consider them. As a matter of fact, you usually can't consider them. That means if you used your marital property to pay off your spouse's premarital debts, both your money and your spouse's debt are now gone. You don't get credit for having paid that bill.

Once you've identified your marital debts, you need to deal with them. The easiest way to deal with them is to get rid of them. If you truly want to start your life fresh after you are divorced, it makes sense to eliminate as much of your debt—and certainly as much of your joint debt—as you can possibly afford. If you and your spouse own a house together, but you have a sizeable mortgage and huge credit card bills, it makes sense to sell the house and use the money to pay off the mortgage and all of your joint credit card bills. If there is anything left, you can divide that. It does not make sense for one of you to keep the house, pay the mortgage, pay half the debts, and still buy out the other person's share of the house. Doing that means that one of you is going to be saddled with an enormous amount of debt, while the other will walk away with enough money to pay off his or her bills and start fresh. While you may think you want to saddle your ex with as many debts as you can just to see your ex suffer, doing that can definitely hurt you in the end.

The problem with allowing any debts to remain in your name, or in the joint names of you and your spouse, after you are divorced is that you will be responsible for paying those debts until they are completely gone—no matter what your divorce judgment says. If the judgment says that your ex is supposed to pay off the car loan that is in both of your names and he or she doesn't do it, the bank can still come after you. If the payments are made late, it will still affect your credit rating. If your ex goes bankrupt on the debts, you and you alone will be left holding the bag. Why? Because when you took out the loan, you and your spouse both agreed to pay it. The bank doesn't care about your divorce. It just wants to be paid. If your spouse doesn't do it, then the bank will come after you. It will then be up to you to chase down your ex and get him or her to pay you back. If you can't find your ex, or if he or she has gone bankrupt, you will be left paying off the debts in your name no matter what your divorce judgment says. That applies to any debts you have jointly taken out with your spouse, including your mortgage, home equity loan, joint credit card bills, or any other joint debt you might have incurred. That is why you want to pay off every joint debt you have with your spouse before you get divorced or as soon after you get divorced as possible. Once the debt has been paid, it can no longer come back to haunt you.

If you don't have the money to completely pay off a joint debt (such as the mortgage on your home), and your spouse wants to keep the home, the other option you have is for your spouse to refinance the mortgage so that it is only in his or her name. If your spouse does that, then he or she will be the only one responsible for making the mortgage payments, and the bank cannot come after you if your ex defaults. Refinancing may also provide you with a way to take some of your equity out of the house. Your spouse can then use that money to buy out your share of the house. For example, if you and your spouse own a home worth $250,000 and you owe $150,000 on it, there is $100,000 in equity in your home. If you are splitting the equity 50/50 with your spouse, that means you are entitled to get $50,000 from your spouse if he or she keeps the home and pays you off. In that case, your spouse could refinance the home and take out a mortgage for $200,000. He or she can then give you the extra $50,000, and you can release your interest in the home to him or her. Your spouse then keeps the house and you get the money. Of course, that means that your spouse will now have a bigger mortgage to pay. However, the home will be your former spouse's sole property, and he or she alone will be entitled to any appreciation it earns in the future.

Sometimes, however, refinancing is impossible. Maybe you and your spouse have a horrible credit rating. Maybe you don't make enough money, or haven't owned the home long enough, to refinance. Maybe the house isn't worth as much money as you need it to be worth in order to be able to take money out to pay off your spouse. In any of these cases and others, the bank may refuse to allow you to refinance. If that happens, you have two choices—keep the mortgage you have, in which case both you and your spouse will remain liable for all of the payments until the mortgage has been paid off in full (which could be thirty years down the road), or sell the house. Those may not be the best choices in the world, but they're pretty much going to be the only ones you have.

What to Do After You Know What You Have

After you've figured out what you have and what it's worth, dividing it up *should* be easy. In reality, it's not. In deciding what you and your spouse should each walk away with in your divorce, not only do you have to consider what you might want, but you also have to figure out what you are going to need, whether you can afford to keep what you get, and what the tax implications will be once you've gotten whatever it is you're going to get. Doing all that is anything but easy. For most people, it's also extremely emotional. Unfortunately, letting your emotions get the best of you is probably the worst thing you could do.

The most productive way to divide up your assets is to use your head, not your heart. Use common sense. Take your list of assets and liabilities, and ask yourself, *What do I really want? What do I need? What does my spouse want? What is fair?* Most people will claim they don't care what their spouses want and would prefer that their spouses don't get whatever they want anyway. However, if that's the approach you take to dividing your property, you are going to be fighting over nonsense for a very long time. Divorce is emotional enough. Fighting over the silverware helps no one. Try to be objective and fair, and be realistic. If you can barely afford your house payments on what you and your spouse make together, what makes you think you are going to be able to make those payments on your salary alone? Yes, you may love the house, and yes, you may want to keep it. But you can't afford it. So sell it, divide the proceeds, and be done with it.

When it comes to dividing your debt, the same principles apply. The more you can keep your emotions out of your decisions, the better off you will be. Because joint debt will follow both of you, it makes sense to get rid of as much of your joint debt as you can. It also makes sense to divide as much of your other debts as possible based upon whose name those debts are in. Obviously, if all the debts are in your name and none of the debts are in your spouse's name, that's not going to work. However, if your credit card bills and your spouse's credit card bills are about the same, it makes sense for you to keep the bills in your name and for your spouse to keep the bills in his or her name. Doing that is just easier. It's also easier, and makes more sense, for the spouse who keeps a piece of property to keep whatever debt is associated with that piece of property. If you keep the car, you should also keep the car loan. If you can't afford the loan, then either your spouse should take the car or you should sell it, pay off the debt, and buy a car that you can afford.

Dividing your assets and liabilities is difficult, not just because you're dealing with money, but because you're dealing with your emotions about money and your emotions about your marriage, your divorce, and your soon-to-be ex. The more you can separate your emotions from what you're doing and approach your property division as you would approach a business deal—rather than treating it as just another fight with your spouse—the better off you will be. Follow your head, take control of your heart, and you will be in the best position to negotiate a deal that you can live with in the future. Just remember—in the end, it really is only money.

9

Negotiating a Property Settlement

Never cut what you can untie.

—Joseph Joubert, Writer

When someone says "it ain' t the money, but it' s the principal of the thing," it' s the money.

—Elbert Hubbard, Author

We cannot negotiate with those who say "What' s mine is mine and what' s yours is negotiable."

—John Fitzgerald Kennedy, Thirty-fifth President of the United States

The thought of negotiating a divorce settlement leaves many people with knots in their stomachs. They think they don't know how to negotiate and that they can't do it themselves. They're afraid that if they start to negotiate with their spouse, they will make a mess of their divorce and their life. Yet, most divorce cases settle, which means that someone negotiated an agreement. Maybe it was the divorcing couple themselves, their lawyers, a mediator, or a minister. Whoever it was, somebody negotiated something—otherwise the case would still be dragging on.

The truth about negotiation is that every human being knows how to do it. Everyone negotiates for things every day. Kids negotiate with their parents to be able to go to the school basketball game with their friends. Parents negotiate with their kids to get them to do their homework before they go to the basketball game. Spouses negotiate with each other over who has to drive the kids to the basketball game, as well as what to eat for dinner, where to go on vacation, how to pay the bills, and hundreds of other issues. Some people negotiate well, others not so well—but everyone negotiates.

It doesn't take an expert to negotiate a deal between you and your spouse in your divorce. Okay—sometimes it does. Sometimes you would be more successful trying to wrestle an alligator in a telephone booth than you would be trying to negotiate a property settlement with your spouse. What's more, if your spouse has a history of bullying or intimidating you, or has been physically abusive towards you or your children in the past, negotiating with him or her directly is generally not a good idea. However, if your spouse has no history of abuse, and you and your spouse have managed to get past the worst of the anger you felt with each other when your divorce began, you may find that the two of you are in the best position to work out a deal that meets your mutual needs and makes both of you less unhappy than you would be if you let a perfect stranger decide your case.

Even if you're not comfortable negotiating a deal with your spouse yourself, and prefer to do it through your lawyer or with the help of a mediator, you still need to understand how negotiation works and what you can realistically expect to get out of it in order to be able to make your best deal. Your lawyer can do your negotiating for you, but you are the only one who can decide what you're willing to accept and what you're willing to give up. A mediator can help you brainstorm settlement options, but he or she can't force you to settle. No matter who negotiates for you, the key to being successful is knowing what you're doing.

Negotiation in a Nutshell

Volumes of books have been written about negotiation. Discussing all of the theories, strategies, and techniques of a trained negotiator is well beyond the scope of this book, but you don't need to get a PhD in conflict resolution to negotiate an acceptable settlement in your own divorce. All you need to do is keep in mind a few basic principles.

PRINCIPLE #1: TO NEGOTIATE SUCCESSFULLY, YOU HAVE TO WANT TO MAKE A DEAL

It seems pretty obvious that in order to negotiate an agreement, you have to want to agree. You have to want to settle. You have to want your divorce to end. While almost anyone who is going through a divorce will tell you that all he or she wants is for the divorce to be over, the truth is that deep down, many people don't want that at all. Maybe they're afraid of being suddenly single again. Maybe they want to fight, get their way, or be right (and what's more, they want their spouses to admit that they're wrong). Maybe they want to continue to live the same way they have always lived and they want their spouses to continue to pay for them to live this way—only they want their spouses to live somewhere else. Sometimes, believe it or not, people going through a divorce still want to be married. People going through a divorce want a lot of different things. The one thing many don't want is to compromise.

Divorce is compromise. Negotiation is compromise. You don't get through either process without it. If you want to reach an agreement with your spouse in your divorce, but you're not willing to give an inch on any of your demands in order to do it, don't waste your time negotiating, because you're never going to make a deal. You cannot reach a settlement agreement with your spouse without giving up some of the things that, in a perfect world, you would want. That's just how compromise works. What's more, when you're going through a divorce, you often have to compromise a lot—or at least, that's how it seems. If you're not willing to do that, your only alternative is to fight. It is impossible for two divorcing people who each want a nice, big piece of the same pie to agree on how to slice it unless they are willing to change the way the pie is cut. In order to negotiate effectively in your divorce, you have to be willing to deal.

Some people aren't willing to compromise in their divorce because they think it's a sign of weakness. Others think that if they are willing to give in on anything, they will end up giving in on everything. Being willing to compromise, however, does not mean that you are willing to be a doormat. There are some things you should be willing to compromise. There are other things that you should not be willing to compromise. The key is to know the difference between the two. How do you do that? Make a list.

PRINCIPLE #2: KNOW THE DIFFERENCE BETWEEN WHAT YOU WANT, WHAT YOU NEED, AND WHAT WOULD BE NICE

Before you can negotiate effectively, you need to know two very important things about your divorce—what you want and what you need. There is a difference. What you want is your wish list. It's everything you would get from your divorce in a perfect world. What you need is what you require to survive, as well as those things that are so important to you that you would be willing to fight to the death for them. A third category of things, which is really a subcategory of what you want, is the *it would be nice* category. This category includes those things that you kind of want, but aren't really excited about. If you got these things, it would be nice, but if you didn't get them, you wouldn't get too upset.

To distinguish between what you want, what you need, and what would be nice, start by making a list of everything you would like to get in your divorce. Write down everything you could ever hope to receive— the house, the car, the kids, a lifetime of support. Write down everything. Then, put your list in order. Take the time to figure out what is the single most important thing to you in the whole divorce. What is the one thing you're willing to go to the wall on? Is it custody of your kids?

Is it sole possession of your house? Is it simply a divorce? Whatever it is, that's number one on your list. Then, figure out your number two, and three, and so on. Once your list is numbered, divide it into three categories—what you need, what you want, and what would be nice. If you've numbered your list properly, you should be able to draw a line that will easily divide your list into these categories. For example, you should be able to say that numbers one, two, and three on your list are the things you really need, numbers four through ten are what you want, and the rest is just what would be nice. After you've done that, take a good, long look at your list.

When you look at your list of needs, wants, and items that would be nice, you should see a pyramid—there should only be a few things that you need, more things that you want, and lots of things that would be nice. If your pyramid is upside down, its time to do a reality check. You don't *need* to get your top twenty-five items in order to get divorced. Depending upon your circumstances, you should only have three, four, or maybe five things that you absolutely need. You may have more wants than that, but your list of wants shouldn't be all that long, either. Again, depending upon your situation, how much you have, and how detailed your list is, your list of wants shouldn't be any more than maybe ten things. Everything else should fall into the category of what would be nice. If you have more than five things listed as needs, or more than ten things listed as wants, go back and redo your list. Pare down what you think are needs and wants until you have a list that is no more than fifteen items—preferably less than that.

You can't negotiate effectively in your divorce unless you know what's important to you. Forcing yourself to recognize the difference between what you need and what you want makes all the difference in your negotiations. If you treat everything you want as something you need, and your list of needs is two pages long, you're going to come off as being so greedy that you will never make a deal. On the other hand, if you focus only on what you want, and let go of what you need, you may make a deal, but it will turn out to be a very bad one for you later on, when you find that you didn't get those few things that, in retrospect, you see were really important. Meanwhile, knowing what falls into the category of things that would be nice is also important. These are the items that you will use to compromise. These are the first things you will be willing to give up in order to get what you need. They will also be the last things that you will be willing to accept in exchange for something you need or something you really want.

PRINCIPLE #3: UNDERSTAND WHAT YOUR SPOUSE WANTS AND NEEDS

Once you have a clear picture of your own wants and needs, it's time to sit down and spend some time thinking about what your spouse wants and needs. If you know that your spouse adores your children, is a fabulous parent, and will never agree to anything in your divorce unless he or she gets at least joint custody and equal time with the kids, then you know that custody of the children is something that would fall into your spouse's list of needs. On the other hand, if your spouse has never been close to the children, travels for work four days a week, and is asking for sole custody just so that he or she doesn't have to pay child support, then you know that custody for your spouse is either a want, an *it would be nice* item, or simply a negotiating strategy. If your spouse knows that custody is something you need, he or she may be asking for it in the beginning of your negotiations just so he or she can give it back to you later on to get something he or she really needs. Knowing the difference between what your spouse wants, needs, and doesn't really care about is extremely important.

When putting together the list of what your spouse wants and needs, try to be as objective, as thorough, and as specific as you can. What has your spouse always cared about? What's important to him or her? Has your spouse always been worried about not having enough money? If so, then you know your spouse is going to want to get enough money in the divorce to feel secure. Has your spouse always worried about ending up as a street person someday? If so, then keeping his or her pension or retirement accounts and money in the bank may be really important to your spouse. Does your spouse own a business, and if so, was creating that business his or her lifelong dream? Then your spouse may be willing to give you more of the personal assets in your divorce as long as you let him or her keep the business. Whatever it is that you think your spouse really wants, list it.

It also helps to think about your spouse's personality, and how your spouse typically goes about getting what he or she wants. If you know that your spouse is a hothead who blows up like a firecracker whenever you say something he or she doesn't like, but calms down later, then you know that when you or your lawyer negotiates with your spouse, you're going to have to make a proposal, give your spouse time to blow up, then talk to your spouse about the proposal a few days later, after he or she had time to think about it. Similarly, if your spouse is the meticulous sort and pays attention to every little detail of anything financial, it doesn't make sense to give your spouse a settlement proposal that just says, "let's split everything 50/50." That's not going to be good enough. If your spouse is a detailed person, give him or her details. If your spouse is a big picture person, give him or her the big picture. Human behavior is consistent. If you know your spouse's personality and you know the way your spouse normally reacts in certain situations, that information will help you and your lawyer know what to expect when you are negotiating with your spouse during your divorce.

When considering what your spouse wants and needs, you need to keep in mind not only your spouse's physical and financial needs, but his or her emotional needs as well. Perhaps maintaining a comfortable home was never that important to your spouse when you were married. Perhaps you were the one who needed the security of owning your own home, while your spouse was the one who was content to move around every year. However, now that you are getting divorced, your spouse insists that all he or she wants is to keep the house. Why? Because your spouse doesn't really want the house at all—what he or she wants is to make you suffer.

UNDERSTANDING EMOTIONAL NEEDS: THE STORY OF DAVID AND ANNE MARIE

David and Anne Marie had been married for five years, the last four of which were awful. Instead of dealing with his marital problems, David had an affair with one of their neighbors, a woman who was much younger than Anne Marie. Anne Marie immediately filed for divorce, threw David out of the house, and started bad-mouthing David all over the neighborhood. Meanwhile, David moved in with the neighbor.

Anne Marie made her divorce with David hell. She and David didn't have any kids, they each earned about the same amount of money, they each had about the same amount in their retirement accounts, and they were each in a position to buy the other out of their share of the house. In theory, their divorce should have been simple. It wasn't.

At first, Anne Marie refused to settle on any terms. She didn't just want a divorce—she wanted David's blood. Finally, when she realized she was going to have to settle for money rather than one of David's body parts, she agreed that David should buy her out of the house. After several months of haggling over the price of the house, they agreed on a value. Then, after David paid to apply for a new loan and refinance, Anne Marie changed her mind and decided she wanted the house. David canceled the refinance and lost $500. Then, after three months went by, Anne Marie changed her mind again and decided they should sell the house. David didn't want to sell the house, but he did want to get divorced, so he agreed. However, when David found a realtor to list the house, Anne Marie changed her mind again. Finally, after over a year of changing her mind, Anne Marie committed (in writing) to let David buy her out of the house, and their case was settled—or so David thought.

On the day their divorce was supposed to be final, Anne Marie came up with a new issue. As a gift, her father had paid for and installed the landscape rocks that were in their front yard. She wanted the rocks back. David went ballistic! He and Anne Marie had argued for months over the value of the house so that he could buy her out. That value included the landscaping. Anne Marie disagreed. They argued. Finally, David agreed to pay Anne Marie an extra thousand dollars to cover the cost of the rocks. But Anne Marie didn't want the money. She wanted the rocks. She wanted David to tear up his entire front lawn and give her back those specific rocks. Anne Marie, who was an intelligent, educated, and otherwise rational human being, stood in open court and proclaimed to the judge, the lawyers, and everyone else in the courtroom that she was emotionally attached to those exact rocks and wanted them back. The judge was not impressed. Needless to say, Anne Marie soon understood that she was better off taking the money and forgetting about both the rocks and her cheating husband, and she got divorced.

David didn't think he and Anne Marie had anything to fight about in their divorce. He didn't think Anne Marie cared about the house. He didn't think she would have any problem letting him buy her out. What David also didn't think about was the fact that Anne Marie was devastated by his affair, and that changed everything. What Anne Marie wanted was an acknowledgment from David that he had done her wrong. When she didn't get that, and David moved in right down the block with the woman he was having an affair with, Anne Marie was beside herself. David should have known that flaunting his affair was the worst thing he could have ever done. Unfortunately, he didn't think about that. As a result, his divorce was a disaster.

As David and Anne Marie's story illustrates, sometimes, when you think you know what your spouse wants, you're wrong. Sometimes you miscalculate. That's why, when you put together your list of what you think your spouse wants, you really have to take some time to put yourself in your spouse's shoes and do your best to be thorough, specific, and objective. If you're not sure you know what your spouse needs and wants, ask. If you can't talk to your ex directly, do it through your attorneys, or do it in a settlement conference, where the two of you and your two attorneys all sit in a room together and try to hammer out a deal. However you can figure out what your spouse wants and needs, do it. In the end, that knowledge will help you as much as, or more than, understanding and acknowledging your own desires.

PRINCIPLE #4: BRAINSTORM AS MANY SETTLEMENT OPTIONS AS YOU CAN

The next key to conducting a successful negotiation is to come up with not one, not two, but as many different settlement options as you can possibly think up. Having many choices and being willing to be flexible in your choices gives you a much greater chance of negotiating an acceptable deal. Don't lock yourself into thinking that there is only one way to settle your case, and that if your case doesn't settle your way, it won't settle at all. In the previous scenario, David was willing to buy out Anne Marie, let her buy him out, or sell the property and split the proceeds. That's three different options for accomplishing the same thing. Even though Anne Marie was determined to drag out their divorce and make David suffer, David's flexibility made it difficult for her to throw him off. If, instead of giving her three choices, David had demanded that Anne Marie let him buy out her share of the house and had refused to settle for anything else, then Anne Marie could have come up with a half dozen seemingly legitimate reasons why that option wouldn't work. She could have then made it seem like David was being unreasonable—and she could have dragged out the case even longer. However, because David was so flexible, the judge could clearly see that Anne Marie was the unreasonable one. If the case had gone to trial, Anne Marie would have been the one in the judge's doghouse.

When you're brainstorming options, look at all of your income, expenses, assets, and liabilities. Look at every possible combination for dividing your property. Include maintenance in the mix as well. Maybe if you give your spouse a bigger share of your property, he or she will agree to waive any claim for maintenance in the future. Maybe if you pay him or her a certain amount of maintenance for a certain number of years, your spouse will settle for a 50/50 property split. Maybe your ex would be willing to make a deal if you paid him or her a lesser amount of maintenance for a longer period of time. There are any number of scenarios that you can create to settle your case. Try to think of them all. Then, decide which ones you would be willing to accept, which ones you would definitely reject, and which ones aren't your favorite, but might be acceptable if that's what you have to agree to in order to be done.

After you've come up with a list of settlement options, discuss them with your lawyer. Obviously, if your lawyer is negotiating for you, he or she needs to know what you want. However, even if you are negotiating yourself or with a mediator, you still need to know what the legal and financial effects of your various settlement options will be. Some of your options might have tax consequences you never thought about. Others might not be legally doable or may create an accounting nightmare. You need to talk to your lawyer before you do anything else. Once you know the legal and financial implications of all of your settlement options, you might find that you have to strike some of your settlement options from your list. By the same token, once you talk to your lawyer or your account- ant, you might come up with more or different settlement options. Whatever options you finally suggest to your spouse, make sure that they are legal, doable, and financially sound before you open your mouth.

Principle #5: Don't Lose Sight of the Big Picture

Coming up with a list of settlement options is fabulous. However, just because you have a list doesn't mean that your spouse is going to like any of them. More than likely, your spouse will choose one of the options you like the least, then change it into something that you like even less. Your spouse may come up with options of his or her own that you will find to be horrible. Your spouse may take weeks to respond to your settlement proposals, or may not respond at all. If any of these things happens to you, relax, breathe, and remember the big picture.

The *big picture*, for purposes of settlement negotiations, means two things—keeping in mind what's really important in life and always negotiating a deal as a whole, rather than trying to negotiate one item at a time. Keeping in mind what's important in life keeps you grounded. It prevents you from getting bogged down in all of the annoying, picky little details of your divorce that drive you insane. It allows you to remember that life is short and no matter how long your divorce takes, it won't last forever. It is a reminder to you that you don't have to control everything. If, in the big picture, something doesn't matter, it's okay to let it go.

Always negotiating a whole deal is also crucial. If you get fixated on settling just one thing, it's easy for your negotiations to get so bogged down that you'll soon be at a stalemate with your spouse. For example, if you and your spouse have a house, and you insist on keeping it and he or she insists on selling it, you can argue in circles forever, but unless one of you gives in, you're never going to get anywhere. You're only dealing with one item, so it's an all-or-nothing proposal—either you keep it or you sell it. If, on the other hand, you don't just talk to your spouse about what to do with the house, but you also include in your discussions the cars, the furniture, and the retirement accounts, you may find that if you give your spouse more of something else that he or she wants, you may be able to convince him or her to let you keep the house in exchange. That's what big picture negotiations are about.

Principle #6: Treat Your Spouse Like a Human Being

It's easy to forget, when you're in the midst of an ugly divorce, that no matter how many truly horrible things your spouse has said, done, or threatened to do to you in the recent (or perhaps not-so-recent) past, he or she is still a living, breathing human being. As such, your ex is entitled to a certain amount of respect—maybe not the same amount of respect that you gave your spouse when you were first married, but he or she still deserves something. What's more, as contradictory as it might seem to you, unless you respect your spouse (or at least respect your spouse's position), you will never be able to successfully negotiate anything with him or her.

Negotiation requires communication. If you want to cut a deal with someone, you have to be able to talk to that person, and he or she has to be able to talk to you. What's more, each of you has to feel like the other is not just talking, but listening as well. That's not an easy thing to do when you're in the middle of a divorce. After all, if you and your spouse were such great communicators, you probably wouldn't be getting divorced in the first place. No matter what happened during your marriage, you can communicate enough in your divorce to settle your case if you just do two things—listen to your spouse when he or she is talking (without interrupting, no matter how outrageous what he or she is saying may be) and respect what your spouse is saying enough to actually consider it. If you can do just that much, you may be truly amazed at what you can work out.

The Power of Respect:
The Story of Deborah and Roger

Roger hadn't exactly been a model husband or father before he and Deborah got divorced. He drank a lot, stayed out all night, and often got into fights. Deborah suspected Roger was doing drugs as well. Even after they were divorced, Roger rarely paid Deborah child support and he blew off a good portion of the visitation he was supposed to have with their son, Tim.

A couple of years after their divorce, Roger got into a terrible motorcycle accident that left him paralyzed from the waist down. Unable to walk without leg braces and crutches, Roger could no longer work, and had to move in with his parents and go on permanent disability. Although he became clean and sober, his brother, who also lived with his parents, did not. When 8-year-old Tim walked in on his uncle smoking marijuana in the basement of Roger's parents' house, Deborah went berserk.

Deborah refused to let Tim go to Roger's house again until Roger's brother moved out. Roger claimed Deborah was trying to ruin his relationship with Tim. Roger and Deborah each got lawyers, who filed a half dozen different motions for everything under the sun, embroiling Roger and Deborah in a fight that was worse than their original divorce. Neither of them could afford the battle, and their situation just kept going downhill. Finally, in desperation, Deborah approached Roger and said, "Let's talk."

Up to that point, Deborah had always treated Roger like a drug-addicted, alcoholic loser. In turn, Roger had refused to talk to Deborah, because all she ever did was criticize him. Their relationship ranged from nonexistent to horrible.

When Roger and Deborah first started to talk, their conversation was awkward and difficult. Roger was convinced that Deborah was trying to cut him out of Tim's life so she could have the perfect family with her new husband. Deborah believed that Roger was exposing Tim to drugs and criminals, and she accused him of suddenly wanting to exercise all the rights of a father without taking any of a father's responsibility. Roger had never paid child support, helped Tim with a school project, gone to Tim's band practice, or seemed interested in Tim's life. You can imagine Deborah's surprise when, instead of arguing with her, Roger started to cry. He said knew he hadn't been a good father, but ever since the accident, he had been trying to change his life around. He hadn't realized how much he had missed in the meantime or how badly he was still screwing up.

Deborah immediately melted. She finally understood just how tough life was for Roger, and that he was in no position to demand that his parents kick his brother out of the house just because Deborah believed the brother was doing drugs. Roger promised to never let Tim be alone with his uncle again. He also gave Deborah the first child support check she had received in years, and he agreed to start paying some of the back support her owed her. In turn, Deborah agreed to decrease Roger's child support so it was in line with his decreased income, and to let him start seeing Tim more often. In the end, Roger got more time with Tim, Deborah started getting some support, and both of them started getting along better than they had in years.

As Deborah and Roger both learned, it is amazing what two people can work out together when they treat each other like human beings. Even if you believe your spouse doesn't deserve your respect, even if you believe he or she is immoral, unethical, unfaithful, or just a blooming idiot, treating your spouse like dirt only makes your own life more difficult. It also makes negotiating a settlement with him or her impossible. So, take the high road. Treat your ex like you would like him or her to treat you. You might be surprised at what happens when you do.

PRINCIPLE #7: GO FOR THE WIN/WIN

The final, and perhaps most important, principle of negotiation is that the best settlement you can make is the one where everyone wins. Of course, in a divorce, no one ever really *wins*. However, just because no one really wins doesn't mean that everyone has to lose. If you can craft a settlement agreement that gives you, your spouse, and your children what each of you needs to continue to live reasonably well after your divorce, that's a win. If you can settle your case in six months rather than fighting in court for years, that's a win. If you can make a deal with your spouse that each of you feels is reasonable, rather than one that either (or both) of you resents, that's a win. In the end, a winning settlement is one that both you and your spouse can live with.

To create a win/win settlement, you must first take into account everyone's needs—not only their physical and financial needs, but their social, emotional, and psychological needs as well. If you want to be effective, you have to look at everything—you have to keep the big picture in mind. Look at your wish list. What do you need? What do you think your spouse needs? What do your kids need? Make a master list that combines what everyone needs so you can easily see, on one piece of paper, what needs your settlement proposal has to meet. (A sample format for a master list of needs is included in Appendix B.)

Before you go any further, examine your list to make sure it is grounded in reality. It should only list needs, not wants. (This is not to say that you won't get anything that you want in your divorce settlement, but when you're starting out, it's more important that you address what you need. What you want will come later.) Your list should also be reasonably balanced. If you've listed ten things you need and only one thing your spouse needs, you're not being fair. If you're not being fair to your spouse and your kids, then you'll end up crafting a settlement proposal in which the only winner is you, and this whole exercise will be an enormous waste of time. The point of this exercise is to come up with win/win settlement proposals. After you do this exercise, even if you throw out the results and go back to fighting like a crazy person, at least you'll know what your best settlement options are.

After you've made your list, you need to organize it in a way that will enable you to see what kinds of issues you need to address in order to meet everyone's needs. To do that, divide your list into four categories: physical, financial, social, and emotional/psychological.

Put everyone's needs into the appropriate category. Physical needs will be things like having a place to live and proper medical care. Financial needs are those that involve money. Social needs are things like having time to spend doing things other than working and taking care of your kids. It's also important for your children (especially if they are teenagers) to have time to spend with their friends, and not just with mom and dad. Emotional and psychological needs are things like your need to feel financially secure, your need to be independent, or your need to have friends and family who support you. All of these kinds of needs, in every category, are important. Some will be more important to you than others, but for the moment, don't judge what you, your spouse, or your children need. Just list those needs, categorize your list, and look at what you've got.

After you've listed everyone's needs, then you have to start brainstorming ways to meet those needs. Start with the physical and financial needs. Look at your income and expense list from Chapter 7, and your asset and liability list from Chapter 8. How can you use the resources you have to make sure that everyone has a place to live, food to eat, and enough money to survive? Whose medical insurance provides better and cheaper coverage for the kids? Where would it be best for the kids to live after you're divorced, and how are you going to handle transporting the kids from one house to another when you and your spouse no longer live together? How can you divide whatever assets you have in a way that will allow both you and your spouse to feel financially secure? Do your best to think of ways to use what you have to meet everyone's needs. When you're done with the physical and financial needs, move on to the other needs. Write down as much as you can.

When you're brainstorming settlement options, it's important to list as many different ideas as you can come up with. Don't limit yourself to creating just one option. There is always more than one way to settle a case. Depending upon what you own, what you earn, how many kids you have, and your overall situation, you may be able to come up with dozens of different settlement scenarios. Write them all down. The more options you can present to your spouse, the better your chances will be that he or she will like one of them. Having lots of options also keeps you from becoming too attached to any one of them. If you allow yourself to believe that your case has to be settled *your* way, you dramatically decrease the chances that it will settle at all. Remember, negotiation means compromise. Be flexible. In the end, the tree that bends with the wind is the one that springs back to life after the storm is over.

Applying the Negotiation Principles

Negotiating any kind of agreement is tough. Negotiating an agreement with your soon-to-be ex-spouse while you're in the middle of a divorce is even tougher. However, doing that still beats going all the way to trial, hands down. If you can apply the principles of negotiation, you should be well on your way towards working out a settlement agreement that suits your family, and that both you and your spouse can live with. If you can't reach an agreement, or if your spouse won't negotiate or won't negotiate fairly, then you may be stuck letting a judge decide your life. If that happens, it happens. Remember, there are some things you can't control. However, if you take the time to put together the information you need and at least try to negotiate a deal with your spouse (even if you do it through your lawyers), you may be amazed at the results you get.

10

Strategies, Games, and Other Things that Will Make You Crazy

Once the game is over, the king and the pawn go back in the same box.

—Italian Proverb

It isn't that they can't see the solution. It is that they can't see the problem.

—Gilbert K. Chesterton, Author

No one can drive us crazy unless we give them the keys.

—Doug Horton, Author

Settling your divorce with your spouse may sound like a grand idea, but just as it takes two people to fight, it takes two people to settle. If one of the people in the fight doesn't want the battle to end, isn't willing to compromise, or is more interested in proving that he or she is right than in moving on with life, then settling the fight can be difficult. Settling can be even more difficult when one of the parties involved in the fight doesn't want to settle, but wants to win.

The Divorce Game

Many people view divorce as a game. There are distinct players, each of whom employs his or her own strategy to achieve a specific goal. In the end, there's a winner and a loser. While the analogy is easy to understand, thinking of your divorce as a game automatically puts you in the position of a player. It also immediately casts your spouse as an opponent. While that may very well be how you feel about your spouse while you're going through your divorce, the problem is that, while most games end and the players shake hands and go home, divorces aren't like that. Divorce isn't a game. It's a part of your life. In most divorces, no one wins. The best outcome you can usually hope for is the one in which everyone's needs are met and everyone loses the least. What's more, once you have spent months or years trying to beat your spouse and defend yourself in the game of divorce, it will be exceedingly difficult to sit next to him or her and make small talk at your child's soccer game or music recital.

The temptation to view your divorce as a game runs deeper than most people think. While there are those who will loudly protest that they would never think that way and that their life is not a game, those same people will continue to do things that drive their former spouse insane, just because they can. They will pick fights, steal money, hide income, ignore court orders, and push their spouse's buttons, while at the same time, they are complaining to the court that their spouse is abusive, cheap, arrogant, and insensitive. No matter what you call that kind of behavior, the truth is, it's game playing—and it's destructive.

Game playing comes in many different forms. If you won't trade visitation weekends when your spouse has a conflict simply because there's no court order saying you have to do so and you'd rather make your spouse squirm, that's game playing. If you purposely throw out every bank statement you've received in the past three years just so your spouse has to spend the money to subpoena them from the bank rather than getting copies from you, that's game playing. If you're unemployed and refuse to look for a job because you want your spouse to continue paying alimony for as long as possible, that's game playing. Similarly, if you're underemployed and refuse to get a better-paying job, even when you could easily do so, because the more money you make, the more you have to pay for child support, that's game playing. No matter how good doing any of these things may make you feel, engaging in that kind of behavior ultimately hurts both you and your family.

There are many variations of the divorce game and innumerable strategies for playing it. Some of the most common games are discussed in this chapter, but many others exist. What's more, people play these games, not only while they are going through a divorce, but often long after their cases have closed. Some people play the games on purpose. They want to make their spouses suffer, cost them money, or just play with their heads. Other people don't realize they're playing a game at all, and would probably deny it if you told them they were. Whether you acknowledge you're playing a game or not, the effect is the same—you cause conflict, grief, and aggravation to your spouse, your children, your family, and yourself. In the end, none of the games are worth playing.

The Scorch and Burn Divorce

The *scorch and burn divorce* is exactly what it sounds like—doing everything in your power to burn your spouse, no matter who or what else you have to burn along the way to do it. It is pure, unadulterated vengeance. It tends to afflict those who feel truly wronged—those whose spouse had an affair, squandered all their money, or destroyed their ideal of the perfect family. To a certain extent, it affects every human being who is going through a divorce. Very few people can honestly say that they made it through the entire end of their marriage and their whole divorce without wanting to rip their spouse's face off at least once. On the other hand, most people allow such feelings to pass, and soon adopt a more rational approach to whatever problems they are facing. Others, however, insist upon extracting a pound of their spouse's flesh in exchange for whatever wrong their spouse has supposedly done. They don't just want a divorce. They want to cause pain. The problem with pain is that it's a lot like water—you can't make it shower down on someone standing close to you without getting yourself just as wet.

VENGEANCE IS NEVER FREE: THE STORY OF TOM AND DEE

Tom and Dee were very well off. After years of struggling, they had built several successful businesses, owned multiple pieces of property, and raised two children. On the surface, it seemed like they had it all. Then Tom, who was 62, fell in love with Monika, a 32-year-old gold digger, who convinced him that if he really wanted to have it all, he would dump Dee and marry her. To further her cause, Monika got pregnant. Tom filed for a divorce.

When Dee got the papers she almost went mad. For years she had turned a blind eye to Tom's infidelity for the sake of their children (and, of course, the lifestyle and money Tom provided her with, although Dee didn't readily admit that), and now, just when she should have been able to relax and enjoy her golden years, she was facing a divorce! Dee hired herself the most obnoxious attorney she could find, and she went after Tom like the scorned woman that she was.

Dee not only fought Tom in court, she fought him in business as well. All of Tom and Dee's businesses were family owned. Dee and her daughter owned the stock in their biggest company; Tom and their son owned the two smaller companies. However, Tom had run them all—that is, until Dee fired him from the company she owned.

Tom went nuts! He had built that company, and had only put Dee's name on the stock for tax and estate planning reasons. If she actually tried to run that company, she'd run it right into the ground—which is exactly what he decided to let her do. As a matter of fact, he went to her suppliers and convinced them to stop selling to her, which made her business start to fail even faster. Dee responded by getting Tom kicked out of the house and telling all of Tom's customers that, for her own safety, she had to get an order of protection against him. Tom turned their son against Dee. Dee turned their daughter against Tom. Tom froze Dee's assets. On and on it went.

For years, Tom and Dee fought over everything—from the value of their real estate to who got the dog. They were in court constantly. They took their case to the appellate court twice. They got to the point where they no longer cared what their fight cost, how long it took, or what their children thought. Each of them only wanted to win. Meanwhile, they spent millions of dollars in attorneys' fees, completely destroyed their family, squandered what should have been their kids' inheritance, bankrupted two of their businesses, and ended up triggering a federal investigation into alleged irregularities in their business operations.

The best thing anyone could say about Tom and Dee's case was that at least their children were grown. Even so, the divorce still deeply affected their children and tore the family apart forever. If, like Tom and Dee, you think that hurting your spouse is worth destroying your family, ruining your business, wreaking havoc on your health, and paying a fortune in lawyer's fees, then perhaps the scorch and burn philosophy of divorce is appropriate for you. For everyone else, adopting such a philosophy is nothing short of insanity.

What should you do, though, if your spouse takes the scorch and burn approach, but you would rather settle amicably? You have two choices—scorch back, or do the best you can do and let go of the rest. Unfortunately, neither one of those is a particularly pleasant choice. If your spouse is determined to destroy you and is willing to destroy him- or herself in the process, no matter what you do, you're going to be faced with a lot of destruction. If you fight back as hard as he or she is fighting you, there won't be much left for either of you to fight about in the end. What's more, it's likely that your relationship, and perhaps even your family, will be destroyed forever. If, on the other hand, you fight as hard as you have to just to get what you need, and let go of everything else, you have at least half a chance of salvaging what's really important to you. That's still not a great choice. It still means that you might have to fight ferociously to get just a fraction of what you should have received. It's likely that you will lose a lot of things that you really wanted, not to mention those that it would have been nice to have. You probably won't feel good about that. As a matter of fact, it's likely that you will harbor bad feelings towards your ex for a long, long time. However, at least you will be able to walk away with some of your sanity and most of your family reasonably intact. If you believe in karma, you can also take comfort in the fact that someday, somehow, your spouse's craziness will come back to haunt him or her.

The Ostrich Technique

Another interesting divorce game is the *ostrich technique*—otherwise known as burying your head in the sand. People who employ this technique believe that if they just ignore the divorce proceedings long enough, the case will magically go away. They don't hire a lawyer, they don't appear in court, and they don't respond to their spouse's attempts to settle the case and move on. They don't do anything until the judge makes them. Then they rush in to court, give the judge a sob story, and beg for even more time to do what they should have done months earlier.

Some people don't ignore their case—they just conveniently neglect it. These people bury their head in the sand a little less deeply. They actually hire a lawyer, but then they become too busy to answer his or her calls. They forget to respond to their lawyer's letters, and they basically don't do anything they're supposed to do to participate in their own case.

When the judge in their case has finally had enough and threatens to hold them in contempt of court, they do what the judge has ordered—but they do it very slowly. What's more, they only do exactly what the judge has ordered them to do, and not one thing more. So, a few months later, they're back in court again, and again, and again.

Whether you refuse to acknowledge that you are going through a divorce, purposely stall every step of the proceedings, or continue to pressure your spouse to go into marriage counseling when you know the only thing he or she wants is a divorce, what you are really doing is burying your head in the sand. Instead of being responsible, facing reality, and dealing with it, you deny what you don't want to see. The problem with using denial as a way to deal with your divorce is that it never, ever works.

People can get divorced relatively easily. Whether you agree with the laws that allow no-fault divorce or not, the truth is that, in most instances, if your spouse wants a divorce, he or she is going to get one. You can make the process take longer. You can make your divorce cost more. However, no matter what you do, you can't stop it from happening. Period. Moreover, once your spouse has decided to get a divorce, chances are that you are not going to change his or her mind by denying that your marriage has failed, trying to make him or her feel guilty for wanting a divorce, or arguing with him or her about every little thing, just to buy yourself more time so that you can work things out in your marriage. What you are going to do by denying reality and acting like your marriage isn't ever going to end is to aggravate your spouse, make life harder on your children, and more likely than not, get screwed yourself. Remember, if your head is buried in the sand, it's pretty hard to see what's coming at you, let alone be prepared to deal with it.

If you find yourself faced with a spouse who refuses to participate in your divorce or who participates so slowly that you're sure you'll be facing retirement before your case is over, the first thing you need to do is to identify where your spouse's behavior is coming from. If your spouse had no idea that you were going to ask for a divorce, while you mentally left the marriage years ago, maybe you just need to give your spouse a little time to catch up. If you do that, it's possible your spouse will stop dragging his or her feet and your case will go much more smoothly. On the other hand, if your spouse doesn't believe in divorce under any circumstances and is burying his or her head in the sand as a way of avoiding the inevitable, or if your spouse has never been great at dealing with what he or she doesn't want to admit exists in the first place, then you may have to be a little bit more aggressive about moving your case forward. Make sure your lawyer stays on top of your case and pushes it forward every chance he or she gets. The lawyer doesn't have to be a pit bull, but he or she also doesn't have to agree to continue the case fifteen times. Do what you need to do, as sensitively as you can, to make sure that your case gets through the system as quickly as possible, and to ensure that, if your spouse insists on burying his or her head in the sand, he or she is not burying you too.

The Refusal of Responsibility Game

Another approach that is similar to burying your head in the sand is the *refusal of responsibility* game—letting your lawyer decide your life. True, you should have a lawyer you trust, and it's generally a good idea to follow his or her advice. However, your lawyer cannot run your life. If you have never seen a household bill in thirty years of marriage, and you have no idea what your assets are or how much money your spouse makes, how can you expect your lawyer to figure out how you're going to support yourself after the divorce or what a reasonable division of your assets should be? Yes, to a certain extent, that's your lawyer's job, and yes, your lawyer can subpoena documents and piece together at least your most recent financial history—but you still have to help. Unless for some reason you are physically or mentally unable to participate in your own affairs, your own case, and your own life, you need to do just that. It will make all the difference in the world.

THE PERILS OF AVOIDING RESPONSIBILITY:
THE STORY OF PAULO AND MARIA

Paulo, an immigrant who lacked any kind of formal education, married Maria, a beautiful young woman from his country, in an arranged marriage. Once she was in this country, Maria got an education, but Paulo did not. Eventually, they bought their own home, as well as several small apartment buildings. Maria managed the properties while Paulo worked. Eventually, Maria, who was many years younger than Paulo, found a new man and started living a much more extravagant life than Paulo had ever dreamed about. Unfortunately, Maria was living it at Paulo's expense.

Paulo was no dummy, but he didn't understand finance or real estate. As long as money was coming in, he never paid much attention to what Maria was doing to get it. He didn't even know what property they owned. All Paulo knew was that when he caught his wife cheating on him, he wanted a divorce. So Paulo took a month's worth of the family mail to a lawyer, dumped it on his desk, and said, "Here's what we have. I want to sell it all and get out."

Paulo was a wonderful, honest man, but when it came to taking charge of his own life, he was completely inept. He knew his wife was playing fast and loose with their property, but he wasn't willing to spend the time or pay the money it took to try to figure out what was really going on. He never visited the properties, collected the rents, or paid the bills, and he didn't want to start just because he was getting a divorce. All Paulo wanted was out, and he wanted someone else to figure out how to get him out.

Unfortunately for Paulo, while he may have been ignorant about real estate, Maria was not. Immediately after Paulo filed for divorce, the tenants in the investment properties suddenly stopped paying the rent. Several of the apartments, which had been rented for years, strangely went vacant. Maria claimed it was bad luck. Paulo knew it had more to do with their divorce than with luck. Yet, he had convinced himself that he would never understand all of the buying, selling, and renting that Maria did, so he didn't even try. Paulo could have hired a private investigator to find out what was going on at the properties, or he could have gone over there himself. However, he had convinced himself that he wasn't educated enough to figure out what was going on, so he didn't even try.

Years later, after Maria had skimmed a nice chunk of rental money from the buildings before they were sold (some at a loss), Paulo found that "half" of their property was considerably less than what he thought it should be. Instead of admitting that his own refusal to become actively involved in the management of his property is what caused him to lose money in his divorce, Paulo ranted about how unfair the court system was and how the divorce laws in this country always favored the woman.

It is your responsibility to participate in your own case. You are in a far better position than anyone—including your lawyer—to find out what you have, what you owe, and whether your spouse is being less than honest with you. Without your help, there's only so much that even the best lawyer can do to help you end your marriage without losing your shirt.

The Expert in Everything Approach

While some people take a completely hands-off approach to their divorce, others mess up their cases by being too hands-on. These are the people who think they know everything. They think they know what's best for themselves, their spouses, and their children. They know more than their accountant, their therapist, and the judge. These people even know more than their lawyers. These are mini-lawyers. They spend hours on the Internet researching the law, only to often get it wrong. They talk to anyone they can find who has gone through a divorce, just so they can compare what they are getting in their case to what everyone else in the world got in their cases, even though every case is different. They insist on coming to every court appearance, reviewing every document, and participating in even the most minute decisions about their case. While that kind of behavior can be helpful to a point, when a mini-lawyer starts telling his or her real lawyer how to run the case, there's a problem.

The reason you hire a lawyer when you're going through a divorce is because you need an educated, objective professional to guide your case through the court system and do what you can't do yourself. You are too emotionally involved in your own case to ever be objective about it. Just as a doctor who operates on him- or herself has a fool for a patient, a divorcing person who represents him- or herself has a fool for a client. (That applies, by the way, even if you are a lawyer yourself.)

A lawyer is in your case to represent you. You need that representation. You need someone to advise you, not only on the law, but on what makes sense in your case and how you can get a fair shake in your divorce. Don't think you can learn all the law you need on the Internet and navigate the court system on your own. It is extremely difficult to handle your case yourself.

Further, if you think your friend has the greatest divorce decree on the face of the earth, and you want your final judgment to say exactly the same thing, then hire your friend's lawyer. Of course, when that lawyer is unable to negotiate the same terms in your divorce judgment as your friend did because you've been married twice as long, make half as much money, have more children, or otherwise have a different life circumstance than your friend does, don't be surprised. No two couples are alike. No two divorces are alike. No two lawyers are alike.

If you've found a lawyer who you think is right for you, then listen to him or her. It doesn't make sense not to. Of course, listening to your lawyer doesn't mean doing everything your lawyer tells you without question. You should not keep your mouth shut if you think something your lawyer has told you is wrong for you or your family. If he or she consistently tells you things that don't sound right to you, you should consider finding yourself a new lawyer. However, realize that when you are getting divorced, you need to give up a certain amount of control over the details of your life. You can't do everything. You can't parent your children, work at your own job, put together a new life for yourself, restructure your entire financial situation, possibly move your home, and run every last detail of your divorce case as well. You will be much better off listening to your lawyer and working with him or her as a team to get through your divorce than you would be by trying to call all the shots yourself.

If you are faced with having to deal with a spouse who thinks he or she knows everything, the best thing you can do is let your spouse know everything. It does you absolutely no good to try to persuade your spouse that he or she is wrong. All you'll do is aggravate yourself, because no matter how much you argue with your spouse, he or she is never going to believe you anyway. Besides, if you play your cards right and can manage to convince your spouse that your settlement proposal is really his or her proposal, and that he or she is the smart one and you are the idiot, both of you will end up getting what you want. You'll get the deal you were looking for and your spouse will get the satisfaction of knowing that, once again, he or she was "right."

The Constant Mind-Changer

Another game divorcing couples get caught up in is *indecision purgatory*. That's what happens when one or both of the people involved in a divorce just can't seem to decide what they want or how to get it. Even if they can decide, they change their minds about what they want at least every other day. (Remember the story of David and Anne Marie from Chapter 9.) Consequently, their case drags on, nothing gets done, and everyone involved gets progressively angrier and more frustrated.

It's understandable that you're often not sure of what you want when you're going through a divorce. Your entire world is changing.

It seems like you have to decide everything all at once. Your emotions are so up and down, and your head is often spinning so badly, that you can't decide what you want for lunch, let alone whether you should refinance the house or sell it. However, if you can't decide what you want or if you change your mind about what you want every five minutes, not only are you going to drive everyone around you completely insane, but you're going to end up having to live with decisions someone else—i.e., the judge—made for you. As the old adage goes, *not to decide is to decide*.

If you have to deal with a spouse who can't make a decision, or who constantly keeps changing his or her mind, you have two choices—you can allow your spouse's eternal indecision to make you crazy, or you can gently but firmly keep the pressure on your spouse (and his or her lawyer) to make as many decisions as quickly as possible, while understanding that your divorce is going to take longer than you want. Remember, you cannot control your spouse. You cannot force your spouse to make decisions if he or she refuses to do so, and you cannot force your spouse not to change his or her mind ten thousand times a day. You can keep pushing your lawyer to move the case forward, but that's about all you can do. Ultimately, the judge will be able to force your spouse to make the decisions that are important in your divorce, or the judge will make them for both of you. In the meantime, you can either drive yourself crazy wishing that your spouse was more decisive, or you can accept the fact that divorces always take longer than anyone wants, and deal with it.

The Righteously Indignant

The game of *righteous indignation* is played when one spouse assumes a position of moral superiority over the other. This game gets played a lot when two parents have different parenting styles. The righteous spouse decides that he or she is the good parent, while the other spouse is a bad parent—and the righteous spouse doesn't hesitate to communicate that fact to the children. He or she makes sure that the children know when their other parent is five minutes late picking them up that if the other parent really cared about them, he or she would never be late. When the children come home after spending the weekend with the noncustodial parent, the righteously indignant spouse asks pointedly whether they have been to church that morning, even though he or she knows that his or her ex isn't religious, just so that the children learn that good parents take their children to church. The righteously indignant spouse clucks his or her tongue when he or she learns that when the children were with their other parent, they had lunch at McDonald's, stayed up past their bedtime, or didn't take a bath because they were out too late having fun. Instead of talking about their different parenting styles with his or her ex-spouse and trying to work out a common set of rules for the children, or explaining to the children that different houses can have different rules and that's okay, the righteous spouse turns every clash of parenting techniques into a moral issue, painting him- or herself as the long-suffering saint and his or her former spouse as a pathetic sinner, or worse yet, the devil.

The purpose of the game of righteous indignation is to allow the righteous spouse to feel morally superior while still ripping his or her ex to shreds. It is a game of anger and vindictiveness, cloaked in the mask of doing what is right. To the outside world, the righteous spouse's only concern is the well-being and moral upbringing of the children. In reality, the righteous spouse's goal is to cut the other spouse out of the children's lives forever so that he or she can be in control. What the righteous spouse doesn't realize is that, of all of the games he or she can play, this one has some of the most dire consequences.

Children need to have healthy relationships with both of their parents. When one parent portrays the other as wicked, evil, or even just consistently wrong, the children become torn. They love both of their parents, but in their minds, if not in reality, they are forced to choose between the two. What's more, children take all of the criticism of their parents very personally. If they love the bad parent (and they do), but that parent is bad (which they know must be true because their other parent tells them so), then they must be bad too. Children hear the criticism of their parent as a criticism of themselves. They are either forced to think of themselves as bad or abandon their bad parent so they can be good. The problem is, abandoning someone you love doesn't make you feel good at all.

If you're faced with a spouse who insists on demonizing you to the children, the first thing you have to remember is not to do the same to him or her. Two wrongs don't make a right, and if you talk as badly about your former spouse as he or she talks about you, you are only going to screw up your children that much more. What you can do is get help. Talk to a counselor or child psychologist to determine how best to handle the situation. Get your children into counseling if you think they need it or that it will help them. If you're still in court, take your issues to your attorney or to the judge. Understand, however, that, unless your ex is blatantly trying to alienate your kids or poison their relationship with you—and you can prove it—there is only so much a judge can do. The judge can't spend twenty-four hours a day with your spouse or strap a tape recorder to your children's bodies to hear all the negative comments your spouse is making to them about you. What's more, as a parent, the last thing you want to do is pump your kids for information. That puts them right into the middle of your fight, which is exactly where you don't want them to be.

Another way you can combat a righteously indignant spouse is to take the moral high ground. While your first instinct will likely be to fight fire with fire, don't do it! Do what you know is right, and set an example for your children. If you have sometimes been less than a model parent in the past, do your best to change. Don't give your ex any ammunition to use against you. This means that you never blow off spending time with your kids. Take an interest in their lives. Attend their soccer games and dance recitals. Go to their school. When it's your responsibility to pick up or drop off the kids for visitation, be on time. Pay your child support so that your ex can't complain that you are not living up to your responsibilities. Resist the urge to bad-mouth your ex, even when you know that's what he or she is doing to you. Take the time to explain to your kids that people are different and that's okay—everyone doesn't need to be the same or to live the same way. Most importantly, make sure you kids know that you love them. In the end, that's the most important thing you can do.

The Eternal Victim

The final divorce game, and one that's played all too often, is the *eternal victim* game. This one is played when one person refuses to take any responsibility for his or her part in the failure of the marriage or in the divorce. That person sees everything as happening *to* him or her. He or she is just a pawn in the chess game of life, and his or her spouse is the king. He or she is the eternal victim.

If a victim is good at playing the game, he or she can make virtually anything his or her spouse does appear to be abusive. The victim claims that he or she got stuck paying thousands of dollars in doctor bills for the kids because his or her deadbeat spouse was too cheap to sign up for an insurance plan that would allow them to get the care they needed. (Translated, this mean the victim spouse took the kids to the emergency room when they had head colds, and the insurance company wouldn't cover the bill.) The victim spouse then wails that the house went into foreclosure because he or she had to use the child support money to pay the doctor bills instead of the mortgage. (Of course, the victim spouse wouldn't have the doctor bills in the first place if he or she had followed the health insurance company's rules.) Ultimately, the victim spouse is forced to go bankrupt in order to save the house, because he or she didn't have the cash to end the foreclosure proceedings, and the victim's good-for-nothing ex wouldn't give an extra dime to save the children's family home. (Of course, the victim spouse conveniently forgets that his or her ex is also paying for the children's school tuition, their medical insurance, half of their extracurricular activities, and a dozen or so other extras that the victim spouse doesn't ever have to pay. The victim spouse also fails to remember that he or she ran up tens of thousands of dollars in credit card debt after the divorce, which was another huge factor in his or her bankruptcy.) From the other spouse's perspective, no matter what he or she does, it's never right and it's never enough.

If you are faced with a spouse who is good at being a victim or a martyr, you might as well accept the fact that, by the time you are divorced, a fair number of sympathetic people are going to believe you are a horrible human being. You can't change that and you can't control it. What you can control are your own emotions and behavior. Again, take the high road and make every effort to do what you know is right. Then, when your spouse attempts to twist situations to make it look like you are abusive, cold-hearted, or just a jerk, you can fight back by calmly proving the facts as they are, and then letting go of what other people choose to think about those facts. Obviously, you are going to care about what some people think—your children, your family, and the judge. If you can manage to let go of what everyone else thinks and maintain your perspective, you will be much better at dealing with your spouse's game than if you let yourself become enraged and end up being sucked into doing the very things you were trying to avoid.

It's Not a Good Idea to Play Games With Your Life

No divorce game is productive. While some of these games may get you what you want for awhile, in the end, every one of them will come back to bite you. Either you will create a horrible relationship with your former spouse or your children, you will cost yourself time and money, or you will drive yourself so crazy that you develop health problems. None of those are good results. When it comes to games, don't play. That may not be an easy choice. You may need to seek out a good therapist to help rid yourself of game-playing behavior or to help you deal with your spouse's game-playing behavior. However, in the end, your reality will be much better than the game you were playing.

11

Dealing with a Difficult Spouse

I imagine one of the reasons people cling to their hates so stubbornly is because they sense, once hate is gone, they will be forced to deal with pain.

—James Baldwin, Author

The best way out is always through.

—Robert Frost, Poet

Going through a divorce rarely brings out the best in anyone. However, divorce and its aftermath seem to bring out more of the worst in some people than in others. While everyone who goes through the process is an emotional wreck at times, some people aren't just emotional wrecks—they're emotional werewolves. In front of other people they appear to be calm, cool, and reasonably together. Yet, when they're out of the public eye, they turn into irrational, emotional, vindictive maniacs who will go to any length to make their spouse or former spouse suffer. These are the people who refuse to settle even the simplest issue. They know every one of their spouse's emotional hot buttons and purposely push them until their spouse explodes. They wheedle, whine, argue, badger, manipulate, control, irritate, and do whatever else they need to do just to prove they are right. These are the people, in other words, who will drive you crazy.

The Two Types of Difficult Spouses

There are two types of difficult spouses—the temporarily difficult and the permanently insane. The temporarily difficult spouse is an otherwise rational human being who gets set off by a certain issue or goes through a phase during which it would be easier to negotiate world peace than it would be for you to talk to him or her. Once your spouse's emotions subside or the trigger issue is resolved, however, he or she usually starts to become a reasonably normal human being again and your divorce settles down into a more standard pattern of ordinary unpleasantness. Dealing with a permanently insane spouse, on the other hand, is an endless nightmare.

The permanently insane spouse never tires of arguing, fighting, manipulating, controlling, or otherwise making your life a living hell. He or she does things on purpose just to make you crazy. The permanently insane spouse uses your children, your home, your finances, your friends, and anything else he or she can think of to cause you pain. He or she drags you to court as often as possible, and won't agree with you on the time of day, let alone anything of substance in your divorce. It is not uncommon for this kind of spouse to go through several lawyers and even a few judges in the quest to ruin your life. The fact that your spouse may lose more fights than he or she wins is irrelevant—this type of spouse would rather fight than win. Even after you are finally divorced, the truly permanently insane spouse will still find ways to get you back into court almost immediately, cooking up some new drama or unsettled issue to fight about. He or she does everything possible to make sure that every contact you have with him or her is aggravating and unpleasant. In short, the permanently insane spouse does whatever it takes to make you crazy.

Identifying Your Difficult Spouse

Distinguishing which type of difficult spouse you are facing is critically important. If your spouse is only temporarily difficult, then you need to focus on the issue that's turning him or her into Mr. Hyde. If you can settle that issue, not only will you be well on your way to restoring your spouse back into the mild-mannered Dr. Jekyll, but you will also have gone a long way towards resolving your entire case. If it's not one particular issue that is making your spouse crazy, but is instead a phase he or she is going through in which everything makes him or her angry, then you need to hang on and ride out the wave of emotion. Eventually, your spouse's anger will burn out and you can start to deal with him or her more normally. Of course, this is terribly difficult to do. When someone is yelling and screaming at you, or doing mean things to you, it is much easier to yell back than it is to calmly maintain your position. However, yelling back or doing something mean to your spouse just because he or she did something mean to you will only make the anger last longer and burn hotter. It is much more productive if you can manage to let your spouse vent without reacting. Doing that has the added benefit of making your spouse feel horribly guilty for being such a jerk once he or she finally does come to his or her senses.

Unfortunately, there's no telling when that might happen. It's not as if your spouse has a certain period of time in which to rant and rave, and when that time is up, his or her emotional outburst will be over and your spouse will return to normal. Emotions don't follow that kind of schedule. If your spouse has always been a fairly reasonable person, at least you can hope that he or she will work through the anger relatively quickly and will return to being a normal human being before you lose your mind, too. If you are dealing with a permanently insane spouse, however, *normal* is not something you are ever likely to see.

Unlike a temporarily difficult spouse, a truly insane spouse was never really normal. That's an important distinguishing feature. Human behavior tends to be consistent. Absent years of therapy, heavy doses of mind-altering drugs, or a full frontal lobotomy, a person's fundamental personality is not likely to change. If you married a lunatic or had the misfortune of marrying someone who turned into a lunatic, you are going to be stuck divorcing a lunatic and dealing with a lunatic after your divorce is done. If you married someone who was mean, sneaky, or combative, then that person is going to continue to be mean, sneaky, and combative all the way through your divorce, and probably forever after. If your spouse was prone to irrational behavior while you were married, or experienced bouts of mental illness, you can't expect that to change while you're going through a divorce. While that is not good news for you, at least it helps you to know what you're dealing with.

Dealing with the Temporarily Difficult Spouse

Dealing with either type of difficult spouse isn't easy. If you have children with one, it's even worse. If your spouse is just temporarily difficult, most of the time you can deal with him or her the same way as anyone would deal with any divorcing spouse, and the advice elsewhere in this book is probably going to be good enough to get you through. If, however, you are dealing with the spouse from hell, or if your spouse's bout of temporary insanity is lasting for longer than you can handle and is starting to make you insane, too, then you're going to need to do more.

Dealing with the Permanently Insane Spouse

The first thing you need to do when you're dealing with someone who is truly crazy is to get yourself a good lawyer. That is not to say that you have to (or even should) hire a shark or any other attorney who is going to make the fight worse instead of better. However, you do need to hire someone who knows the law, has a strong personality, and won't shrink from a fight. Some lawyers are better at negotiating, and some are better at fighting. You need a fighter.

The next thing you need is a good therapist. While the therapist won't solve all your problems, he or she will help you stay sane while you try to resolve your problems yourself. It also wouldn't hurt to put together a good support group of family and friends, or join a divorce support group where other people are trying to deal with their own crazy spouses. Of course, no support group can fix your life, but it can provide you with the support and understanding you need to get through the process without losing your own sanity along the way. Your support group will also provide you with a good dose of reality checks in times when you're not sure that you haven't already lost your mind.

After you line up a solid base of support, you need to take a step back, and as best as you can, analyze your situation. Try to figure out exactly what your spouse does that sends you into orbit. What pushes your buttons? What pushes your spouse's buttons? What is your spouse afraid of? What leverage, if any, do you have? What leverage does your spouse have on you? Look at every aspect of your relationship and every fact involved in your divorce. After you've gathered all that information, you are ready to make a plan.

DEFINE THE INSANITY YOU FACE

The problem with trying to deal with a crazy spouse is that there isn't just one kind of insanity. There are control freaks, screamers, manipulators, humiliators, liars, the impossible to please, and those who just won't agree to anything. How you deal with a truly insane spouse depends upon what type of insanity you are facing. The way you would handle an ego-driven, manipulative screamer is very different than the way you would handle a passive-aggressive control freak. What's more, if your spouse is violent, or has physically abused you or your children in the past, then that changes everything.

Dealing with a Physically Abusive Spouse

Domestic violence, including physical assault, rape, stalking, and homicide, is a serious social problem that affects millions of people around the world. Estimates of the number of women who are victims of violence committed by an intimate partner in the United States alone range from 588,490 to 3,000,000 per year. While men can be the victims of domestic abuse, women and children are the most frequent victims. According to the United States Bureau of Statistics, family violence accounted for 11% of all violence between 1998 and 2002. Approximately 22% of murders in 2002 were family murders. With numbers like these, it is clear that domestic violence is not a rare or isolated event, and it is not something that happens once in a great while. It happens every day.

Domestic violence is an extremely complex issue, and one that should not be treated lightly. Dealing with such violence effectively takes a great deal of education, planning, and support. Discussing this issue in any kind of meaningful or in-depth way is something well beyond the scope of this book. However, a multitude of other books, websites, hotlines, and organizations exist that can provide you with a tremendous amount of information and support regarding domestic violence in all of its various forms. A list of some of these resources is contained in Appendix D. If you are, or have been, the victim of physical violence by a spouse or intimate partner, use these resources to get help for yourself and your children as soon as possible. In the meantime, the following are a few rules you should keep in mind.

RULE #1: YOUR PERSONAL SAFETY IS PARAMOUNT

Maintaining your personal safety and the safety of your children is the single most important job you have. Nothing else matters more than that. Period. If you fear that your spouse will act violently towards you or your kids, leave. Get out of the house. Get away from your spouse. If for some reason you can't leave or you have nowhere else to go, then at least make sure you keep a cell phone with you at all times—and don't be afraid to use it. If your spouse is attacking you, call 911. When the police come, tell them what happened. Ask the police to take your spouse out of the house and keep him or her out for as long as the law allows. If your spouse has committed a crime, don't be afraid to press criminal charges and get an order of protection. While doing all that still is no guarantee of your safety, at least by calling the police and getting your spouse taken away from you and the children until he or she has time to cool down, you will buy yourself the time and space to do what it takes to make sure that you are safe.

RULE #2: USE YOUR HEAD

When dealing with any kind of violence, you have to keep your wits about you and use common sense all the time. Make sure that you are never alone with your spouse in an isolated place, or even in a room that only has one exit door. Never leave the children alone with your spouse. If there are guns in your home, hide them, get rid of the bullets, or remove a piece of the gun so it won't work. Get an order of protection if you can, but remember that an order of protection is just a piece of paper. It won't stop a bullet or shield you from a knife. So, even if you get an order of protection against your spouse, you still need to use your common sense to make sure that you are safe in other ways as well.

Make sure your friends, your boss, your children's teachers and day care providers, and anyone else who needs to know about your situation, knows about it. This is not the time to be shy. If your children's teachers don't know you have an order of protection against your spouse, they will let your spouse come and take the children home from school, and you may never see your children again. If your boss doesn't know you have an order of protection against your spouse, he or she may let your spouse into your workplace, where your spouse can be a danger to you and others around you. You have to tell other people what is happening for your own protection.

RULE #3: ALWAYS HAVE A PLAN

Along with using your head, you need to make a safety plan for yourself and your children. Think about what you would do to maintain your safety in all kinds of different situations. Keep a bag of essentials with a change of clothes for you and the kids, a week's supply of any medications you might need, and as much money as you can manage to tuck away for an emergency, packed and ready to grab in case you need to leave quickly. Contact a domestic violence hotline and ask them to help you plan a way to get out of your situation safely and to stay safe until you are ready and able to get out. Learn basic self-defense techniques. Do whatever you need to do to plan a safe future for you and for your kids. In the end, that's the most important thing you can do.

Nonviolent Abusive Spouses

If your spouse is not physically violent, but is verbally, emotionally, or financially abusive, then your approach to the situation will be somewhat different. While dealing with verbal abuse or other vindictive behavior can be almost as difficult as dealing with physical abuse, at least when your personal safety is not an issue you are free to focus on the emotional and legal issues inherent in your divorce. Still, doing so is far from pleasant. When your spouse is standing in front of you, screaming that you are fat, stupid, lazy, or whatever else he or she can think of, you're not going to feel much better by thinking, *at least he or she is not beating me*. When your spouse is so controlling that you are forced to try to skim a few dollars from the grocery money just to be able to buy your kids a new toy or get yourself a small treat, you're probably not going to be thinking about how fortunate you are that your spouse is not stalking you. Getting through these and countless other difficult situations isn't easy for anyone.

The first thing you need to do when dealing with a verbally or emotionally abusive spouse is to take responsibility for yourself. Taking responsibility for yourself means taking care of yourself. As much as possible, get yourself out of the abusive situation. When your spouse starts screaming at you, leave. If you can't leave, see if you can get a friend to drop by and spend some time with you. Your spouse is less likely to use you as a verbal punching bag if there is someone else around watching. If no one can (or wants to) be with you, then find a way to tune out the abuse as best you can. In the meantime, find things that you can do to start moving yourself forward, so that you can get away from the abuse as soon as possible. Focus on saving some money, finding a job, finding a new place to live, and above all, finding yourself a good therapist. All of those things will help you start to regain control over your life. But remember, no matter what you do, you're never going to be able to control your spouse.

Letting go of your urge to control your spouse is particularly difficult in the context of an abusive spouse, because you want so desperately just to make the abuse stop. However, you have to realize that, no matter what you do, your spouse is never going to act or react the way you want. The more you try to make your spouse do so—the more you try to reason with your spouse or make him or her act normal—the more frustrated you will become. What's more, as long as you focus on controlling your spouse instead of controlling yourself, you will be trapped in your spouse's insanity—he or she will be acting, and you will be reacting. Your spouse will push your buttons and you will respond. Whether you respond in anger, pain, stony silence, or complete hysteria, your response fuels your spouse's insanity and keeps both of you playing the same game. It's not a game you can ever win. However, choosing not to play is often the hardest thing you could ever do.

FIGHTING FIRE WITH FIRE BURNS YOU BOTH: THE STORY OF HANNAH AND ROY

Roy was a moderately successful, 50-year-old artist. His wife of twenty-five years died, leaving him heartbroken. That's when he met Hannah, an attractive, divorced, 30-year-old artist groupie, who he married after a whirlwind romance. Immediately after the wedding, Hannah got pregnant. Shortly thereafter, Roy's honeymoon was over.

It turned out that Hannah was embroiled in a bitter custody battle with her former spouse, whom she claimed was crazy. In her fight for sole custody of their daughter, Hannah accused her ex of everything from drug dealing to sexual abuse. At first Roy believed Hannah's horror stories about her ex. As time went on, however, Hannah started to contradict herself, and her stories became harder and harder to believe. When Roy questioned Hannah about what was really going on, Hannah immediately started a fight with him, then called the police and told them Roy had threatened to kill her and their unborn child. Then she got an emergency order of protection against him.

Roy did not handle Hannah's actions well. He was angry and hurt, and mad at himself for having married a crazy lady. When he got to court, he ranted and raved and behaved so badly that the judge extended the order of protection for two years. Meanwhile, Hannah, who claimed she was afraid of Roy, refused to tell him which hospital she was going to have the baby in. She refused to allow him to be near her, or near their baby after he was born. She wouldn't allow Roy to attend the baby's baptism without a court order. In short, she made Roy's life hell.

For the first few months, Roy reacted emotionally to everything Hannah did. He yelled and screamed and went back and forth to court so many times that the judge knew him by name. He cried to his friends, argued with his lawyers, and drove his pastor crazy trying to get him to mediate his divorce. Yet, the angrier and more desperate Roy got, the more court battles he lost. Finally, Roy changed his approach. Instead of ranting and raving when Hannah pushed his buttons, Roy kept his mouth shut. He got a counselor and learned to control his temper. Instead of running to court constantly, he picked his battles and only fought the most important issues. In short, he took control of his emotions. Not long after that, Hannah lost control of hers.

Once Roy started acting reasonably, Hannah's attempts to paint him as a raving lunatic no longer worked. The judge modified the order of protection. He granted Roy visitation. Infuriated, Hannah tried every trick she could think of to make Roy lose his temper. She canceled Roy's visitation on a moment's notice, claiming the baby was sick. She made sure her mother (who hated Roy) was present whenever Roy came to see the baby, making Roy's visits tense and unpleasant. She spread horrible rumors about Roy, and embarrassed him in front of his family and friends. Through it all, Roy stayed calm. He also pushed for the court to force Hannah to undergo a psychological evaluation. When she finally did, the results were not surprising.

The psychiatrist found that Hannah had a personality disorder. He also found that she was not stable, not truthful, and not a good person to be granted custody of an infant. Roy, who had also had an evaluation performed, turned out to be the better parent. In the end, he got custody of his son.

If You Want to Win, Stop Playing the Game

The only reason Roy finally succeeded in court was because he stopped playing Hannah's game. Instead of reacting to what she did, he took control of himself and acted responsibly. Instead of spending his time trying to get back at Hannah, he focused on doing what he needed to do for himself. He stayed in counseling, took parenting classes, and set up a nice home for his son. Focusing on his own issues rather than becoming obsessed with Hannah's behavior took an enormous amount of work and self-control. Hannah baited him to do otherwise every step of the way. Sometimes, Roy couldn't help himself and he took the bait. Whenever he did, he immediately found himself back in court facing Hannah's trumped-up accusations. Getting through those accusations, and getting custody of his son, took years. It cost him every penny he had. Even after he got custody, Roy still faced having to put up with Hannah's antics in one way or another for the rest of his life. However, Roy got what was important to him—his son. In the end, he decided that doing that was worth more to him than continuing to play a game he would never win.

Roy changed the rules of Hannah's game. He got the help he needed, then he patiently worked within the court system until he achieved the result he wanted. He used his head instead of his heart. To survive your own battle with an insane spouse, you need to do the same thing. When your spouse pushes your buttons, try changing the way you normally react. If your spouse always goads you into starting an argument, don't let yourself get sucked in. Instead of screaming at your spouse, try talking calmly. Change the subject. Politely end the conversation. Don't take the bait and don't bait the hook yourself. Let the argument go. If your spouse is a control freak who always has to have his or her way, instead of fighting, let your spouse have his or her way! Let your spouse "win," then walk away. That will make your spouse crazier than if you fight to get your own way. Look at whatever you normally do in response to your spouse's insanity, and then try doing something different. By changing your reaction, you completely change the game. When that happens, you may find that you no longer need to try to change your spouse.

Act, Don't React

One of the most difficult things to do when dealing with someone who is making you miserable is to resist the urge to make that person miserable in return. It's even more difficult when you know all of the buttons to push that will set your spouse off. Unless you stop your spouse's misery (or at least stop intentionally causing your spouse's misery), your own misery will never end.

Not making your spouse miserable seems like the opposite of what you should want to do while you're going through a divorce. Many people actually stay up at night trying to think of things to do to make their spouse miserable while they are going through a divorce. What those people don't understand is the law of karma. What goes around comes around. When you do something mean to your spouse, your spouse reacts by doing something mean to you. Then you get hurt, so in turn, you do something else to hurt your spouse. Then your spouse hurts you back. On and on it goes until you're both writhing in pain. If you like being in pain, that's fine. If you don't, then you have to stop inflicting pain on your spouse. Like it or not, that's the only way you stand even the tiniest chance of being able to stop bringing down the pain on yourself.

The next thing you need to do in order to make your life easier when dealing with a difficult spouse is to stop accepting the pain your spouse sends your way. Understand that just because you stop causing pain to your spouse does not necessarily mean your spouse will stop causing pain to you. Your spouse might stop causing you pain or might cause you less pain. On the other hand, your spouse might not stop doing anything at all, and may just continue doing whatever it was that he or she was doing to make you miserable. Either way, just because your spouse causes you pain doesn't mean that you have to take it.

If your spouse is screaming at you and it's making you crazy, leave. Walk away and let your spouse scream alone. If your spouse threatens to destroy your family photos or other sentimental items, get the ones that are important to you out of the house. If your spouse wants to destroy the rest of them, either get those out of the house too, get a court order stopping the destruction, or just let your spouse go. (Which is not to say that you won't ask the judge in your case to compensate your for your spouse's destruction later.) If your spouse spreads horrible lies about you to his or her family and friends, as much as you can, let it go. No matter what you do or say, you are never going to convince your spouse's family that you are a wonderful person and your spouse is a dirtbag, so why worry about it? Take the high road. Let everyone believe what they want to believe, and don't waste your time and energy worrying about it or trying to convince your friends and family that your spouse is the one with a problem. They'll figure it out.

Not accepting the pain your spouse sends your way goes hand in hand with not accepting the guilt your spouse tries to lay on you. Regardless of whose fault it is that the marriage ended, the truth of the matter is that both you and your spouse played a role in getting married, and both you and your spouse are responsible in some way for getting divorced. Even if the divorce was mostly your doing or is mostly your fault, feeling guilty about it for the rest of your life serves no useful purpose. What's more, even though you should not try to cause your spouse unnecessary pain, it is not your responsibility, or even within your power, to make your spouse happy. That's your spouse's job. Going through a divorce is rarely a happy time for anyone. If you want to feel guilty about getting divorced, you can. On the other hand, you can also do what you need to do to get over your guilt and get on with your life.

Action, not reaction, is the key to your own happiness. If you want your life to change, start acting in a healthy way and stop reacting in anger or frustration. Stop trying to make your spouse miserable and start trying to make yourself happy. Focus on yourself, not your spouse. Rearrange your priorities. Do what's best for you instead of worrying about what's worst for your spouse. Then let the rest go. It's a subtle shift of attitude, but one that makes all the difference.

CHANGING YOUR PERSPECTIVE CAN CHANGE YOUR LIFE: THE STORY OF PAMELA AND KIRK

Pamela and Kirk went through a bitter divorce. They ended up with joint custody of their three children, with Pamela as the primary residential parent. Pamela and Kirk continued to fight even after the divorce, although they managed to stay out of court until Pamela remarried. Kirk didn't like Pamela's new husband. He started planting seeds in the children's minds that it might be time to come and live with dad. The oldest two kids were teenagers, and they were rebelling against Pamela's rules anyway. Their relationship with Pamela was rocky, at best. It wasn't difficult for Kirk to convince them that life with him would be way more fun.

Pamela refused to let the kids live with Kirk. Since he had no legal grounds to take the kids away from Pamela, Kirk just kept manipulating their emotions until one day their daughter, Rose, took matters into her own hands. She ran away to her dad's house, crying and distraught. She said that Pamela's new husband had gotten into a fight with her, pushed her across the room, and threatened her. Their oldest boy backed up Rose's story. Without even calling Pamela, Kirk immediately got a restraining order against Pamela and the kids moved in with him.

When the police came and took the children from Pamela, she was beside herself. Rose's story was entirely made up. Nothing had happened. Pamela's initial reaction was to go to court, prove the truth, and get her kids back. However, after she watched her two oldest children purposely lie to the judge, she changed her mind. Instead of putting her children through months of court battles, psychological evaluations, and everything else that goes along with a contested custody fight, Pamela listened to what they told her. She realized that making the kids stay with her would only make them want to live with their dad even more. So Pamela made the most difficult and courageous decision a mother could make—she let her kids go. She sat down with Kirk, worked out a visitation schedule, figured out what she was going to have to pay in child support, and she allowed Kirk to become the children's residential custodian.

Pamela's decision was radical and extreme. It was a decision very few mothers would be willing to make. However, after she made it, Pamela's life, and her relationship with her children, immediately improved. Pamela's daughter admitted that the story she told had all been a lie. Since the kids were no longer living with Pamela, they stopped rebelling against her and their relationship flourished. What's more, because of the liberal visitation schedule Pamela had worked out with Kirk in exchange for letting the children live with him, she saw the children almost as much as she had when they lived with her. In the end, everyone was better off.

Doing the Right Thing

Allowing your teenage children to go live with your ex just because that's what they think they want is not always the best idea. However, in Pamela's case, it was the right thing for her to do, and she knew it. Instead of fighting Kirk because that's what a mother is supposed to do, or holding on to the children because that's what she—not they— needed to do, Pamela let go. Suddenly, her difficult ex-spouse had his hands full raising two teenagers and a 10-year-old. Kirk no longer had time to make Pamela's life difficult. He was too busy trying to handle the kids and deal with his own life. While Pamela's situation still wasn't perfect after Kirk took the kids, it was definitely better. A few years later, the kids ended up back with her.

Doing what's right isn't always easy. However, doing the right thing is something you are capable of doing. Making your spouse do what you think is right, on the other hand, is impossible. Remember, the only person you can control is yourself. If you focus on your own actions, you can create results. If you focus on your spouse's actions, all you will create is frustration.

If you find that no matter how hard you try, you still long to drive your spouse crazy just for the sheer fun of it, consider trying a new approach—kill your spouse with kindness. Instead of doing something to purposely aggravate your spouse, do something that you know will make him or her happy. It doesn't have to be something big—a small gesture will suffice. Perhaps you help the kids pick out a nice present for your spouse's birthday. Maybe you arrange to pick the kids up from school yourself when they have a half day off for parent-teacher conferences and your spouse can't get off work early to pick them up. Whatever it is, just do something simple and kind. However, you must be genuine (or as genuine as you can manage to be under the circumstances). Do the best you can to put your own emotions aside, and just do the right thing. Then, let it go. Don't wait for your spouse to thank you. Don't expect your spouse to lavish you with praise. Just do something nice, and move on.

When you first start changing your behavior toward your spouse, you may have to force yourself to do the right thing. It might not feel normal, and you may not always succeed. However, little by little, changing your behavior will change you. It may never change your spouse, but it will definitely change you. You will start to feel better. You will know (even if no one else does) that you are doing the right thing, and you will be able to hold your head high. You will feel even better once you let go of your need to have your spouse acknowledge that you did something nice for him or her. Whether or not your spouse ever thanks you is not the point. The point is that you did what was right, and you know it. That's enough.

Pick Your Battles

One of the most important strategies for dealing with a difficult spouse is to pick your battles. Fight for what's really important. Let everything else go. Who cares if your former spouse forgot picture day and sent the kids to school in old t-shirts instead of their good clothes? Having decent school pictures may be nice, but in the grand scheme of life, it's not that important. Instead of arguing with your ex about how irresponsible he or she is, let it go. The same thing holds true when your daughter wants to go to the prom, and without asking you, your ex pays $200 for the dress and $50 for the shoes, splurges on a haircut and a manicure, then expects you to kick in half. Instead of arguing with your former spouse over whether your daughter needed to spend that much money on one dance or whose responsibility it is to pay for things like that, it won't kill you to just give your ex a few extra bucks to help defray the expenses. If you treat your former spouse with a bit of compassion and avoid fights instead of picking them, you may be amazed at how the quality of your own life improves.

WHAT TO DO WHEN EVEN KINDNESS DOESN'T HELP

Sometimes, no matter how much you try to take the high road, your spouse insists on dragging you down to the lowest possible level. When you do something nice for your spouse, he or she responds by doing something mean to you. When you try to walk away from an argument, your spouse causes a scene. When you decide it's not worth it to fight and you give your spouse what he or she wants, your spouse only wants more. You find that you are knocking yourself out to try to work things out, and your spouse is still being as difficult as ever. What should you do then? Unfortunately, sometimes the answer is fight. Sometimes, some things are just so important that fighting for them is worth everything you've got. If that's the case, then get yourself a good lawyer and give it your best shot. Remember, though, that there's an enormous difference between fighting as a last resort and fighting for any other reason.

If you find yourself facing a fight, the first thing you need to ask yourself is, *is this fight worth it?* To answer that question, you need to figure out exactly what it is that you are fighting for. Are you fighting over something that's really important to you, or are you fighting because your spouse just pushed all of your buttons? Are you fighting over an issue that is facing you today, or are you fighting because you're still angry at some evil thing your spouse did to you six months ago, and you still want to make your spouse pay? Is the issue that you are facing critical to the health, safety, or well-being of you or your children, or are you fighting because your spouse always seems to get his or her way and you're just tired of it? Is the real issue the thing that you are fighting about, or is the real issue the fight? In order to answer these questions, you need to take a look inside yourself, and examine your own motives and your own ego.

There is no quicker way to get yourself embroiled in an endless battle, especially if your spouse is purposely trying to wage an all-out war with you, than to let your ego get in the way of your better judgment. No matter how much you want to fight with your spouse just to prove that you are right, the bottom line is that being right doesn't matter—being happy does. What's more, sometimes the only way you can find happiness for yourself is to let your spouse win.

Allowing your spouse to win a fight, even when he or she clearly deserves to lose, takes an incredible amount of self-control and maturity. It's not easy to agree to accept less money per month in child support than your cheapskate spouse should pay, even though you know you (and your children) are being cheated. It's frustrating to have to rearrange your schedule to accommodate your spouse's visitation times, and then not get angry when your spouse is late. It's aggravating to have to give your spouse the wedding china in the property settlement, when you know the only reason your spouse wants it is so that you cannot have it. Sometimes, letting go of those kinds of issues makes sense. They're just not worth it. In the long run, sometimes giving in a little bit makes much more sense than launching into a battle that will only cause you years of grief and aggravation.

How to Cope When the Insanity Won't Stop

Sometimes, no matter how much you give in, no matter how often you compromise, no matter what you do, your spouse still wants to fight. He or she does things on purpose just to make you crazy. Your spouse constantly calls and interrupts your time with the children, or drags you into court on motion after motion over every aspect of your behavior and every penny of your finances. Your spouse purposely does whatever he or she can do to try to control you, your life, and your children. In short, your spouse is obsessed with making you miserable—and it works.

One of the most difficult types of insanity to cope with is the obsessive and all-consuming craziness created by the spouse or ex-spouse who has the time, the money, and the desire to focus on making you miserable for the rest of your life. While this type of spouse is rare, he or she is also absolutely impossible to deal with. Logic and reason don't work on this type of person. He or she doesn't seem to care about spending a fortune on legal fees. Typically, an ex-spouse who is really this obsessive does not have physical custody of the children. Yet, that does not stop him or her from giving you constant, detailed, and completely unsolicited advice on how you should raise your children on an almost minute-by-minute basis. He or she provides you with a running commentary of insults and criticisms of your parenting style. He or she chides you for not dressing the children properly, not taking them to the right doctor, feeding them fast food, and doing a host of other things that most other people would consider normal. This kind of spouse insists on talking to the children at the most inconvenient time every day. If you're not home when he or she calls, your voice mail gets filled with irate messages and threats that your spouse is going to take you to court and get custody taken away from you if you to continue to alienate the children from him or her. In short, this kind of spouse's behavior is verbally abusive, obsessive, and relentless.

Dealing with this type of insanity, particularly if you have to work for a living, raise your children, maintain a household, and try to have a life of your own, can be exhausting. Your ex wears you down with constant criticism, which he or she makes sure to deliver to you via telephone messages, faxed documents, mail, and email. You find yourself wishing you could do something—anything—to stop him or her. However, stopping your spouse is the one thing you will never do. As a matter of fact, the more you try, the more you will get sucked into your ex's insanity. So, instead of trying to control his or her behavior, you need to focus on controlling your own.

The best way to cope with an obsessive ex-spouse is to set boundaries and stick to them. As much as you can, try to limit your contact with your ex. Communicate via email rather than telephone. Be clear that you will not put up with profanity, verbal abuse, or name-calling. If your ex can communicate within those boundaries, fine. If not, you need to let your ex know that while you want to try to work things out on whatever the issue of the moment may be, you are not willing to be abused in the process. If your ex is screaming, advise him or her that you will only talk when he or she is calmer. Then hang up. If your ex's emails are filled with profanity, send a response telling your ex to clean them up and then you will read them. You don't want to cut off all communication altogether—that only leads to worse problems. You don't want to respond in kind or in anger—that also accomplishes nothing. You do need to limit your communication to what is helpful and productive, and then, calmly and politely, ignore the rest.

Effectively dealing with an insane ex-spouse requires you to set boundaries, not only with him or her, but with yourself as well. Don't let yourself do things that serve no purpose other than to make you crazy. If reading your ex's ten-page, single-spaced letters sends you rocketing into the stratosphere with rage, then don't read them. Skim them, or have someone else read them and tell you if there's anything in the letter that you really need to know. If your ex sends you mounds of abusive emails, exercise your finger and hit the delete button before you read every word and raise your blood pressure so high that you feel like a geyser is about to erupt out of the top of your head. If your ex leaves you scathing voice mail messages, fast forward through them and delete those as well. Of course, you need to listen enough to know if there's a real issue in there somewhere or a problem that you need to discuss with him or her. However, if your ex leaves you ten messages about the same thing, or if he or she is yelling and screaming uncontrollably, then don't torture yourself by listening to the entire tirade. Finally, no matter what else you do, don't treat your ex in the same way that he or she is treating you. The last thing you need to do is throw fuel on the fire. Limit the abuse you will allow yourself to take, and limit your urge to initiate any abuse yourself. Your sanity and your psyche will both be better off.

The Role of Compassion

Dealing with a difficult spouse is never easy and never fun. Dealing with a difficult spouse with compassion and understanding may seem impossible. It may also seem wrong—if your ex spends his or her time driving you insane, why should you not return the favor? The reason is that if you do, the insanity never ends. You will be far better off if you take the high road, knowing that what your ex does will come back to him or her without any help from you.

12

The Realities of Custody, Visitation, and Child Support

Your children will see what you're all about by what you live rather than what you say.

—Dr. Wayne Dyer, Psychotherapist

Even a minor event in the life of a child is an event of that child's world and thus a world event.

—Gaston Bachelard, Scientist and Philosopher

Of all the battles that are waged in the war of divorce, none is more heart-wrenching than a custody fight. Battles over visitation and other issues involving what's best for the children are not much better. Children who are caught in these types of domestic combat are dragged into court, interviewed by attorneys, analyzed by experts, bounced between angry parents, and still expected to function as normal kids. While many of them manage to do so, that is more a testimony to the strength of the children than it is to any virtue on the part of their parents. Yet, most parents who are willing to fight bitterly over visitation, custody, and other child-related issues honestly believe that what they are doing is not only right, but necessary for the good of their children. In reality, these kinds of fights are anything but good for the children.

Not fighting over your children is a wonderful idea in theory. In practice, keeping your mouth shut and not fighting when it comes to your children is nearly impossible. If you are like most people, you value your children more than anything else in the world. They are what is most important to you—not just in your divorce, but in your life. You want them to be happy and well-adjusted, and most of all, you want to continue be an important part of their lives even after you are divorced. At the same time, you are afraid that, because of your divorce, none of this will happen. So you fight to keep them, to control what happens to them, and to make them happy. Unfortunately, in most cases, fighting over them is what makes them the most unhappy in the long run.

There are times, of course, when you have no choice but to fight over your children. If your spouse has physically abused your children, fighting to maintain custody of them (or to keep your spouse away from them unless and until your spouse has received counseling, gotten his or her temper under control, and is no longer a danger to them) is worth whatever pain or problems it may cause. If your spouse is verbally or emotionally abusive to your children, the same thing applies. If your spouse is truly mentally unbalanced or uncontrollably mentally ill, then it makes sense for you to fight to maintain as much control over your children's lives as possible. In most other circumstances, however, fighting over custody, visitation, child support, and other child-related issues is rarely a good choice. Before you can make a better choice, however, you have to know exactly what it is you are fighting for.

Understanding Legal Custody

There are two aspects to child custody—legal custody and residential custody. *Legal custody* is what gives you the right to make important decisions regarding your children, such as what school they will attend, what religion they will be raised in, and what medical treatment they will receive, should they need it. *Residential custody* refers to where the children will live most of the time. While parents are married, they each have legal custody and residential custody of their children. That is, each parent has the right to make important decisions about their children's lives, and presumably, the children live with both of them. When parents divorce, they must decide whether one or both of them will have legal custody over their children. They must also decide where their children will live.

Legal custody can be either joint or sole. If you have sole legal custody of your children, you will have the right to make most (but not necessarily all) of the important life decisions regarding your children, without having to get any input from your former spouse. You can consult with your ex if you choose, but you aren't required to do so and you don't need your ex's permission to do anything. On the other hand, if you and your former spouse have joint legal custody of your children, you will be obligated to consult with your former spouse when making these kinds of decisions regarding your children, and you and your ex will have to reach some sort of agreement on whatever decision faces you before you can do anything.

Unlike sole legal custody, joint legal custody requires parents to communicate with each other frequently and consistently about anything that affects the children. In order to make joint custody work, therefore, parents have to get along. They don't have to like each other. They don't have to spend a lot of time with each other. However, they do have to be able to work together for the benefit of their children. Otherwise, having joint custody just doesn't work.

Because of the level of cooperation that joint custody requires, courts are not likely to grant joint custody to parents who are fighting over the children so much that they end up going all the way to trial to get the judge to decide the issue of custody for them. If two people can't agree on who should have custody of the children in the first place, they will never be able to agree on the other, larger issues surrounding their children's education, religion, upbringing, and medical treatment that they absolutely need to agree on in order to make joint custody work. That's an important fact to keep in mind when you're deciding whether to engage in a custody war with your spouse. You need to understand that if you and your spouse agree that you should have joint custody, then you will have it. If you and your spouse can't agree that you should have joint legal custody, then one of you is going to be granted sole legal custody.

While the definition of joint and sole custody seems fairly straightforward, determining what decisions regarding your children you can and cannot make on your own, even if you have sole custody, is not always easy. Obviously, if you and your spouse have joint custody, you will be consulting with each other about almost every issue that comes up that involves the children, from deciding what church they will attend to working out whether they should be enrolled in soccer or swimming after school. However, even if you have sole legal custody, you will still have to include your spouse in more decisions than you may think.

If your divorce judgment requires your ex to pay for certain things for the children, such as after-school activities or extraordinary medical expenses, then the judgment probably also gives your ex the right to have some input into deciding whether you can incur those expenses in the first place. You cannot enroll your children in every after-school activity possible without so much as mentioning it to your ex, and then expect your ex to pay for half of those activities. You cannot have an orthodontist put braces on your child's teeth without your ex's consent and then stick your ex with half of the bill. You can't single-handedly decide to send your kids to private school, and then expect your ex to pay a tuition bill the size of the national debt. Sole custody or not, that kind of behavior just won't fly.

Understanding Residential Custody

Residential custody, which is sometimes referred to as *physical custody*, is custody over the body of your child or children. Residential custody determines the place where your children will live most of the time. If you are your children's *residential custodian*, that means, technically and legally, they will be deemed to live with you. They will be enrolled in the school district in which you live. They will use your address on all of their important forms. You will be deemed to be the primary caretaker of your children.

Legal custody and residential custody are two different things. Typically, if you have sole legal custody of the children, you will also have residential custody of them as well. That means the children will live with you, and you alone will have the right to make the major decisions that affect their lives. When you and your spouse have joint legal custody, however, it's a different story.

Even if you and your spouse have joint legal custody of your children, the children still have to live somewhere. Most courts will require either you or your spouse to be designated as the children's residential custodian. Children cannot be deemed to live in two places at once. Typically, if the children spend more time living with you, then you will be their residential custodian. If they spend more time with your spouse, then he or she will be their residential custodian. A problem arises, however, when you and your spouse want to equally share residential custody of your children; that is, if you want the children to live half of the time with you and half the time with your ex.

Shared custody, or joint legal and joint residential custody, is a fairly new concept in the area of family law. It means that two parents equally share time with their children, as well as decision-making authority over them. In a shared custody arrangement, children live half of their lives with one parent, and half of their lives with the other parent. Shared custody is not something that courts look upon favorably, because it is such a difficult situation to make work. In order to do so, two parents really have to get along well, have to communicate with each other almost daily, and have to be willing to put their own differences aside and work together for the benefit of the children. Not many divorced couples can pull that off. What's more, shared custody only works if former spouses live very close to each other. If parents have to commute for an hour or more to pick up their children, then bouncing the kids back and forth between houses several times a week just doesn't make sense. What's more, judges often discourage any kind of shared custody arrangement, because they believe that shuffling children between homes disrupts their routine, undermines their sense of stability, and is usually not in their best interests. Thus, shared custody, while it exists, is still rare.

Visitation

Visitation, as a legal concept in dealing with divorce and children, is not tough to understand. Visitation is time spent with your kids. If your children live with your former spouse, then you have a right to have visitation time with them, so that you and your kids can be together and maintain a relationship with each other. Unfortunately, while the concept of visitation is simple, its application often is not.

Every parent (except those who have abused their children) has the absolute right to have visitation time with their children. What's more, courts are starting to acknowledge that every parent has the right to have *substantial* visitation time with their children, and that it's in the children's best interests to spend the time it takes to have a relationship with both of their parents, not just the one with whom they live. Judges will, therefore, do their best to grant nonresidential parents as much visitation time as they can, including holiday and vacation visitation, as well as regular visitation.

Your visitation schedule is a blueprint of the time you will get to spend with your children. While, in the past, visitation schedules simply said that the noncustodial parent would be granted *reasonable and liberal* visitation, and the divorced couple was left to figure out what that meant, courts now tend to require that you set forth a precise schedule that lays out in great detail when each of you gets to spend time with your children. (A sample holiday and vacation visitation schedule is included in

Appendix C.) The reason for that is simple—the more detailed your visitation schedule is, the less room there is for argument in the future.

The reason your schedule is just a blueprint of your time with your kids is because, if you and your spouse agree, you can change the schedule between yourselves whenever and however you want. You don't need to go back to court to do it. You both just agree that from now on, you're going to make certain changes, and that's it. You can make changes from week to week if that works for both of you. However, if you two don't agree to make changes, or if one of you doesn't abide by your informal agreement, then the visitation schedule that's part of your judgment is the schedule you have to follow.

What Happens When Parents Fight

If you and your spouse can't agree on who should get custody of the kids or what your visitation schedule should be, and you can't work out your disagreements on your own, through your lawyers, with a mediator, or any other way, then the only choice you are left with is to fight your battle in court. That, however, is an expensive battle in more ways than one.

Once you and your spouse become locked into a custody battle, or even just a visitation battle, the court will often appoint an attorney to represent your children. This attorney may be called a *guardian ad litem*, a *child representative*, or simply an *attorney for the children*. While there are some technical differences between what each of these different types of attorneys do, no matter what you call them, their job is essentially to represent your children and advise the court of what they think would really be in your children's best interest. They interview your children, you, and your spouse. They may interview your children's teachers or other professionals. They may visit your home. They recommend experts that the court should require to be hired in order to evaluate you, your spouse, and your children. Ultimately, they recommend whether you or your spouse should get custody of your children, and what your visitation schedule should be. For the most part, the judge listens to their recommendations.

Given the extraordinary power and influence that the attorney for your children will have over your life, it is not a good idea to aggravate him or her. When the attorney makes appointments with you or your children, you need to keep them and show up on time. It's also important that you put your best foot forward when you are with him or her. On the other hand, it's also pretty transparent when you try make it seem like you're parent of the year when you can really barely cope with your kids. The best thing you can do is to be honest. However, remember, no matter how nice that attorney might seem, or how sure you are that he or she is on your side, the truth of the matter is that he or she represents your kids. The children's attorney is not your attorney, and you shouldn't confide in him or her as if he or she was your attorney. Be honest, but don't spill your guts.

Your children's attorney is the eyes and ears of the court. That attorney does the legwork with your family that the judge doesn't have time to do. However, the amount of time that your children's attorney spends on your case is still not that great. Like every other attorney in the world, your children's attorney has other cases to handle. He or she cannot be with you twenty-four hours a day. What's more, since you are paying for every hour of his or her time, you wouldn't want him or her to be with you twenty-four hours a day. You couldn't afford it.

A conservative estimate of what a contested custody battle will cost you ranges between $20,000–50,000—and that's just what it will cost *you*. Your spouse will pay a similar amount. You will both pay more if you fight a lot. The reason that the battle is so expensive is that you have to pay for everything. Every time anyone goes to court, you have to pay the fee. You have to pay for your attorney. You have to pay for your children's attorney. If you have to pay for your spouse's attorney as well, you're really going to get socked! You have to pay for the psychologist or social worker the court appoints to evaluate your children, not to mention the therapist you have to start taking your children to see because they're so stressed out by your divorce. (A child custody evaluation alone will run you between $5,000–15,000.) If the attorney for your children, or the judge, recommends that you see a mediator to try to work things out, you will have to pay the mediator. If the judge decides that you need to attend parenting classes or any kind of therapy yourself to deal with whatever issues you may have, you'll have to pay for that. Basically, you have to pay for everything. However, what you have to pay for a contested custody battle in money is nothing compared to the emotional cost of your fight.

What to Do about the Absentee Parent

Dealing with conflicting parenting styles is a challenging problem. Having no conflicts at all because your spouse has bailed out on you and the kids can be equally challenging. Unfortunately, the sad truth is that there is no court in the world that can force your ex to be a parent if he or she doesn't want to be one. You can have the most detailed visitation schedule possible, but if your former spouse never shows up, there's not much you can do about it. Rather than wasting your time and energy trying to force your ex to be a parent, you would be much better off focusing on making your children's lives as normal and whole as you possibly can.

Dealing with an absent ex-spouse is never easy. Dealing with an absent ex-spouse who suddenly reappears and wants to get back into your life and your children's lives as if nothing happened and nothing has changed is even harder. Often, the formerly absent ex expects that he or she can go back to being a normal part of your life, without giving you any explanation as to where he or she has been, and without paying the support and other expenses for the children that went unpaid while he or she was off in the great unknown. What's more, the formerly absent ex often expects you to let him or her immediately start seeing the kids overnight and on weekends, even though he or she hasn't had any kind of relationship with the kids in months or even years. Not surprisingly, you're probably not willing to let that happen. You don't think its good for your children to go off for the weekend with a total stranger, even if that stranger does happen to be their parent. You are also not about to let your children get hurt again by re-forming their relationship with your ex, and risking that he or she will disappear again and only cause them more pain. Before you throw your ex out completely, however, think carefully about who you are hurting, what you are doing, and what your chances are of winning this kind of fight.

Unless a court has terminated your former spouse's parental rights, your ex is legally entitled to see and spend time with your children. He or she may not be entitled to take them on a week's vacation to Mexico after not having seen them in eight months, but he or she will be allowed to meet them for dinner. What's more, even though your ex may have abandoned you and the kids for awhile, it may be important for your children to repair their relationship with your ex now, rather than to wait until they're adults and they've spent years in therapy working on their abandonment issues. How you deal with the reappearance of your ex after a period of absence is critically important.

If you find yourself faced with the problem of the vanishing and reappearing ex-spouse, the best way for you to handle the situation is to get yourself, your kids, and your ex (if you can swing it) into therapy. Let a trained professional deal with the issues that have arisen since your ex went AWOL, and get the therapist's advice on how to reestablish a relationship, not just between your ex and your kids, but between the two of you as well. Whether you want to reestablish any such relationship for yourself is, unfortunately, not important. If your ex is going to be back in your children's lives, you need to be able to communicate with him or her for the good of the kids. It doesn't matter that your ex ended all communication when he or she fell off the face of the earth. It doesn't matter that you're the one who has to be the mature adult again. If you care about your kids, and you want to do what's best for them, you will do what it takes to communicate with your ex and to guide your children's relationship with your ex back into comfortable territory. In the end, your children will be better off because you put aside your own anger and ill feelings, and did what was truly in their best interests.

The Realities of Supporting Your Child

The last main issue involving children revolves around money. It primarily involves child support, but also includes such things as medical insurance, the payment of uncovered medical expenses, the payment of day care and extracurricular activity expenses, and life insurance. Determining who pays these kinds of bills for your children after you are divorced is an enormous issue, and one that can have consequences long into the future. Deciding this issue fairly is therefore critically important to you, your ex-spouse, and your children.

The first thing to remember when considering any issues of money and children is that, as a parent, you have an absolute obligation to support your children. Period. It doesn't matter if you are divorced. It doesn't matter if your spouse earns more money than you do. It doesn't matter who your children live with. If you brought children into this world, then you are responsible for taking care of them until they are legally and physically old enough to take care of themselves. Hiding money, lowballing your income, or repeatedly changing jobs just to get out of paying child support is wrong. Spending money that you are given to support your children on luxuries for yourself while your children do without the things that they need is wrong. If you are a parent, your first priority must be your children.

Understanding that you have an obligation to support your children, and determining the limits of that obligation, however, are often two different things. Most often, states set guidelines for what child support should be, or they have a formula they use for calculating the appropriate amount of child support in each case. While each state handles child support somewhat differently, most states base the amount of child support a noncustodial parent should pay on fairly standard factors: the amount of the noncustodial parent's income; the number of children who need to be supported; and, the physical, emotional, and educational needs of those children, among other things. Some states also consider the amount of the custodial parent's income and assets, as well. In special circumstances, the court can deviate from its formula or guidelines and order the noncustodial parent to pay either more or less child support than what would otherwise be required. Once the court determines the appropriate amount of child support, the judge will then enter an order requiring the noncustodial parent to pay that amount of support to the custodial parent. That court order can be served on the noncustodial parent's employer, who will then be required to withhold the amount of child support due from the noncustodial parent's paycheck, or the noncustodial parent can simply pay that amount voluntarily.

In addition to paying child support, a noncustodial parent may also be required to provide medical insurance for the children, as well as to contribute towards the payment of the children's uncovered medical expenses, day care costs, extracurricular activities, and educational expenses. In addition, one or both parents may be required to maintain a life insurance policy on their lives to make sure that if anything happens to them, there will be money available to care for their children. It's easy to see how all of these things can quickly add up and become an enormous financial burden, which is one reason why it's so important to try to be reasonable while you are getting divorced and maintain the best relationship you can with your spouse even after the divorce. Children are expensive. They were expensive before you got divorced, and they're sure not going to get any cheaper afterwards. If you and your ex can work together after your divorce to make the best and most economical decisions regarding your children, everyone will benefit. On the other hand, if you do whatever you want, without worrying about whether your ex can afford it, you will soon find your-self back in court, waging yet another war that nobody will win.

What do you do, though, if you've tried your best to be reasonable, and still your former spouse won't pay what he or she is supposed to pay to support your children? If your ex has a steady, salaried job, your answer is simple. You can go to court, get an order from the judge that calculates the amount of back child support and expenses that are owed to you (this is called an *arrearage*), and have a withholding order entered that garnishes a certain amount of money from your former spouse's paychecks. That money will then be sent to you until the debt has been paid. If, however, your ex is self-employed, works for cash, changes jobs constantly, or is unemployed, collecting past due child support may not be so easy.

Many states now have child support collection agencies that help custodial parents collect past due child support and other child-related expenses. States are also toughening up the laws surrounding the collection of child support, and now provide that income tax refunds can be intercepted from those parents who owe past due child support. They have laws requiring employers to report when a parent leaves his or her job, where that parent lives, and the name of the parent's new employer to the state agency responsible for overseeing the collection of child support. That way, the state agency can contact the new employer to make sure it withholds child support from the parent's new paycheck, so there is no lapse in the payments the custodial parent receives. There are also laws in place that make collecting child support from parents who live in other states easier than it had been in the past. The services each state provides vary, and you should check to see what's available in your area. If you can't or don't want to have a state agency try to collect your child support, you can also hire your own attorney to do it. While hiring a private attorney may cost you more money in the short term, private attorneys will typically handle your case much faster and will give you more personalized attention than what any state agency could do.

You can also go after your deadbeat ex yourself. Handling your case yourself, however, is not easy. Just as you are better off getting a lawyer to handle your divorce, so too will you be better off getting a lawyer to collect your back due child support. Lawyers do it all the time. You don't.

Custody, Visitation, and Child Support—How They Relate and How They Don't

Understanding custody, visitation, and child support is not particularly difficult. What is difficult is understanding how they do and don't work together, and what that means to you. First of all, it is important to understand that custody, child support, and visitation are all separate. Just because your ex is screwing up on one doesn't mean you have the right to play with another. Even if you have sole custody and your ex is months behind in his or her child support payments, you cannot refuse to let your ex see the kids. He or she is entitled to visitation. Similarly, you can't make a deal that you agree not to ask your ex for child support as long as he or she leaves you alone and never comes to see the kids. You can't trade child support for visitation (or the lack of visitation). On the flip side, even if you never see your kids or never want to see your kids, you still have an obligation to support them. It doesn't matter that you feel like your children only want your money. Regardless of whether you ever wanted to be a parent, and regardless of whether you actually act like a parent, if biologically you are a parent, you have an obligation to support your children.

YOUR CHILDREN ARE YOUR RESPONSIBILITY: THE STORY OF JIM AND HELEN

Jim and Helen were still in high school when Helen got pregnant with twins. They decided to "do the right thing," so Helen dropped out of school and they got married. Within two weeks of the children's births, Jim had filed for divorce.

Jim resented the fact that Helen had refused to get an abortion and had "trapped" him into getting married. Even though Jim stayed in school and went on to college, he still thought that having children so young ruined his life. Consequently, he never gave his children the time of day. He never visited them. He never kept in touch with their mother, whom he considered to be beneath him. Most of the time, he acted like they didn't exist.

Jim was in school for many years, so Helen didn't even get the paltry $25 per week that he was supposed to pay for child support. As soon as Jim graduated from college and got a job working as an accountant at a small firm, Helen immediately took him back to court.

When Jim realized how much he was going to have to pay in child support, medical insurance, and other bills, he almost fainted. Yes, he finally had a good job, but as far as he was concerned, he had worked hard for that job and he deserved to be able to enjoy the benefits of it just like all the rest of his peers did. Plus, he had student loans to pay and he wanted to be able to get a new car. It just didn't seem fair that more than one-third of his paycheck was going for child support and medical insurance, when Helen was too lazy to go out and get a decent job and support the kids herself. After all, she was the one who wanted children.

Luckily for Helen, the judge was not impressed by Jim's complaints, and did not care that Jim never wanted children or that he was barely more than a child himself when he had had them. What's more, the judge found that Jim was in arrears almost $8,000 for all of the child support he hadn't paid while he was in school.

The judge ordered him to come up with $3,000 within a week, and pay the rest off in payments, on top of paying his regular child support. One week later, when Jim hadn't made the payment and failed to show up in court, the judge sent the sheriff to get him. Needless to say, Jim was mortified when he got called out of a business meeting, only to get hauled off in handcuffs on a citation for contempt of court. He paid the $3,000 that day.

Like Jim, many people have a blind spot when it comes to complying with child support orders. Somehow, they think that child support orders aren't real court orders, and therefore, they don't really need to be followed. They don't realize that a child support order is just like any other court order, and that if you blow it off, it will come back to haunt you. They also don't realize that they actually have to pay the amount they have been ordered to pay, and pay that amount when it's due, just like any other bill.

For some reason, many noncustodial parents who are supposed to pay child support treat their obligation with the *it's close enough* approach. That is to say that, if the child support order says that they have to pay child support on the first day of each month, then as long as the check is in the mail at some point during the first week of the month, that's close enough. If they get laid off or become unemployed, they think it's acceptable to pay only a small portion of what they owe (usually without bothering to tell the custodial parent that there won't be any money coming in for awhile) because, as long as they are paying something, it's close enough. They don't bother petitioning the court to cut down the amount of their child support obligation while they look for a new job (which they certainly could do). They don't worry about the fact that their children's expenses haven't changed one cent, and that the kids still have to eat, sleep, and have their other needs met. They just think that they can do whatever they want, and it's good enough. It's not.

If you are faced with a spouse who believes that doing only a part of what the court ordered him or her to do for the children is close enough to be acceptable, you have two choices: let your spouse go or take him or her back to court. Deciding which option to take depends upon exactly what's at stake and what your remedies are. If your spouse or former spouse consistently pays your child support a few days late, you may be able to get a withholding order that enables you to get the child support money directly from your spouse's employer. That will help you get your money on time and solve your problem. If your spouse is self-employed and always pays child support late, a withholding order won't work. Then you have to decide whether it's worth your time and money to go back to court, only to have the judge order your spouse to do what your spouse has already been ordered to do—make the child support payments on time—or whether it makes more sense for you to just bite your tongue and plan your budget around what you know will be late payments. On the other hand, if your problem isn't that your spouse is paying you late, but that your spouse is shorting you money, then going back to court might be worth it. Again, whether it will be worth it to go back to court depends upon how much money is involved. If your spouse owes you $100, and it will cost you $500 in attorneys' fees to go back to court, then fighting over the $100 doesn't make sense. You will lose more than you will win. If your spouse owes you $1,000, however, then going back to court may be worth your time. In the meantime, you need to keep track of everything your spouse owes you. Sooner or later, even the little things will add up. When they do, it may be worthwhile to tell your spouse that he or she either needs to settle up with you, or go back to court and explain to the judge why he or she shorted you money.

Fighting Over Money—Again

Even though most parents understand that they have an obligation to support their children, and most parents are willing to live up to that obligation, they still fight with their other spouse over child support because they don't believe their spouse is paying his or her fair share. That applies to both the custodial and the noncustodial spouse. Many custodial parents believe their ex-spouses are hiding income and living the high life while they struggle just to get by. Noncustodial parents believe that their ex-spouses are just trying to squeeze them for every dime they have, and that their ex-spouses don't really need as much money as they are getting. Because of their beliefs, each spouse or ex-spouse feels justified in trying to get or receive more than what the judge has ordered, and they use the children to do it.

When it comes to money and children, there is no end to the games that people play with each other. Custodial parents send their children for visitation in rags, and when the children come back with new clothes that the noncustodial parent bought for them, the custodial parent keeps those new clothes. The next time the children visit their noncustodial parent, they go in rags again. The same thing happens with toys, books, and every other kind of possession the children may have. Another common game is for one parent to refuse to buy the children what they need—for example, their school supplies—and tell them to ask the other parent to get it for them because he or she has more money. When the children do that, the other parent explodes and sends them back to the first parent to tell that parent that he or she should buy the kids their stuff. In the meantime, the children are forced to shuttle back and forth between both parents, begging them for what they need, and stressing out about the fact that they won't get it from either parent and that they will be the only kid in school without any notebooks, because their parents are divorced and can't get along.

Don't put your children through that kind of insanity. Being the children of divorced parents is hard enough on them already. Don't make it worse—and don't think that fighting over money doesn't affect your children in the same way that fighting over custody and visitation affects them. It's all the same to kids. They don't want to be in the middle of your fights, and as a responsible parent, you shouldn't put them there. Give your kids a break. Really do what's best for them. It will make all of the difference in their world.

13

The Best Interests of Your Children

Nothing has a stronger influence psychologically on their environment and especially on their children than the unlived life of the parent.

—Carl Jung, Psychiatrist

The pressures of being a parent are equal to any pressure on earth. To be a conscious parent, and really look to that little being's mental and physical health, is a responsibility which most of us, including me, avoid most of the time, because it's too hard.

—John Lennon, Singer and Songwriter

A torn jacket is soon mended; but hard words bruise the heart of a child.

—Henry Wadsworth Longfellow, Poet

Deciding who should have custody of your children, and arguing over how they are going to spend the rest of their childhood while you and your spouse live separate lives, is incredibly difficult and often very painful. When making decisions about custody, visitation, support, and anything else involving the children, everyone in a divorce—parents, lawyers, child representatives, and the judge—is supposed to do what is in the best interests of the children. The problem, of course, is deciding just what those best interests are. Not surprisingly, divorcing parents often disagree on what's best for their children. What's more, they are usually so angry at their soon-to-be former spouse that even if they could agree on what was best for the children, they'd still find a way to disagree on principle. As a result, kids get manipulated, used, and emotionally beat up in a way that most parents never intend. It's not surprising, therefore, that so many children have such a difficult time when their parents divorce.

Your Divorce Does Not Have to Ruin Your Children's Lives

Contrary to what most people think, divorce itself does not necessarily ruin children's lives. True, divorce can cause children the same kind of emotional upheaval and psychological trauma it causes their parents. It changes the family structure, and undeniably can cause kids problems or make the problems that they already have much worse. Yet, given a supportive environment, a little bit of time, and if necessary, some counseling, most children manage to adapt fairly well to their parents' divorce. The one thing that children don't adapt well to, however, is conflict. That, more than anything else, will wreak havoc on both their psyche and their lives.

Children want their parents to be happy. They don't want them to fight. Unfortunately, it is usually far easier for you to fight than it is for you to swallow your pride and keep the peace. If you want to, you can fight with your ex over everything from what time the kids come home to what they eat for dinner. You can drag your kids through the court system until they're 18 years old, and, if you really work at it, for the next four or five years after that as you fight over college expenses. You can spend thousands of dollars, and immeasurable amounts of emotional energy, fighting over every detail of your children's lives. In the end, what you will get for your trouble is a lot of stress, countless headaches, enormous legal bills, and some seriously messed up kids.

Obviously, your divorce will affect your children. You can't help that. What you can help, however, is how much it affects them and how negatively it affects them. The way you can minimize that negative effect is to shield your children as much as possible from the conflicts you are having with your spouse. That means not only should you not fight with your spouse in front of your children, but you should try not to fight when the children are in a position to overhear the two of you screaming at each other. It doesn't matter if your kids are in the room or not when you and your spouse argue. If they can hear your voice, they know you're fighting, and they're probably listening to everything you say. None of that is their business and none of it should be their concern. If you and your spouse have to fight, do it when the kids aren't around.

Shielding your children from conflict also means keeping them out of your divorce. Your children do not need to know the details of your divorce, your finances, or your spouse's bad behavior. Your children are your children—not your peers, your friends, or your counselors. It is not your children's job to support your emotional and psychological needs. It doesn't matter that your lousy bum of an ex hasn't paid child support in six weeks and now you're struggling to make the mortgage payment. Your children love that parent anyway and they don't need to be told he or she is a deadbeat. It only makes them feel bad. Children love their parents, and they want to think the best of their parents. The more you try to make them think otherwise, the more you're going to hurt them.

YOUR CHILDREN DON'T WANT TO SEE YOU FIGHT: THE STORY OF DOUG AND DIANE

Doug and Diane's divorce wasn't horrible, but it wasn't all that great, either. Like so many other couples, their main issue was money. Doug was a doctor. Diane was a nurse. They had two children, who were 8 and 10 years old at the time of their divorce.

Doug and Diane fought often over money, both during and after their divorce. Diane accused Doug of hiding money and cheating her out of the child support she should have been getting for the kids. Doug, who paid thousands of dollars a month in child support, all of the kids' private school tuition, and a lot of other things as well, was angry that Diane told the kids he was a cheapskate and forced the kids to ask Doug to buy them things when they were with him. From his perspective, Doug was paying way more than his fair share for the kids, yet he was being made out to be the bad guy. What was even worse in Doug's eyes was that the kids seemed to believe Diane. The more Doug and Diane fought, the more the kids sided with Diane.

In spite of Doug and Diane's fights over money, they managed to raise their children reasonably well. The children got through college and eventually established good relationships with both of their parents. One day, years after the divorce, Doug and his kids started talking about it. It was then that the kids confided in Doug that, when he and Diane fought over money all those times, they knew all along he was right. They knew he was a good father and not a cheat, they knew he was doing his best to take care of them, and they knew their mother was lashing out at him unfairly. Doug was astounded. He asked them why they hadn't ever taken his side in a fight if they knew he was right. Their answer was simple: we knew you were right, but it didn't matter. We just didn't want to you to fight.

Doug and Diane's story illustrates that it is not just divorce that hurts children, but the conflict after a divorce that causes them distress. As Judith Wallerstein and her colleagues have found in the landmark 25-year study of the children of divorce that they discussed in "The Unexpected Legacy of Divorce":

Adult children of divorce are telling us loud and clear that their parents' anger at the time of the breakup is not what matters most. Unless there was violence or abuse or unremitting high conflict, they have dim memories of what transpired during this supposedly critical period.... It's the many years of living in a postdivorce or remarried family that count....

Thankfully, most battles involving children, like most divorce cases in general, settle. The fact that most parents finally manage to work out a compromise regarding their children at some point before they go all the way to trial, however, rarely reduces the trauma the kids experience in the meantime—trauma that often leaves them with long-lasting emotional scars. What divorcing parents often fail to realize is that it's not just a trial that hurts children—it's the constant battle leading up to the trial, not to mention the never-ending war that rages afterward, that throws children into an emotional uproar. Even if parents finally settle before they go all the way to trial, the damage to their children is often already done. In most cases, if parents really want to do what's best for their children, they won't fight over them in the first place.

Your Children are Not Pawns in the Chess Game of Your Divorce

Conflict alone, both during and after a divorce, is not the only thing that hurts children. Involving children in adult issues, using them to relay information to your spouse, or getting information from them about your spouse can hurt them just as badly. It is both inappropriate and unfair to your children to use them to relay messages to your former spouse just because you don't want to have to talk to him or her any more. It is also wrong to use your children to deliver your child support check, find out who your spouse is dating, or bring you things from your spouse's house that your spouse wouldn't give you. All of those things are what you— the parent—should be doing or dealing with yourself. Take the responsibility that belongs to you and keep your children out of your mess.

Taking responsibility also means keeping your mouth shut when opening it would do nothing other than hurt your children. Your children do not need to know about your finances, your divorce, your legal issues, or the details of your former spouse's infidelity. You may think it's important to be honest with your kids, but honesty to the point of causing your children pain or damaging their relationship with their other parent is both unnecessary and unfair to them. What's more, it is clearly not in their best interests. Of course, you don't want to lie to your children. There will be certain information they need to know. However, there are some things that your children—even your adult children—don't need to know about your divorce or about your ex-spouse. It is your responsibility to keep quiet about those things. If you need to vent, talk to your friends. If you have problems you can't solve, find a good therapist. Don't use your children to make yourself feel better when doing so will only make them feel worse.

If you truly want to do what's best for your children, not only will you be responsible enough to keep them out of your conflicts and away from issues they have no business being involved in, but you will also do whatever you can to minimize your conflicts with your spouse in the first place. That means you have to communicate with your spouse without involving your children. If you don't communicate with your spouse, you will have problems with him or her. It's that simple. Misunderstandings will arise, problems will develop, and arguments will inevitably occur. Keeping the lines of communication open, however, is not always easy.

Communicating with Your Spouse is the Most Important Thing You Can Do for Your Children

If communication with your spouse was a problem during your marriage, don't expect it to be any easier after you are divorced. Human behavior is consistent. For that reason, you and your spouse will likely fall into the same communication pattern after your divorce that you had while you were married. If, before the craziness of your divorce set in, you were able to talk to your spouse reasonably well, then chances are the same thing will be true after the dust settles on your divorce and you both move on with your lives. On the other hand, if, during your marriage, you found that it was easier to talk to the wall than it was to your spouse, then you will likely have problems communicating with your ex after your divorce. What you need to realize, however, is that no matter how badly you and your spouse communicated while you were married, you have the power to change that communication pattern now and to turn it into something productive instead of something destructive.

You are the only one who can set boundaries with your spouse after your marriage has dissolved. Doing so is your responsibility. If your spouse was a screamer during your marriage, and you allow your now ex-spouse to continue to scream at you after your divorce, then you (and your children) are going to have to deal with that screaming forever. If you decide that you are no longer willing to let your ex yell at you, verbally abuse you, hang up on you, or argue with you in public, then you need to tell your spouse that this behavior is not acceptable. You need to explain that you are no longer willing to be treated the way you were treated in the past. What's more, you need to tell your ex not only what you don't want (i.e., that you don't want him or her to scream at you any more), but also what you do want (i.e., to be spoken to in a normal tone of voice). You also need to tell your ex what you are going to do if he or she doesn't do what you ask (i.e., you will walk away and come back later, when your ex is calm). You need not and should not put this in terms of an ultimatum. You're not saying, *Do this or else*. You're simply saying, *This is what I need you to do, and if you can't do it, that's okay, but you need to understand that then what I'm going to do is leave* (or whatever it is you decide you are going to do). Then you need to do what you said.

Setting boundaries with your ex takes work and it takes time. It's not easy to break out of a communication pattern that the two of you established years ago. At first, changing the way you react will seem strange. It won't feel right. However, if you stick to your guns, little by little, your new mode of action will feel better, and you will begin to feel better. Whether or not your spouse will feel better or get the hang of your new system is another story.

No matter how many boundaries you set with your former spouse, or how much you change the way you react to your ex or try to communicate with him or her, you cannot control your ex. So, don't be surprised if you set your boundaries, stand your ground, and your ex still screams at you. The point of setting boundaries is not to change your ex. It is to change you. If you change yourself, then maybe your ex will change too, but that is something you can't control. If, in spite of all of your best efforts, you find that your ex just won't change, and communicating with him or her in person is still unbearable, then you're going to have to find a way to exchange information that does not involve face-to-face interaction.

There are many different ways to communicate with your ex when you can't manage to talk one-on-one without making yourself insane. You can write each other notes, send each other letters, leave each other voice mail messages, or communicate via email. If none of those options works, you should probably try going to a counselor—with your former spouse if you can manage it—so that the two of you can establish some method by which you can communicate with each other for the benefit of the children without turning yourselves into emotional wrecks doing it. Understand that you don't have to call each other and chat every day. You just need some way of working out the details of life that every parent, married or single, needs to work out. You need to know who's going to pick the kids up when they only have a half day of school. You need to know whether your son's fever has gone down or whether you're going to have to take him to the doctor in the morning. You need to talk about how your daughter is going to get home from soccer practice if you have to work late. You just need to be a parent and talk to your children's other parent.

It is, of course, possible to be super-parent, and juggle your children's schedules and activities by yourself without ever consulting with your former spouse. Sometimes it's easier to do everything alone rather than having to deal with the inevitable conflict that arises when you talk to your ex. However, if you do everything on your own and don't communicate with your former spouse, not only are you bound to exhaust yourself, but you are guaranteed to create gigantic interpersonal problems between you and your former spouse, and you will ruin what little relationship the two of you may have left. If you don't communicate with your ex, he or she will get angry and frustrated when he or she doesn't know what's going on with the kids. Your ex will attribute motives to your behavior that never even occurred to you. Eventually, you will blow up at each other in yet another world-class fight, simply because neither one of you bothered to talk to the other. While you may think that you don't care anymore if your ex picks a fight with you or if the two of you have any kind of relationship at all, allowing a bad relationship to develop will cause more trouble for you and your children in the future.

Your Children Have Two Parents

Sometimes, even if you and your spouse or former spouse are communicating, that's still not enough to make your parenting relationship run smoothly. Parenting styles and values differ. In fact, those kinds of differences may have played a role in your decision to divorce your former spouse in the first place. Even so, your children were born of the union of two people. They do not belong only to you. For better or for worse, both you and your spouse have the right to decide, at least to some extent, how your children are raised, what values they will be taught, what religion they will participate in, and what schools they will attend. True, one parent may give away his or her rights—or in cases of abuse or neglect, a parent may have his or her rights taken away—but in most cases, both parents have the right to have input in their children's lives. How do you deal with the conflicts that inevitably arise when two very different people try to raise the same set of children? The answer is to remember the law of control.

You May be Able to Control Your Children, but You Will Never be Able to Control Your Spouse

Raising children is difficult enough when the only ones you're trying to control are the children. When you are trying to control your spouse or former spouse on top of it, especially when you're using the children to do it, life gets really complex. Legally speaking, if you have sole custody of your children, you probably have more of a right to raise your children the way you want, without consulting your former spouse, than you would if you had joint custody. Even with sole custody, however, you will still probably have to consult with your ex on certain issues, primarily those involving your child's health, safety, and major medical treatment. If you don't agree on those sorts of issues, you can fight about them, mediate them, or go back to court and let a judge decide them. Custody aside, if you and your ex don't have the same values, your kids are still going to learn very different things from each of you. Whether you like it or not, unless what your children are doing at your ex's house is illegal, grossly immoral, or dangerous, you're going to have to deal with those differences.

YOUR EX WILL ALWAYS BE YOUR CHILD'S OTHER PARENT: THE STORY OF MICHELLE AND JOHN

Michelle married John three weeks after meeting him in a bar. Michelle was a fairly devout, conservative Christian. John was a wickedly handsome, motorcycle-riding, party-loving bad boy. The two stayed married just long enough to conceive a child. Then John left. Michelle was crushed. She thought that this was not how things were supposed to be.

John and Michelle never saw eye to eye on much of anything. Once their baby, Nicole, was born, they agreed on even less.

Michelle decided that John (who was already living with his new girl-friend by the time Nicole was born) didn't have the kind of values that the father of her child should have, so Michelle did everything she could to exclude John from Nicole's life.

When Nicole was an infant, Michelle wouldn't let her out of her sight. She convinced the court-appointed attorney for Nicole that John couldn't be trusted to spend time alone with Nicole because he didn't know anything about infants. So John took parenting classes. Then Michelle accused John of being a drunk and doing drugs. So John submitted to random drug tests—all of which came out clean. Then Michelle breast-fed Nicole for over a year, and argued that John couldn't have visitation for more than a few hours at a time because Nicole needed to eat. Eventually, Nicole was weaned and John pushed for overnight visitation. That's when Michelle fell apart.

Michelle accused John of sexually abusing Nicole. Six months later, after John had been through a grueling investigation and all of Michelle's allegations turned out to be untrue, not only was John given liberal overnight visitation with Nicole, but Michelle almost lost custody of Nicole completely.

Everything Michelle did looked legitimate on the surface. In her own mind, Michelle had convinced herself that she wasn't trying to limit John's time with his daughter, she was trying to make sure her daughter was safe, well-fed, and properly cared for. While Michelle's stated concerns were valid, her actions were aimed more at controlling John's behavior and getting back at him for leaving her than they were at looking out for Nicole's best interests. John had to fight in court for every minute of time he got to spend with his daughter. Michelle wouldn't agree with him on anything. It wasn't until the judge threatened to take Nicole away from Michelle and give custody to John based upon Michelle's pretty obvious attempts to alienate Nicole from her father that Michelle finally had no choice but to let John become an active part of his daughter's life.

When it Comes to Your Children, Always Take the High Road

Using your children to hurt your former spouse can be extremely effective. The only problem with doing it is that not only do you hurt your former spouse, but you hurt your children as well. While it may not seem that way to you when you're doing it, screwing up a parent/child relationship is guaranteed to cause your kid problems in the future. If you really love your children, you will always take the high road. This means that even if you don't approve of your former spouse's lifestyle or values, you will resist the urge to bad-mouth your ex to the children. If your kids are young, hearing bad things about their parent will be hurtful and confusing. If they are teenagers, you run the risk of alienating them altogether as they rebel against your authority and decide to side with your ex. Either way, demeaning your former spouse, or his or her values or parenting style, in front of the children is always a bad choice.

Instead of tearing your ex down in front of the children, try a different approach. Talk to your children and talk to your former spouse. Use the differences in your parenting values or approaches to life as a springboard for a discussion with your children. Talk to them about why you do what you do and why you believe what you believe. The discussion will not only help them to understand your point of view, but it may help them start forming their own values and beliefs.

If your children are too young to talk about your rules for them, your values, and what you think is right, then just let them know that it's possible in life to have two sets of rules—one for your house and one for your ex's house. Make sure they know your rules and leave it at that. If your ex is doing something that you find completely wrong or offensive, talk to him or her about it. Communication is key. You may not ever agree to change your parenting styles to be alike. However, if you both genuinely consider the children's best interests, you may be able to compromise on certain issues, or work things out in a way that won't send mixed messages to your kids.

While everyone talks about doing what's in the best interests of the children, what is best for your children is often a matter of opinion. Sometimes there is no one best thing—there are two or three equally good choices of things you could do, one of which would work perfectly for everyone, and the others which will work well for you, but will cause your former spouse to suffer all kinds of unnecessary grief and aggravation. Of course, it's tempting to choose the latter course of action—watching your ex suffer can be amazingly satisfying. However, it also drives another wedge between the two of you and makes dealing with your former spouse that much more difficult in the future. Plus, next time, when it's you that needs the break, don't be surprised if your former spouse refuses to accommodate you. In the end, you, your ex, and your children will be far better off if you treat your ex-spouse like a human being and cut him or her a break (even if he or she doesn't deserve it), instead of doing things to purposely push your ex's buttons.

Fighting Hurts Your Children

Conflict hurts children. It damages and sometimes even destroys relationships. Conflicts over children, whether they involve custody, visitation, or both, damage your children's relationships with you, their other parent, and at times, their siblings. Not only is conflict horrible for children, but battles involving your children can never be won. No matter who gets custody or what kind of visitation schedule is put in place, your children will still have to suffer through the conflict that it took to decide those issues. They will carry the scars from that battle for a long time. What's more, no matter how much you fight, both you and your ex will still be parents of your children forever. That means after you have just spent years trying to annihilate each other in court, you will be expected to sit next to each other at your children's sporting events, school plays, and graduations, trying to pretend you don't hate each other's guts. You will have to talk to the same teachers, consult with the same doctors, and deal with each other as parents for the rest of your lives. It doesn't matter if you can't stand each other. It doesn't matter if you don't share the same values. It doesn't matter if your parenting style is like Ozzie Nelson and your former spouse's is like Ozzy Osbourne. Parents are parents for life.

As a parent, the best thing you can do for your children is not to fight over them, about them, with them, or in front of them. Even if you think the children don't know you're fighting, they do. Children are far more aware of what's going on in their lives than you might think. What's more, children are not possessions to be fought over in a divorce like any other piece of property. They do not *belong* to one parent or to the other. They are products of both parents. Chances are, they love both parents. Unless they're teenagers, they probably want to spend time with both parents. If you deny your spouse the right to see or talk to your children, you're hurting your children. If you tear down your spouse in front of your children and do other things to hurt their relationship with him or her, you're hurting your children. If you purposely exclude your spouse from your children's lives and activities, you're hurting your children. Everything you do to hurt your spouse affects your children.

People fight over their children for all kinds of reasons. Some people fight to gain custody or to limit their spouses' visitation because they don't think their spouses make good parents, or they don't approve of their spouses' values or parenting styles. Others might admit that their spouses make decent parents, but they believe they are better parents because they have more time, more money, or more interest in their kids. Still others hate their spouses so badly that they want to exclude them from their lives, and from their children's lives, forever. Then there are people who want custody just because their spouse wants custody, and they don't want their spouse to "win" anything. Other people use the children as leverage or want custody so that they can get the child support money that comes with it. Other people, especially women, can't imagine giving up custody because it's just not something they are supposed to do. Whatever the reason for the fight, when you dig to the bottom of it, you will usually find that most fights over the children are really not about the children at all.

Children need to have a relationship with both of their parents. What most parents don't understand when they are dueling over what's best for the children is that spending time with their other parent is usually what's best for the children. It doesn't matter if you think your ex is immature and doesn't make the best decisions for the children. It doesn't matter if you don't approve of the movies your ex takes the children to see, the food he or she buys them to eat, or the hour at which he or she puts them to bed. Your children are your spouse's children, too. Like it or not, your spouse has as much of a right to raise the children as you do. Unless your spouse is physically abusing them, putting them in danger, or doing things that are clearly and obviously inappropriate, then it doesn't matter whether you agree with what your spouse is doing or not. What matters is that the kids grow up with both of their parents in their lives. So, if you really want to do what's best for your kids, you will bite your tongue and find a way to get along with your ex for their sake.

The Reality of Getting Along with Your Children's Other Parent

If the concept of getting along with your former spouse sends you into fits of laughter, shock, or disbelief, you're not alone. For many people, it's a tough thing to do. After all, if you got along with your former spouse, you probably wouldn't have gotten divorced in the first place. However, if you are sincerely concerned about doing what is best for your children, then you will do for them the single most difficult thing anyone could ever ask you to do—get along with your ex.

What does getting along with your ex mean? It means putting into practice the same strategies you would use for handling any difficult spouse—keep in mind the big picture, pick your battles, and use your head. If your spouse brings your children home from visitation covered in mud from head to toe because they just came back from the park and they didn't have time to bathe, don't scream. Bite your tongue, send the kids off to the bathroom, and let it go. It's only dirt. It doesn't matter. The same thing applies if your ex shows up late, brings the children back home hungry, or forgets to return half of their stuff when he or she brings them back to you. In the big picture, none of that matters. If your ex forgets to tell you about the children's school play and you miss it, don't launch into a tirade in front of the children about how he or she is purposely trying to ruin your relationship with them—simply explain to the kids that you had a miscommunication and you'll make it up to them. Then, go to the school and make sure you get notices about that sort of thing directly from the school in the future, so that you don't have to rely on your ex to keep you informed. Do what you need to do to take care of your needs and the needs of your children, while also doing what you have to do to keep the peace and to get along with your ex. The price you pay if you don't is just too high.

THE PERILS OF NOT GETTING ALONG WITH YOUR EX: THE STORY OF KARL AND ANNA

Karl, an established scientist, married Anna, a social worker, late in his life. They each desperately wanted kids. After a brief courtship and almost immediately after their wedding, Anna became pregnant with Eric, their son. As soon as Eric was born, Anna announced to Karl that she was gay and filed for a divorce.

Karl and Anna had never been madly in love, but they were bound together by the one and only thing that each of them wanted—their son. While neither one of them wanted to share Eric with the other, each of them also realized that the risk of losing custody in a contested court battle was too great to bear. Karl didn't want to fight over custody because he understood that most judges would be reluctant to grant custody of an infant to a father, and Anna didn't want to do it because she was afraid that a judge would deny her custody of her son because she was gay. So, out of mutual fear of losing, Karl and Anna settled on joint custody.

Unfortunately, while fear motivated Karl and Anna to settle, once their case was over, the real battles began. If Karl was ten minutes late to pick Eric up, Anna would refuse to open the door and would pretend she wasn't home. Then Karl would come back with a police escort, and Anna would be standing at the door, waiting, pretending Karl had never been there in the first place and acting like he was crazy. For his part, Karl had nothing good to say about Anna, her mothering abilities, or her lifestyle, and he started trying to persuade Eric to move in with him almost as soon as Eric was old enough to talk. Karl and Anna rarely talked to each other, and Eric grew up being the go-between in all of their disputes.

Eric was a very smart child, and he learned how to manipulate his parents at a very young age. He played his parents off each other, and pretty much managed to get anything he wanted. Not surprisingly, by the time Eric was 10 years old, he was acting out in school and barely passing any of his classes. Not long after that, he started experimenting with drugs.

Karl and Anna's constant conflict made Eric a mess. Even though each of them truly believed that he or she was doing what was best for Eric, any outsider could see otherwise. What's more, it wasn't just the court fight that was a problem—their entire relationship was the problem. Both of them wanted Eric all to themselves, and neither could have him. Each one wanted to be in control—both of Eric and of the other. Each of them did things their own way and refused to even talk to the other one about what was best for Eric. While they never would have admitted it, their fight was not about Eric. It was about power and control. As happens so often in a divorce, their fight for control lasted well beyond the date they got divorced.

Fighting Over the Kids is a Never-Ending Battle

One of the biggest problems with child-centered battles is that, regardless of who wins, the battle never ends. It may not always be waged in the court system, but it doesn't go away. No matter what your divorce decree says, no matter whether or not you have sole custody, joint custody, or no custody, unless you make a conscious effort to work together with your spouse or former spouse on the issues that involve your children, you are going to have problems—and your children are going to have problems—for the rest of everyone's collective lives. What's more, if you don't maintain at least a civilized relationship with your former spouse after your divorce, or you don't communicate with him or her on a reasonably regular basis, it won't be long before you end up dealing with your problems in the one place that is the least suited to resolve them in a way that ends the conflict forever—the courts.

The battles that people fight over their children in a public courtroom are nothing less than shocking. Because these issues involve children, they are always emotionally charged, and resolving them is challenging. One way or another, however, they must and will be resolved. The only question is whether the parents will find a way to do it themselves, or whether they will let their lawyers and the judge do it for them.

Leaving the fate of your family to be decided by a total stranger is never a good idea. No matter how well-intentioned the judge is or how hard your lawyer works to present your case, in the end, the judge will be making a decision about your life based upon a few hours or days of testimony. You and your spouse, if you are able to communicate and compromise, will almost always be able to work out an agreement that is better suited to each of your needs and the needs of your children than any judge would ever be able to do. Before you go to court and before you make your personal family argument a matter of public record, you will almost always be better off trying to work out a solution to your problem.

Deciding not to fight over your children, in theory, is easy. Actually not fighting over them is not. Doing what's truly in their best interests is even harder. The problem with figuring out what is really in your children's best interest is that it's terribly difficult not to mix up what is in your own best interest with what you believe is best for the kids. It's difficult to analyze your own behavior to determine whether what you are doing is genuinely motivated by your concern for your children, or whether, subconsciously, you're really trying to torture or control your ex.

An easy way to figure out your true motivation is to look at the effect of your actions. If you know that what you are doing for the good of the children is guaranteed to transform your ex into a raging lunatic, chances are that what you're doing has more to do with hurting your ex than it does with doing what's best for the children. (Of course, it could also mean that your former spouse is an irrational maniac who responds to anything you do with rage, but most people tend to calm down after awhile and only react poorly to actions that truly irritate them.) Either way, your life, as well as your children's lives, will be infinitely easier if you can find a way to act that both works for your children and doesn't cause such an emotional reaction in your ex. In the end, whether you want to admit it or not, doing what is best for the children often requires you to also consider what is best not only for you, but for your ex as well.

14

Creating Good Post-Decree Karma

I first learned the concepts of non-violence in my marriage.

—Mahatma Gandhi, Indian Philosopher
and leader of the nonviolent struggle
for independence

It is better to conquer yourself than to win a thousand battles. Then the victory is yours. It cannot be taken from you, not by angels or by demons, heaven or hell.

—Siddhartha Buddha, Spiritual Leader

We fail to see that we can control our own destiny; make our-selves do whatever is possible; make ourselves become what-ever we long to be.

—Orison Swett Marden, Author of Motivational Books

The principles in this book are based upon three simple, universal laws—responsibility, control, and karma. If you take responsibility for your own life and your own divorce, and if you control your actions and emotions and stop trying to control everyone else, then you will get through your divorce in the best possible way—with your dignity, sanity, and integrity intact. With any luck, your children will be intact as well. That is not to say that your journey will be easy, or that there won't be huge bumps along your road. At times, you, like every other person who is going or has ever gone through a divorce, will feel like a failure. You will be angry, upset, frustrated, depressed, and lonely. You will wish you could just wave some magic wand and make the whole thing go away. But you will get through it. Nothing lasts forever—not even a horrible divorce. What matters, and what you have to decide, is how you will get through it.

Divorce is not a game. There are no winners. If you're lucky, and both you and your spouse do your best to act like civilized human beings and get through the process with the least amount of damage to everyone involved, you might make sure that at least there are no losers— but that's generally about as good as it gets.

Divorce is a process—a process of change. It starts long before you or your partner dares utter the word *divorce* out loud, and it ends long after the judge has signed your divorce decree and you and your ex have gone your separate ways. The legal part of the divorce—the legal process—is perhaps the most stressful portion of the entire ordeal. Yet, the legal process is but one part of your divorce. The other parts of your divorce—the emotional trauma, the new financial situation, the revised family structure, and the changed relationships you will have with everyone from your former spouse to your dearest friends—are all as much a part of the process as the courtroom drama. What's more, while you can suffer from the legal ramifications of your divorce for years, the nonlegal parts of the process can affect you for a lifetime. Indeed, you probably won't be able to appreciate the full effect of your divorce until years after the final order is entered and both you and your ex have moved on with your lives (or not). Although, if your divorce was particularly bitter and ugly, you will undoubtedly feel its effects right away.

Louise and Peter hadn't gotten along for years before Peter finally filed for divorce. Louise was very religious and Peter was trying to do the right thing, so they stayed together for the sake of their three children. When Peter finally decided he couldn't take it anymore, Louise was devastated. Her religion frowned upon divorce in all but the most extreme circumstances, such as when a spouse was unfaithful and would not repent, or if there was violence involved. Peter didn't have a girlfriend, but he did have a temper. So, when their youngest child came home from visitation at Peter's new apartment with bruises on her body, Louise was immediately ready to conclude that Peter had beaten her and sexually abused her. Without even calling Peter to get an explanation, Louise called the Department of Children and Family Services and demanded an investigation.

When the investigator called, Peter became outraged. He had never laid a hand on any of his children, and would never even dream of sexually abusing them. He deeply resented the accusations against him. Unfortunately, Peter's angry outburst did nothing to convince the investigator that Peter's daughter had accidentally fallen down the stairs when she tripped on a wayward toy, and that's why she was bruised. As for the alleged sexual abuse, Peter didn't know what to say, other than to deny the charges and to blurt out to the investigator that he didn't know how Louise could be so twisted as to accuse him of that sort of thing. Not only was it a lie, but as far as Peter was concerned, it was sick. Louise pressed charges, and within hours, had a criminal indictment against Peter and an order of protection prohibiting Peter from seeing any of his children.

After more than a year of fighting, the judge finally threw the case against Peter out for lack of evidence. By that time, Peter, a blue-collar worker who lived paycheck to paycheck, was so far in debt from all of his attorney's fees and everything else he now had to pay for that he had to go bankrupt. That, in turn, forced Louise to also go bankrupt, because she became liable to pay all the marital bills that Peter couldn't pay. Neither of them had any money to pay the mortgage and their home went into foreclosure. Meanwhile, their son, Joe, became angry and withdrawn and started acting out in school, their daughter, Geri, developed an eating disorder, and none of their family relationships were ever the same.

Louise and Peter's story is an extreme example of the effects of karma in life. When Louise jumped to conclusions about Peter and accused him of abuse before she even knew his side of the story, she started a series of events in motion that ultimately destroyed her entire family. When Peter reacted in anger, he made the case against him worse. What's more, his anger and his pride prevented him from petitioning the court for supervised visitation while the child abuse investigation was pending in court. In the end, he lost all contact with his children, and that only hurt them more.

Both Louise's and Peter's actions created reactions that they didn't desire and couldn't control. Both of them acted out of anger, and that anger came back to affect each of them in the worst ways. Each of them could blame the other, but in truth, they each created their own mess, and together they created a disaster.

What Goes Around Comes Around, So Take the High Road

What you do comes back to you. Getting divorced, as painful as it may be, is no excuse for bad behavior. What's more, bad behavior at any time tends to only make your situation worse. If you barrel through your divorce without concern for your spouse's feelings, your children's welfare, or anything other than your own greed and self-interest, you shouldn't be surprised when your relationship with your kids falls apart, your ex-spouse constantly drags you back to court, you pay a small fortune in attorney's fees, and you end up miserable. If you fail to understand that getting divorced doesn't end your relationship with your spouse, and you go about ending it yourself in a wicked court battle, then you will have no one to blame but yourself when the rest of your life becomes ten times more difficult because every interaction with your ex is an ordeal.

If you are like most human beings, and definitely most Americans, you want to see the results of your actions, and you want to see them now. If, instead of spending your divorce making your spouse squirm, you exercise every ounce of self-restraint that you have and you do the right thing, you want to know that you're going to get a reward. If you let go of all the wrong things that your ex has done and is doing to you, you want to know he or she is going to get paid back as well. You don't want to have to wait twenty years before you see your ex suffer. You want him or her to be writhing in agony now. You want your ex to realize his or her mistakes, and to either regret causing you such pain or regret being stupid enough to divorce you in the first place. Not only do you want your ex to regret all that, you want him or her to admit the mistakes as well, preferably in a public place with you and all of your friends as witnesses. That's what you think karma is, or at least what it should be. Unfortunately, that's not karma—that's a delusion.

Karma, like so many other things in life, happens in its own way, in its own time. You can't direct it and you can't control it. That means you aren't the one who gets to choose what happens to your ex for treating you poorly. You also don't get to choose what happens to you for swallowing your anger and treating your ex better than he or she deserves to be treated. You may bend over backwards to compromise with your former spouse in ways you don't believe you should have to compromise, only to have your ex react by still being a complete jerk. That's not what you want to have happen after you made the effort (often to your own detriment) to control your own urge to be a jerk. You want to know that if you treat your ex well even if he or she doesn't deserve it, your ex will treat you well in turn, because you do deserve it. Yet, just as bad results sometimes take time to evolve, so too do good results. Just as your bad actions in one area of your life may cause a bad reaction in another, unanticipated area, so too do your good actions cause reactions in places you wouldn't expect. One way or another, the good that you do comes back to you.

SOMETIMES GOOD THINGS HAPPEN, TOO: THE STORY OF TIM AND JOAN

Tim and Joan's marriage had always been stormy, and their divorce was no different. By the time they were done, neither one of them could stand to be in the same room with the other. It didn't help that they had two children and had to deal with each other on a fairly regular basis. At least they did until Tim got thrown into jail.

Tim was an alcoholic. After his third drunk driving conviction, the judge threw him in jail for a year. When he got out he had no job, no driver's license, a felony conviction, and a lot of past-due child support.

It took awhile, but eventually Tim started to get his life together. He started going to Alcoholics Anonymous and was actively looking for a job. When he tried to start seeing his kids again, though, Joan balked. She immediately filed a motion asking the judge to hold him in contempt of court and throw him in jail again, this time for not paying child support.

Tim and Joan's relationship had not improved since their divorce. Even though they hardly ever talked, Joan knew that Tim was scared to death of having to go back to jail, and she hoped that when he got her motion he'd just leave her and the kids alone. She was having a hard enough time keeping both of the kids, who were now teenagers, under control and trying to get them to pick up their grades in school. She didn't want or need Tim's help, although she certainly wouldn't have turned down his money.

At the first court hearing on Joan's motion, the sparks flew. Joan accused Tim of being farther behind in payments than he actually was. Tim couldn't understand why Joan wouldn't give him a break when he was struggling to stay sober and get a job. Neither one of them had an attorney, and by the time they got done fighting, the judge was ready to hold them both in contempt of court. So the judge sent them off to get lawyers and come back in six weeks.

Even though neither of them had much money, both Tim and Joan brought lawyers with them to their second court appearance. When their case was called, the judge made all of them sit in a conference room and try to work things out. No one, especially Tim and Joan, thought they would actually be able to do that. However, once they started talking, a funny thing happened. For some reason, they paid attention to each other. They may only have been talking because the judge made them do it, and they may only have been talking civilly because their attorneys wouldn't let them scream at each other, but for the first time in years, each one of them was able to explain his or her position and explain how he or she felt without getting screamed at by the other. So, for the first time in years, not only did they talk to each other, but they listened.

During their conversation, Tim and Joan started to realize that each of them had problems. Tim was struggling at overcoming his addiction each and every day. Joan was struggling to work full-time and raise two teenage children who had lots of their own issues all by herself. Both Tim and Joan had issues, and both of them had limitations—and both of them were just doing the best that they could, given the situation they were in. After about an hour of talking, they struck a deal. Joan gave Tim a break on how much money he owed her. Tim, in turn, made a payment schedule and even gave Joan a little money right there in court. They walked out, not as friends, but at least no longer as enemies.

It would be a wonderful postscript to this story to be able to tell you that, from that point forward, Tim and Joan's relationship became perfectly fabulous and they never had an argument again. Of course, that didn't happen. They were still divorced. They still didn't like a lot of things about each other. They still didn't trust each other, and they still fought a lot. However, they also talked to each other—it was a start. Over time, they did manage to rebuild a relationship that was at least civilized enough to keep them out of court and working together (more or less) for their children until they were grown.

Dealing with Your Divorce

Life doesn't always work out the way you want it to. You don't always get to see the results of what you do or what your spouse does. In the big picture, it doesn't matter. The results are there, and they affect you. Even if you never see any outward affect of the action you took, you hold the truth of your activity in your heart, and that affects you as much as any outside event in your life. It affects your self-image and your self-esteem. It affects who you are as a person, and who you believe yourself to be.

It is extremely difficult when you are going through a divorce to take the high road. You are so angry, upset, and emotional, that you naturally want to lash out from your place of pain and hurt your spouse too. However, hurting your spouse ultimately hurts you. It hurts your children. Helping your spouse, which is typically the last thing you feel like doing, ultimately helps you and your children. It helps you even when you think that it doesn't.

Whatever you do, even while you're going through a divorce and you feel like your guts are being ripped out, your head is spinning, and you don't know how you and your kids are going to survive—even then, what you do matters. If anything, it matters more because it sets the stage for how you will get through the rest of your life. Once you understand that, you begin to also understand that the manner in which you conduct yourself while you are going through your divorce will determine the quality of your family relationships after the legal process is over. When you look at your divorce with that in mind, suddenly being selfish, greedy, spiteful, or wicked to your former spouse doesn't make nearly as much sense as it did when you viewed your divorce as a once-in-a-lifetime event.

Appendix A:
Financial Worksheets

This appendix includes worksheets to help you organize your financial life. These guide you what financial information you need to gather for your divorce.

The first two worksheets are designed to assist you in creating a budget. The second two worksheets will give you a clear picture of your assets and liabilities (or debts).

Monthly Income Worksheet

GROSS MONTHLY INCOME

a. Salary/Wages/Base pay $_____

b. Overtime $_____

c. Commissions $_____

d. Bonuses $_____

e. Draws $_____

f. Pension and retirement benefits $_____

g. Disability benefits $_____

h. Workers' compensation benefits $_____

i. Social Security benefits $_____

j. Unemployment benefits $_____

k. Investment income $_____

l. Rental income $_____

m. Interest income $_____

n. Dividend income $_____

o. Trust income $_____

p. Annuity income $_____

q. Business income $_____

r. Partnership income $_____

s. Royalty income $_____

t. Fellowship/Stipends $_____

u. Spousal support received $_____

v. Child support received $_____

w. Public aid/Food stamps $_____

x. Other income (specify) $_____

Total Gross Monthly Income $_____

Required Monthly Deductions from Income

a. Federal Tax (based on ___ exemptions) $_____

b. State Tax (based on ___ exemptions) $_____

c. FICA (or Social Security equivalent) $_____

d. Medicare tax $_____

e. Self-employment tax $_____

f. Mandatory retirement contributions
required by law to be deducted $_____

g. Union dues
(name of union) _____ $_____

h. Health/Hospitalization premiums $_____

i. Prior obligations of support actually paid
pursuant to court order $_____

j. Medical expenditures necessary to
preserve life or health $_____

k. Expenditures for the repayment of debts
necessary for the production of income
(specify) _____ $_____

Total Required Deductions from Income $_____

NET MONTHLY INCOME $_____

Additional Nonmandatory Deductions

a. Retirement/401(k) contributions $_____

b. Deferred compensation contributions $_____

c. Charity contributions $_____

d. Other items deducted from paycheck
(specify) _____ $_____

Total Optional Deductions from Income $_____

NET MONTHLY INCOME WITH
OPTIONAL DEDUCTIONS INCLUDED $_____

Monthly Expense Worksheet

HOUSEHOLD EXPENSES

a. Mortgage or rent $_____

b. Home equity payment $_____

c. Real estate taxes, assessments $_____

d. Homeowners or renters insurance $_____

e. Heat/Fuel $_____

f. Electricity $_____

g. Telephone (land lines) $_____

h. Telephone (cell phones) $_____

i. Water and sewer $_____

j. Garbage removal $_____

k. Laundry/Dry cleaning $_____

l. Maid/Cleaning service $_____

m. Furniture and appliance repair/Replacement $_____

n. Home repairs and maintenance $_____

o. Lawn and garden/Snow removal $_____

p. Food (groceries, household supplies, etc.) $_____

q. Liquor, beer, wine, etc. $_____

r. Cable/Satellite TV $_____

s. Internet Service Provider $_____

t. Pet care expenses $_____

u. Other (specify): _____ $_____

Subtotal Household Expenses $_____

TRANSPORTATION EXPENSES

a. Gasoline $_____

b. Repairs and maintenance $_____

c. Insurance $_____

d. License/City stickers $_____

e. Payments/Replacement $_____

f. Alternative transportation $_____

g. Parking $_____

h. Other (specify): _____ $_____

Subtotal Transportation Expenses $_____

PERSONAL EXPENSES

a. Clothing $_____

b. Grooming $_____

c. Medical (unreimbursed expenses) $_____

    Doctor $_____

    Dentist $_____

    Optical $_____

    Medication $_____

    Therapy $_____

d. Insurance $_____

    Life (term) $_____

    Life (whole or annuity) $_____

    Medical/Hospitalization $_____

    Dental/Optical $_____

e. Other (specify): _____ $_____

Subtotal Personal Expenses $_____

MISCELLANEOUS EXPENSES

a. Clubs/Social obligations/Entertainment
    (including dining out) $_____

b. Newspapers, magazines, books $_____

c. Gifts $_____

d. Donations, church or religious affiliation $_____

e. Vacations (cost for you, not kids) $_____

f. Computer/Supplies/Software $_____

g. Other (specify): _____ $_____

Subtotal Miscellaneous Expenses $_____

CHILDREN'S EXPENSES

a. Clothing $_____

b. Grooming $_____

c. Education $_____

 Tuition $_____

 Books/Fees $_____

 Lunches $_____

 Transportation $_____

 School-sponsored activities $_____

d. Medical (after insurance proceeds) $_____

 Doctor $_____

 Dentist $_____

 Optical $_____

 Medication $_____

e. Allowance $_____

f. Child care/Preschool care/After-school care
(not included elsewhere) $_____

g. Baby-sitters $_____

h. Lessons/Extracurricular activities/Supplies $_____

i. Clubs/Summer camps $_____

j. Vacations (children only) $_____

k. Other activities $_____

l. Entertainment $_____

m. Gifts children give to others $_____

n. Other (specify)_____

Subtotal Children's Expenses $_____

TOTAL MONTHLY LIVING EXPENSES $_____

Assets Worksheet

As of Date: _____

CASH OR CASH EQUIVALENTS

Type of Account	Where Account is Held	Account Number	Held by H, W, or Both	Balance
Savings or Interest-Bearing Accounts				
Checking				
Checking				
Checking				
Certificates of Deposit				
Money Market				
Other				

INVESTMENT ACCOUNTS AND SECURITIES

Type of Account	Where Account is Held	Account Number	Held by H, W, or Both	Balance
Stock				
Bonds				
Any Other Securities				
Investment Accounts (Other than Retirement)				
Other				

REAL PROPERTY

Type of Property	Address of Property	Amount of Mortgage & Other Loans	Current Market Value
Residence			
Secondary or Vacation			
Investment or Business			
Vacant Land			
Other			

Motor Vehicle(s)

Type of Vehicle	Year, Model, Make	Name of Loan Company	Amount of Loan	Current Value

Business Interests

List any corporations, partnerships, sole proprietorships, etc.

Name & Address of Business	Type of Business Entity (Corporation, Partnership, etc.)	Name of All Owners	Percent of Ownership or Number of Shares Owned	Current Value

INSURANCE POLICIES

List any life, disability, business overhead, property, etc.

Name & Address of Policy Holder	Type of Policy	Name of Insurer	Policy Number	Beneficiary	Face Value of Policy

RETIREMENT ACCOUNTS

List any IRAs, 401(k) plans, pension plans, etc.

Type of Plan	Name & Address of Company	Account Number	Beneficiary	Vested Amount	Value

STOCK OPTIONS/EMPLOYMENT BENEFITS

List any stock options, ESOPs, other deferred compensation, or employment benefits

Type of Benefit	Name of Owner	Name & Address of Company or Holding Benefit	Account Number	Number of Shares and Value

VALUABLE PERSONAL PROPERTY

List and describe any collectibles you or your spouse may have, such as jewelry, gold or silver, stamp collections, antiques, artwork, etc.

Type of Item	Name of Owner	Date Purchased	Value

ALL OTHER PROPERTY (PERSONAL OR REAL, NOT PREVIOUSLY LISTED, VALUED IN EXCESS OF $1,000)

List any other property not mentioned above and provide its current value

Type of Property	Name of Owner	Date Purchased	Value

TOTAL VALUE OF ASSETS $_____

Liabilities Worksheet

As of Date: _____

HOME

Type of Account	Name and Address of Creditor	Account Number	Owed by H, W, or Both	Total Balance Due	Monthly Payment
Mortgage					
Home Equity Loan					
Line of Credit					

VACATION HOME OR INVESTMENT PROPERTY

Type of Account	Name and Address of Creditor	Account Number	Owed by H, W, or Both	Total Balance Due	Monthly Payment
Mortgage					
Home Equity Loan					
Line of Credit					

STUDENT LOANS

Name and Address of Creditor	Account Number	Owed by H, W, or Both	Total Balance Due	Monthly Payment

CAR LOANS

Name and Address of Creditor	Account Number	Owed by H, W, or Both	Total Balance Due	Monthly Payment

OTHER LOANS

Name and Address of Creditor	Account Number	Owed by H, W, or Both	Total Balance Due	Monthly Payment

CREDIT CARD DEBT

Name and Address of Creditor	Account Number	Name on Account (H, W, or Both)	Purpose of Debt	Total Balance Due	Monthly Payment

TOTAL BALANCE DUE $_____

TOTAL MONTHLY PAYMENT $_____

Appendix B: Checklists

The checklists in this appendix are provided to help you keep track of all the things you need to remember in your divorce. The first check-list will help you organize your documents in preparation for your divorce, while the second will help you keep everyone's needs in mind when working towards a settlement agreement.

Document Checklist

- ❑ Your W-2 Form for the past three years.
- ❑ Your spouse's W-2 Form for the past three years.
- ❑ Federal Income Tax Returns for the past three years.
- ❑ At least one year of checking account statements for any account held in your name, your spouse's name, or both of your names.
- ❑ At least one year's worth of savings account statements for any account held in your name, your spouse's name, or both of your names.
- ❑ At least one year's worth of market account statements held in your name, your spouse's name, or both of your names.
- ❑ At least one year's worth of investment account statements for any account held in your name, your spouse's name, or both of your names.
- ❑ Current statements showing the value of your pension plan, IRA account(s), deferred compensation, annuities, and 401(k) plan(s).
- ❑ Current statements showing the value of your spouse's pension plan, IRA account(s), deferred compensation, annuities, and 401(k) plan(s).
- ❑ All document(s) regarding any stock option account(s), ESOPs, other deferred compensation or employee benefits held in your name, your spouse's name, or both of your names.
- ❑ Your current home mortgage statement showing the account number, the total amount due, and your monthly payment.
- ❑ Current statements from your home equity loan or any line of credit on your home.
- ❑ Current statements for any other mortgage on any property you, your spouse, or both of you own.
- ❑ All motor vehicle titles held in your name or jointly with your spouse.
- ❑ The leases for any vehicles you or your spouse may have.
- ❑ A copy of any life insurance policy held either in your name, your spouse's name, or your children's names.
- ❑ A current fair market value appraisal of your home.
- ❑ Any partnership or business agreements regarding any business you, your spouse, or both of you have an interest in.
- ❑ Stock certificates for any corporation you, your spouse, or both of you own shares of.
- ❑ All credit card bills for the past year.

Sample Needs Checklist

YOUR NEEDS

❑ Financial Needs
   a. Monthly income
   b. Monthly expenses
   c. Money in the bank

❑ Physical Needs
   a. Home
   b. Food
   c. Clothing
   d. Exercise
   e. Sleep

❑ Social Needs
   a. Time with the kids
   b. Time without the kids
   c. Time with your friends
   d. Time to date again

❑ Emotional/Psychological Needs
   a. Therapy
   b. Time alone
   c. Other needs

YOUR SPOUSE'S NEEDS

❑ Financial Needs
   a. Monthly income
   b. Monthly expenses
   c. Money in the bank

❑ Physical Needs
   a. Home
   b. Food
   c. Clothing
   d. Exercise
   e. Sleep

❑ Social Needs
   a. Time with the kids
   b. Time without the kids
   c. Time with his/her friends
   d. Time to date again

❑ Emotional/Psychological Needs
   a. Therapy
   b. Time alone
   c. Other needs

YOUR CHILDRENS' NEEDS

❑ Physical Needs
   a. Home
   b. Food
   c. Clothing
   d. Exercise
   e. Sleep

❑ Educational Needs
   a. Tuition paid
   b. Books/fees/etc.
   c. Extracurricular activities
   d. Special educational needs

❑ Social Needs
   a. Time with Mom
   b. Time with Dad
   c. Time with their friends
   d. Time to participate in their extracurricular activities

❑ Emotional/Psychological Needs
   a. Time alone
   b. Ability to talk to someone
   c. Other needs

Appendix C: Sample Holiday Visitation Schedule

This sample schedule includes every major U.S. holiday, as well as those for the Christian and Jewish religions. You can strike out the holidays that don't apply to you, and use as many or as few of these holidays as you like.

Sample Holiday Visitation Schedule

The parties agree to alternate all major secular and religious holidays with the first year's schedule, set forth as follows:

Holiday	Father	Mother
Christmas Eve 10 a.m.–10 a.m. On Christmas Day	Odd Years	Even Years
Christmas Day 10 a.m.–10 a.m. On Dec. 26	Even Years	Odd Years
Easter 9 a.m.–9 p.m.	Even Years	Odd Years
Yom Kippur	Odd Years	Even Years
Rosh Hashannah	Even Years	Odd Years
Hanukkah	Odd Years	Even Years
Passover	Even Years	Odd Years

Holiday	Father	Mother
Purim	Odd Years	Even Years
Thanksgiving 9 a.m.–9 a.m. Following day	Odd Years	Even Years
Father's Day	10 a.m.–6 p.m.	N/A
Mother's Day	N/A	10 a.m.–6 p.m.
New Year's Eve 5 p.m.–9 a.m. New Year's Day	Even Years	Odd Years
New Year's Day 9 a.m.–9 a.m. Jan. 2	Odd Years	Even Years
Martin Luther King Day 9 a.m.–9 p.m.	Even Years	Odd Years

	Odd Years	Even Years
President's Day 9 a.m.–9 p.m.	Odd Years	Even Years
Lincoln's Birthday 9 a.m.–9 p.m.	Even Years	Odd Years
Columbus Day 9 a.m.–9 p.m.	Even Years	Odd Years
Memorial Day 9 a.m.–9 p.m.	Even Years	Odd Years
July 4 9 a.m.–9 a.m. Following Day	Odd Years	Even Years
Labor Day 9 a.m.–9 a.m. Following Day	Even Years	Odd Years
Halloween 9 a.m.–9 a.m. Following Day	Odd Years	Even Years
Father's Birthday	5:30 p.m.–8:30 p.m.	N/A
Mother's Birthday	N/A	5:30 p.m.–8:30 p.m.

The parties agree that the parent who does not have scheduled visitation with a child on that child's birthday shall have two hours' visitation with the child on his or her birthday, at times that are mutually agreeable to the parties and do not disrupt the child's activities.

The parties also agree that they each may have two weeks' vacation time with the children, which may be taken consecutively or in increments. The parties further agree that they each shall have telephone contact with the minor child at all reasonable times and places during the vacation period. The parties agree to consider the plans and activities of the minor children when scheduling vacations.

Each party agrees to give the other party thirty days' advance written notice prior to his or her intended vacation with the minor children, along with his or her destination and a complete itinerary, telephone number, and address where he or she can be reached during the vacation with the minor children.

Appendix D: Resources

Books

For Divorcing Spouses

A Man's Guide to a Civilized Divorce: How to Divorce with Grace, a Little Class, and a Lot of Common Sense. Sam Margulies, PhD, JD, 2004

Boomer's Guide to Divorce (and a New Life). Marlene M. Browne, 2004

Crazy Time: Surviving Divorce and Building a New Life, revised edition. Abigail Trafford, 1992

Divorce and Money: How to Make the Best Financial Decisions During Divorce. Violet Woodhouse and Dale Fetherling, 2004

Divorce & New Beginnings: A Complete Guide to Recovery, Solo Parenting, Co-Parenting, and Stepfamilies. Genevieve Clapp, 2000

Divorce for Dummies. John Ventura and Mary Reed, 1998

Divorce Hangover: A Successful Strategy to End the Emotional Aftermath of Divorce. Anne Newton Walther, MS, 2001

Money and Divorce: The First 90 Days and After. James Gross and Michael Callahan, 2006

Not Your Mother's Divorce: A Practical, Girlfriend-to-Girlfriend Guide to Surviving the End of an Early Marriage. Kay Moffet and Sarah Touborg, 2003

Rebuilding: When Your Relationship Ends, 3rd Ed. Dr. Bruce Fisher and Dr. Robert Alberti, 2005

Spiritual Divorce: Divorce as a Catalyst for an Extraordinary Life. Debbie Ford, 2002

Surviving Separation and Divorce. Loriann Hoff Oberlin, 2005

The Complete Idiot's Guide to Surviving Divorce, 3rd Ed. Pamela Wentraub and Terry Hillman, 2005

The Good Divorce: Keeping Your Family Together When Your Marriage Comes Apart. Constance Ahrons, PhD, 1998

The Healing Journey through Divorce: Your Journal of Understanding and Renewal. Phil Rich and Lita Linzer Schwartz, PhD, ABPP, 1999

The New Creative Divorce: How to Create a Happier, More Rewarding Life During and After Your Divorce. Mel Krantzler and Patrician B. Krantzler, 1999

The Unexpected Legacy of Divorce: The 25 Year Landmark Study. Judith S. Wallerstein, Julia M. Lewis and Sandra Blakeslee, 2001

Transformational Divorce: Discovery Yourself, Reclaim Your Dreams & Embrace Life's Unlimited Possibilities. Karen Kahn Wilson, 2003

Uncoupling: Turning Points in Intimate Relationships. Diane Vaughan, 1986

What Every Woman Should Know About Divorce & Custody: Judges, Lawyers, and Therapists Share Winning Strategies on How to Keep the Kids, the Cash, and Your Sanity. Gayle Rosenwald Smith, JD and Sally Abrahams, 1998

Your Divorce Advisor: A Lawyer and a Psychologist Guide You Through the Legal and Emotional Landscape of Divorce. Diana Mercer, JD and Marsha Kline Pruett, PhD, MSL, 2001

FOR PARENTS

Child Custody, Visitation and Support in Illinois. Linda A. Connell, 2003

Divorce Casualties: Protecting Your Children from Parental Alienation. Douglas Darnall, 1998

Divorce Poison: Protecting the Parent-Child Bond From A Vindictive Ex. Richard A. Warshak, 2003

Helping Children Cope With Divorce. Edward Teyber, 2001

Joint Custody With A Jerk: Raising a Child with an Uncooperative Ex. Julie A. Ross, MA and Judy Corcoran, 1996

Juggling Act: Handling Divorce Without Dropping the Ball: A Survival Kit for Parents and Kids. Roberta Beyer and Kent Winchester, 2001

Parenting After Divorce: A Guide to Resolving Conflicts and Meeting Your Children's Needs. Phillip Michael Stahl, PhD, 2000

The Co-Parenting Survival Guide: Letting Go of Conflict after a Difficult Divorce. Elizabeth Thayer, PhD, 2001

FOR CHILDREN

Dinosaurs Divorce: A Guide for Changing Families. Laurie Krasny Brown and Marc Brown, 1988

Divorced But Still My Parents. Shirly Thomas, et al, 1997

Helping Your Kids Cope with Divorce the Sandcastles Way. M. Gary Neuman, 1999

I Don't Want to Talk About It. Jeannie Franz Ransom, 2000

Its' Not Your Fault Koko Bear: A Read-Together Book for Parents & Young Children During Divorce. Vicky Lansky, 1998

Mom's House, Dad's House: Making Two Homes for Your Child. Isolina Ricci, PhD, 1997

The Divorce Helpbook for Teens. Cynthia MacGregor, 2004

The Suitcase Kid. Jacqueline Wilson, 1998

The Truth About Children and Divorce: Dealing with the Emotions so You and Your Children Can Thrive. Robert E. Emery, PhD, 2004

ON MEDIATION

Guide to Divorce Mediation: How to Reach a Fair, Legal Settlement at a Fraction of the Cost. Gary J. Friedman, 1993

The Divorce Mediation Answer Book: Save Time, Money, and Emotional Energy With a Mediated Separation or Divorce. Carol A. Butler, PhD, and Delores D. Walker, MSW, JD, 1999

The Divorce Mediation Handbook: Everything You Need to Know. Paula James, 1997

Organizations

ATTORNEYS

American Academy of Matrimonial Lawyers
150 North Michigan Avenue
Suite 2040
Chicago, IL 60601
312-263-6477
Fax: 312-263-7682
www.aaml.org

American Bar Association
321 North Clark Street
Chicago, IL 60610
312-988-5000
Fax: 312-988-6281
www.abanet.org

Association of Family and Conciliation Courts
6525 Grand Teton Plaza
Madison, WI 53719
608-664-3750
Fax: 608-664-3751
www.afccnet.org

COUNSELORS AND THERAPISTS

American Association for Marriage and Family Therapy
112 South Alfred Street
Alexandria, VA 22314
703-838-9808
www.aamft.org

National Association of Social Workers
750 First Street, NE
Suite 700
Washington, DC 20002
202-408-8600
www.naswdc.org

DOMESTIC VIOLENCE

Child Abuse Listening and Mediation (CALM)
P.O. Box 90754
Santa Barbara, CA 93190
805-965-2376
24-hour listening service (bilingual): 805-569-2255
www.calm4kids.org

Child Welfare League of America
440 First Street, NW
Suite 310
Washington, DC 20001
202-638-2952
Fax: 202-638-4004
www.cwla.org

National Coalition Against Domestic Violence
1120 Lincoln Street
Suite 1603
Denver, CO 80203
800-799-7233 (SAFE)
www.ncadv.org

MEDIATION AND MEDIATORS

Association for Conflict Resolution
  1015 18th Street, NW
  Suite 1150
  Washington, DC 20036
  202-464-9700
  www.acrnet.org

PARENTS AND CHILDREN

Children's Rights Council
  6200 Editors Park Drive
  Suite 103
  Hyattsville, MD 20782
  301-559-3120
  Fax: 301-559-3124
  www.gocrc.com

National Organization of Single Mothers
  P.O. Box 68
  Midland, NC 28107
  704-888-5437
  www.singlemothers.org

Parents Without Partners
  1650 South Dixie Highway
  Suite 510
  Boca Raton, FL 33432
  561-391-8833
  Fax: 561-395-8557
  www.parentswithoutpartners.org

Stepfamily Association of America, Inc.
  650 J Street
  Suite 205
  Lincoln, NE 68508
  800-735-0329
  www.saafamilies.org

Websites

COLLABORATIVE LAW

Collaborative Divorce
   www.collaborativedivorce.com

Collaborative Professional Center
   www.collablaw.com

The Coalition for Collaborative Divorce
   www.nocourtdivorce.com

International Academy of Collaborative Professionals
   www.collaborativepractice.com

Collaborative Divorce in Canada
   www.collaborativedivorce.ca or www.collaborativedivorce.org
   www.collaborativedivorce.com
   www.collaborativelaw.ca
   www.divorcenet.com/canada

DIVORCE, IN GENERAL

Divorce Care
   www.divorcecare.com

Divorce Headquarters
   www.divorcehq.com

Divorce Information
   www.divorceinfo.com

Divorce Links
   www.divorcelinks.com

Divorce Net
   www.divorcenet.com

Divorce Support
   www.divorcesupport.com

Divorce Support Groups
   www.smartdivorce.com/resources/support.shtml

Divorcing as Friends
   www.divorceasfriends.com

Family Law Source
   www.familylawsource.com

Family and Relationship Organizations
www.menstuff.org/resources/resourcefiles/families.html

Fathers and Divorce
www.dadsdivorce.com

Transitioning from Divorce
www.divorcetransitions.com

Your Are Not Alone—Divorce Advice
www.enotalone.com

DOMESTIC VIOLENCE

Abuse Counseling & Treatment, Inc.
www.actabuse.com

National Coalition Against Domestic Violence
www.ncadv.org

National Domestic Violence Hotline
www.ndvh.org
800-799-7233
800-787-3224 (TTY)

Violence Against Women Online Resources
www.vaw.umn.edu

FINANCIAL ISSUES

Divorce and Credit
www.ftc.gov/bcp/conline/pubs/credit/divorce.htm

Credit Reports
www.annualcreditreport.com
www.equifax.com
www.experian.com
www.transunion.com

MEDIATION AND MEDIATORS

Divorce Mediation
www.mediate.com

Information about Divorce and Mediation
www.allny.com/divorce

Divorce Mediation Resources
www.mediationnow.com

Divorce Mediation
http://womansdivorce.com/mediation.html

Parents and Children

American Academy of Child and Adolescent Psychiatry
   www.aacap.org/publications/factsfam/divorce.htm

Child Support
   www.supportguidelines.com

Coping with Divorce and Helping Children
   www.nlm.nih.gov/medlineplus/divorce.html

Dealing with Divorce for Kids and Teens
   http://kidshealth.org/teen/your_mind/families/divorce.html or
   http://kidshealth.org/kid/feeling/home_family/divorce.html

Divorce and Stepfamily Support
   www.divorcestep.com

Divorced Father's Network
   www.divorcedfathers.com

Effects of Divorce on Children
   www.helpguide.org/mental/children_divorce.htm

Index

P

pain, 5, 8, 16, 34, 40, 74, 107, 148, 163, 164, 171, 175, 176, 186, 194, 208, 227, 230

paranoid, 110

parents, 6, 7, 11, 18, 21, 22, 25, 43, 53, 57, 64, 72, 79, 80, 90, 93, 94, 105, 128, 132, 140, 141, 156, 157, 158, 159, 173, 176, 178, 182, 185, 186, 187, 189, 190, 191, 192, 193, 194, 195, 196, 197, 198, 200, 201, 202, 203, 204, 205, 206, 207, 208, 210, 211, 212, 213, 214, 215, 216, 217, 219, 220

patience, 41, 51

paychecks, 92, 111, 196, 197, 199, 226

pension, 118, 119, 120, 133

personalization of reality, 33

perspective, 27, 28, 31, 33, 34, 35, 36, 37, 56, 72, 92, 161, 176, 206

Petition for Dissolution of Marriage, 48

picking your battles, 179, 218

police, 14, 80, 168, 169, 172, 177, 219

premarital agreement, 116, 117

prioritizing property, 131, 142

private investigators, 47, 111, 113, 154

professionals, 36, 62, 64, 68, 69, 78, 81, 102, 155, 191, 194

property, 9, 13, 24, 25, 46, 47, 61, 62, 68, 96, 104, 106, 107, 108, 112, 113, 115, 116, 117, 118, 120, 122, 123, 124, 125, 127, 128, 129, 131, 133, 135, 136, 137, 139, 141, 143, 148, 153, 154, 181, 216
  commingled, 117
  community, 68, 115, 116
  equitable distribution, 116
  marital, 46, 47, 68, 116, 117, 118, 122

psychological effects, 3, 7, 102, 142, 143, 173, 177, 204, 205

psychologist, 1, 60, 64, 71, 159, 192

R

reality check, 28, 35, 37, 72, 131

receipts, 22, 42, 114

reconciliation, 71, 72

referrals, 75

refinancing, 53, 123, 124, 134, 157

relationships, 2, 3, 4, 5, 6, 7, 11, 12, 25, 28, 29, 30, 31, 32, 33, 34, 40, 53, 56, 57, 63, 64, 70, 71, 74, 85, 88, 93, 140, 150, 158, 159, 161, 167, 177, 178, 190, 194, 195, 196, 206, 208, 211, 214, 215, 216, 217, 218, 219, 220, 224, 226, 227, 228, 230, 231

relatives, 36, 112, 116

religion, 186, 187, 211, 225

respect, 7, 8, 26, 41, 72, 139, 141

responsibility, 4, 5, 11, 13, 14, 15, 16, 17, 18, 19, 26, 35, 39, 43, 56, 57, 72, 75, 93, 97, 98, 120, 121, 122, 123, 140, 151, 152, 153, 154, 159, 160, 170, 173, 176, 179, 195, 197, 198, 202, 203, 207, 208, 209, 223

retirement, 5, 17, 30, 31, 62, 66, 101, 104, 106, 110, 114, 115, 117, 119, 133, 134, 138, 151

rules, 2, 3, 13, 14, 18, 40, 42, 45, 46, 55, 56, 57, 65, 66, 77, 81, 86, 158, 160, 168, 174, 177, 214

S

safety, 149, 168, 169, 170, 180, 212

salary, 9, 90, 115, 119, 124

scheduling, 11, 79, 80, 83, 165, 177, 178, 181, 190, 191, 192, 193, 215, 230

school, 6, 9, 10, 11, 25, 38, 53, 79, 81, 89, 90, 95, 96, 97, 104, 128, 140, 159, 160, 169, 178, 179, 186, 188, 189, 198, 199, 202, 206, 210, 216, 218, 219, 226, 229

scorch and burn divorce, 147

self-defense, 170